The Year 2000 Software Problem

The Year 2000 Software Problem

Quantifying the Costs and Assessing the Consequences

Capers Jones

ACM Press
New York, New York

ADDISON-WESLEY

An Imprint of Addison Wesley Longman, Inc.

Reading, Massachusetts • Harlow, England • Menlo Park, California
Berkeley, California • Don Mills, Ontario • Sydney
Bonn • Amsterdam • Tokyo • Mexico City

Many of the designations used by manufacturers and sellers to distinguish their products are claimed as trademarks. Where those designations appear in this book and Addison-Wesley was aware of a trademark claim, the designations have been printed in initial caps or all caps.

The author and publisher have taken care in the preparation of this book, but make no expressed or implied warranty of any kind and assume no responsibility for errors or omissions. No liability is assumed for incidental or consequential damages in connection with or arising out of the use of the information or programs contained herein.

The tables in this book contain numbers that have been rounded to the nearest integer. The author and publisher acknowledge that this may cause minor inconsistencies in the totals and averages.

This book is published as part of ACM Press Books—a collaboration between the Association for Computing, Inc. (ACM) and Addison Wesley Longman, Inc. ACM is the oldest and largest educational and scientific society in the information technology field. Through its high-quality publications and services, ACM is a major force in advancing the skills and knowledge of IT professionals throughout the world. For further information about ACM, contact:

ACM Member Services
1515 Broadway, 17th floor
New York, NY 10036-5701
Phone: 1-212-626-0500
Fax: 1-212-944-1318
E-mail: acmhelp@acm.org

URL: http://www.acm.org

ACM European Service Center
108 Cowley Road
Oxford, OX4 1JF, United Kingdom
Phone: +44-1865-382388
Fax: +44-1865-381388
E-mail: acm_europe@acm.org

The publisher offers discounts on this book when ordered in quantity for special sales. For more information, please contact:

Computer and Engineering Publishing Group
Addison Wesley Longman, Inc.
One Jacob Way
Reading, Massachusetts 01867-3999

Library of Congress Cataloging-in-Publication Data

Jones, Capers.
    The year 2000 software problem : quantifying the costs and
assessing the consequences / Capers Jones.
        p.   cm.
    Includes bibliographical references and index.
    ISBN 0-201-30964-5
    1. Software maintenance.   2. Year 2000 date conversion (Computer
systems)   I. Title.
QA76.76.S64J65   1998   97–31806
005.1'6—dc21   CIP

ISBN 0-201-30964-5
Text printed on recycled and acid-free paper.
2 3 4 5 6 7 8 9 10—MA—0201009998

Second printing, February 1998

Find Addison-Wesley on the World Wide Web at: http://www.awl.com

Find the author's company, Software Productivity Research, Inc., on the World Wide Web at: http://www.spr.com

Contents

Chapter 6: Testing, Test Case Errors, and Repairing Software Regression Test Libraries — 131

Chapter 7: Repairing Databases, Repositories, and Data Warehouses — 149

Chapter 8: Litigation and Liability Potential for the Year 2000 Problem — 153

List of Tables

Chapter 7

Chapter 8

Chapter 10

Chapter 11

Chapter 12

Chapter 13

Chapter 14

Appendix A

Appendix D

Foreword

An acute awareness of the potential severity the year 2000 problem has now surfaced on the agenda of every executive responsible for information management. This includes not only CIOs and computer operations managers, but also boards of directors, audit committees, and computer steering committees. Such consciousness is only of a recent origin. Judging from articles in the press, professional papers, and technical meetings, the year 2000 has become a topic worthy of focused discussion only in the last two years. Such a recent awakening of threats to the operational and financial health of organizations may be puzzling, especially in retrospect. The delays in dealing with what are now likely widespread damages will surely be argued when litigation suits base their compensatory claims as incontrovertible proof of managerial negligence.

The coming of a new century has been predictable for at least a thousand years. Why then the delays, surprises, and the rapidly escalating panic that a year 2000 debacle may not only jeopardize the financial health of a firm, but also destroy careers and reputations?

I find that the principal reason for the current confusion and dismay has been the absence of a thoughtful and well-documented analysis of the severity of the problem. The early warnings about the incipient year 2000 problems were dismissed with incredulity. They lacked sufficient and substantive documentation about the amount and quality of the work that had to be accomplished. Even headline-grabbing research service pronouncements were greeted with skepticism because they could not explain how they arrived at their estimated expenditures to fix the problem. Individual organizations had no way of coming up with a budget that would assure their management that any proposed spending was based on demonstrable and sound cost-estimating principles. Multiplying the inventory of lines of code under control of the CIO—if such an inventory was available at all—by one of the wide-ranging cost quotes per line of code yielded numbers that very few financial executives could accept for redirecting funds.

This book stands out as the best, most thorough, and monumental contribution in defining what the year 2000 problem is all about. In painstaking detail it describes what is the scope of the year 2000 problem and what are the most likely approaches that could lead to alleviating its damage. It documents the dimensions of the software defects, organizational problems in managing year 2000 projects, and resource limitations in much greater detail than anything that has been published so far by anyone. For that reason, it should receive immediate acceptance as a much sought-after reference for anyone who wishes to check the adequacy of their year 2000 protective measures.

This book is required reading for all executives who may have to account for their custodianship of the year 2000 solutions whenever the inevitable after-the-fact recriminations occur. In the same way as the fall of the Berlin Wall became the symbolic event marking the downfall of a mismanaged Soviet Empire, it is likely that the enormous costs, litigation, and adverse publicity of any year 2000 failures will be seen as the end of trust in the management of information technologies. What will follow are inevitable changes in organization, budgeting, and accountability. There is still a preciously small amount of time to get a grip on dealing with the year 2000 challenges, but that must be done with the aid of rational and comprehensive analysis. I trust that this new book by Capers Jones will provide those insights and guidance.

Paul A. Strassmann
New Canaan, Connecticut
July 1997
paul@strassmann.com

Preface

For more than twelve years my company has done research on a variety of software issues. Our consulting work includes performing qualitative assessments and collecting quantitative data on software costs, productivity, schedules, quality, and a number of related subjects. We collect this data to develop and tune the algorithms for our main commercial software tools, which are software cost and quality estimation tools: CHECKPOINT and the more recent KnowledgePLAN, which were produced just as this book was being drafted.

Because we have a substantial volume of information on software maintenance and quality, both of which are relevant to the year 2000 issue, I decided to write a short technical report for our clients in 1996 on the probable costs of repairing the year 2000 problem. We have been working for several years to estimate the costs of the software portions of the year 2000 problem, although neither our tools nor anyone else's can handle topics such as the litigation costs for year 2000 damages.

As I began to assemble the information and write the first draft, it quickly became obvious that the year 2000 problem was going to be a major issue for the world software community and also for the world business community. Once I realized the vast significance of the year 2000 problem, I continued to expand my initial report roughly every six weeks through eight additional versions.

By the time I reached version 5 early in 1997, other year 2000 authors had seen my data on our Web site (http://www.spr.com) and requested permission to use some of it in their books. For example, Dr. Leon Kappelman, Dr. Dick Lefkon, Dr. Howard Rubin, Dr. Keith Jones, and Bryce Ragland have all used some of my cost and economic findings in their own excellent books on the year 2000 problem.

By the time my report reached version 7 it had grown to more than 120 pages, and I began to think in terms of a book of my own, since it was obvious that the year 2000 problem is almost unique in human history. There has never been a man-made technical problem that will impact so many businesses, so many government groups, and cause so many problems at a personal level.

Since I've reviewed four books, six book drafts, and another dozen book proposals for the year 2000 problem, I know that there is a great deal of valuable information already in print on this subject, or being printed in 1997. It is a fair question to ask what my book might discuss that is not already available in the books of other authors. The primary information contained here, but not available in other books, is the quantification of two key topics:

1. What will it cost to fix the year 2000 problem by country, by industry, by programming language, and by application?
2. For the year 2000 problems that slip through and are not fixed, what will the costs be for immediate damages, and then for long-range recovery?

There are a number of excellent books on the technical year 2000 problems, on how corporations might address and deal with those problems, and on some of the sociological and technical damages that might occur if the year 2000 problem is not fixed in time. However, there is no other readily available published source of information that addresses the full gamut of year 2000 costs, including:

- Portfolio analysis
- Software repairs
- Database repairs
- Test library repairs
- Hardware upgrades
- Litigation expenses
- Potential damages from litigation
- Year 2000 failure costs
- Year 2000 recovery costs

My data for the entire spectrum of the year 2000 issue has a significant margin of error. However, by the time the errors could be eliminated and the data validated in order to achieve high accuracy, it would already be the year 2000, and hence, far too late for the data to have any value. There are other sources of quantitative data on the year 2000 problem, but they are not readily available to the general public. Several information service providers such as Gartner Group, Meta

Group, and Giga Group provide quantitative data to their clients, but not very much of this data is available to non-clients.

The structure of this book is far from perfect because the book grew organically and spontaneously rather than as a planned document. *Chapter 1* is a short executive overview of the year 2000 problem and why it is significant. *Chapter 2* discusses the origins of the year 2000 problem and some related problems caused by attempts to conserve storage (a goal that is still causing problems even today). *Chapter 3* introduces the key terms and concepts that describe the nature of the organizations and applications that must deal with the year 2000 issue. *Chapter 4* deals with a very important but controversial point: the use of *lines of code* (LOC) metrics or *function point* metrics—or both—for quantifying the year 2000 problem. This chapter concludes that the very common LOC metric is actually hazardous, and that some of the common ways of enumerating this metric can lead to severe overcharges by contractors and outsource vendors. *Chapter 5* deals with the size of the year 2000 problem for the United States, including some special liability issues for US corporations and US executives. *Chapter 6* deals with the important topic of year 2000 testing, and the underreported topic of errors in year 2000 test cases. *Chapter 7* deals with the impact of repairing databases, repositories, and data warehouses. The year 2000 problem is particularly severe and expensive in the data arena, and the costs cannot be measured using LOC metrics or function point metrics. *Chapter 8* deals with the risks of litigation associated with the year 2000 problem. Unfortunately the risks of litigation are both plentiful and severe, and may include personal suits for violation of fiduciary duty against many senior executives. *Chapter 9* deals with risks of business failure associated with the year 2000 problem. Here, too, the risk of bankruptcy or business failure due to the year 2000 problem is alarmingly high. *Chapter 10* discusses the emergence of the year 2000 repair industry, which has expanded faster than almost any industry in history. It has gone from nonexistence to having a set of 18 companies summarized as a new stock market indicator in less than 24 months. *Chapter 11* discusses *masking,* or some of the evolving forms of concealing, the year 2000 problem over and above simply expanding the date fields from two to four digits. Topics such as encapsulation, bridging, and compression are discussed. *Chapter 12* expands the year 2000 problem from the United States to the world, and summarizes the probable expenses individually for large countries, and then in aggregate for the entire world. This chapter also discusses the conflict for resources between the year

2000 problem and the European currency conversion problem, which are on a collision course in terms of both schedules and resource requirements. *Chapter 13* discusses some of the complex issues with the costs of the year 2000 problem, and explains why the costs will vary widely from company to company, country to country, industry to industry, and even from city to city. *Chapter 14* is based on the assumption that many organizations will not successfully achieve year 2000 compliance before the end of the century. This disturbing chapter is speculative, since the end of the century is in the future. However, it attempts to quantify the damages and recovery costs for almost 1,700,000 software applications that will still have latent year 2000 errors as the dawn arrives on January 1, 2000. *Chapter 15* builds upon the gloomy scenario in Chapter 14, and discusses the defenses that companies, government agencies, and private citizens might take to minimize the risks and problems that the year 2000 issue will bring to pass. All of us will have problems and will need to take some evasive and corrective actions, but hopefully by the end of the century we will fully understand what needs to be done.

At the end of the book are several appendices, a glossary of common year 2000-related terms, and an index. *Appendix A* provides a short overview of the sources of data used to construct the book. *Appendix B* is an annotated listing of other year 2000 sources of information. *Appendix C* details a number of Web sites containing year 2000 information. *Appendix D* lists the programming languages that will be affected by the year 2000 problem. Lastly, *Appendix E* contains an annotated bibliography of other year 2000 books.

Acknowledgments

First and always, thanks to my wife, Eileen, for her patience and support in having an author for a husband. Thanks also for her handling of all of my publishing agreements and knocking off the usual rough edges.

Thanks to the personnel and management team at Software Productivity Research, Inc. (SPR) for providing useful information in large volumes. Special thanks to Jan Huffman and Mark Beckley for making a number of helpful suggestions as this book evolved. Thanks also to Ajit Maira of the SPR Board of Directors for his recognition that the year 2000 topic would become a major factor for SPR.

I'd also like to express appreciation for the information and helpful comments received from some of the other year 2000 researchers who have provided data, offered suggestions about my data, or both: Watts Humphrey, Dr. Leon Kappelman, Bob Kendall (whose far-seeing ideas may yet come to pass), Keith Jones, Dr. Richard Lefkon, Lauris Nance, Ken Orr, Peter de Jager, Bryce Ragland, and Dr. Howard Rubin. Special thanks to Paul Strassmann for his Foreword, and also for the clarity and excellence of his own economic work.

It is sad when a great software researcher passes away at a fairly young age, when discoveries are yet to be made. Appreciation is due for the many contributions to the science of software engineering made by the late Thom Peters—a friend and colleague from IBM, who later worked at Carnegie Mellon—who passed away in May 1997 in Pittsburgh.

Introduction

To conserve storage space software applications historically used two digits for recording calendar years—for example, the year 1990 would be stored as 90. When the twentieth century ends, many software applications will either stop working or produce erroneous results since their logic cannot accept the transition from 1999 to 2000, when the dates change from 99 to 00. The costs of fixing the year 2000 problem appear to constitute the most expensive single problem in human history.

Even worse, year 2000 problems might lead to the most expensive litigation in human history. The costs of repairing this problem may equal or exceed 30% of the annual software budgets of typical corporations. But the damages and recovery costs from *unrepaired* year 2000 problems may exceed a year's software budget. The costs of defending against litigation and lawsuits can approximate half a year's software budget, but damages and penalties from suits that are lost can reach multiples of annual software budgets and lead to bankruptcy. Individual executives may also be sued personally.

The end of 1997 is approximately the last point at which year 2000 repairs can start with a reasonable probability of finishing before 2000. Unfortunately, current data indicates that at least 15% of software applications will not be repaired in time.

1 | Introduction and Executive Overview

THE YEAR 2000 software problem concerns the widespread practice of storing calendar year dates in two-digit form. For example, the year 1997 is stored as 97. At the end of the twentieth century many software applications will stop working or create erroneous results when the year switches from 1999 to 2000 at midnight on December 31. This is because many applications use dates for time-sensitive calculations, and the sequence of 99 followed by 00 can cause software crashes or incorrect results for many important calculations such as interest rates and mortgage payments.

The year 2000 problem will be one of the most expensive problems in human history. For the United States, more than four months of effort may be needed on the part of every software professional in the country to repair the year 2000 problem. The year 2000 repair costs may exceed $2,000 for every working person in the United States, or more than $900 for every citizen of the United States. This problem is not trivial and will not go away if ignored. Failure to correct it could lead to serious consequences, including several kinds of litigation, possible bankruptcy, and possible business failure. Software and corporate executives may be held personally liable for some of the consequences of the year 2000 problem unless prompt and energetic actions are taken to correct the problem. The year 2000 problem may lead to lawsuits against corporate executives for violation of fiduciary duty, and against software executives for professional malpractice, and these may occur even if these individuals retire or change jobs prior to the year 2000.

A variety of tools and services are now available to assist in finding and repairing the year 2000 problem. However, October 1997 is the last month and year in which there is a reasonable possibility of finding and repairing all year 2000 instances before the end of 1999 as a normal business activity. Extraordinary measures such as canceling all other projects or moving to 24-hour-a-day repairs can shift the starting point into early 1998, but may cause other kinds of serious problems. Executives and managers are urged to explore the year 2000 situation in their own enterprises as rapidly as possible.

Although the year 2000 problem is very serious, the companies and organizations that are able to resolve the problem will find some significant benefits too. Software applications that are year 2000 compliant should be much easier to extend and maintain than their predecessors. Also, the work of solving the year 2000 problem will give enterprises a much better understanding of how much software they own, and its business value, than has yet been possible.

Potential Year 2000 Problems that Affect Daily Life

Unfortunately, the year 2000 problem does not just affect a few financial records. It is a widespread problem with many implications. Consider the kinds of hazards that might occur in the 10 industries listed in Table 1.1.

Table 1.1: Year 2000 Damage Possibilities in 10 Industries

Industry	Major Year 2000 Hazard

Airlines
    Air traffic control malfunctions
    Flight schedule confusion
    Navigation equipment failures
    Maintenance schedule disruption
	Safety hazards

Defense
    Base security compromised
    Computer security compromised
    Encryption compromised
    Strategic weapons malfunction
    Command and communication network
        problems
    Aircraft maintenance records disrupted
    Logistics and supply systems disrupted
    Satellite malfunction
	Security hazards

Continued on next page

Table 1.1: Year 2000 Damage Possibilities in 10 Industries, continued

Industry	Major Year 2000 Hazard
Finance	*Financial transaction hazards*
Interest calculations in error	
Account balances in error	
Credit card charges in error	
Funds transfers disrupted	
Mortgage/loan interest payments in error	
Lease records in error	
Health care	*Safety hazards*
Patient monitoring devices malfunction	
Operating room support systems disrupted	
Medical instruments malfunction	
Patient billing records in error	
Medical insurance billing in error	
Insurance	*Liability and benefit hazards*
Policy due dates in error	
Benefits and interest calculations in error	
Annuities miscalculated	
Payment records in error	
Year 2000 damages underestimated	
Local government	*Local economic hazards*
Property sales misdated	
Jury records in error	
Real estate transactions misdated	
Divorce records misdated	
Marriage records misdated	
Birth records misdated	
Death records misdated	
Traffic ticket dates incorrect in computers	
Traffic light synchronization disrupted	
Court dates in error	

Continued on next page

Table 1.1: Year 2000 Damage Possibilities in 10 Industries, continued

Industry	Major Year 2000 Hazard

Manufacturing
    Subcontract parts delivery
        disrupted
    Just-in-time arrivals disrupted
    Assembly lines shut down
    Aging of accounts receivable and
        cash flow
    Aging of accounts payable and
        cash flow
    Pension payments miscalculated
	Operational hazards

National government
    Tax records in error
    Annuities and entitlements
        miscalculated
    Pensions miscalculated
    Disbursements miscalculated
    Retirement benefits miscalculated
	Citizen record hazards

Public Utilities
    Electric meters malfunction
    Gas meters malfunction
    Distribution of electric power
        disrupted
    Billing records in error
    Nuclear power plants malfunction
	Safety hazards

Telecommunications
    Intercontinental switching disrupted
    Domestic call switching disrupted
    Billing records in error
	Service disruption hazards

The obvious aspects of the year 2000 problem may well be repaired in time. What is most troubling are the hidden manifestations of the year 2000 problem that will escape notice in time for repair prior to the end of the century. Some of the unexpected problems associated with the year 2000 issue that affect daily life might include the following, although these are from a worst-case scenario and hopefully will not occur at all.

- At midnight on December 31, 1999, your electric power may shut off either because the generating plant has malfunctioned (hopefully not a nuclear power plant) or because the distribution of electricity is thrown off. Your electric meter may malfunction too.
- If you attempt to telephone to report the electric problem, your phones may not work because switching systems have malfunctioned. If you are able to place a call, the billing information may not be correctly recorded.
- If you decide to drive toward your office or into a town to see what other damages might have occurred, traffic lights may not be working or may no longer be synchronized.
- If you need to stop to purchase gasoline, your credit card may not be recognized at the gasoline pump.
- If you need to stop to get money from a cash machine, the automatic teller machines may not be working.
- If your office building has a security system, you may not be able to get in the door because the date may not be recognized.
- If your computer network has a security system, you may not be able to log on because the date may not be recognized.
- If you need to travel, airline flight bookings may be confused and, even worse, air traffic control may have malfunctioned.

These serious problems will probably not occur, but they illustrate how pervasive computers and software have become to industrialized countries in the twentieth century. Almost every industry and service use computers and software as invisible agents to perform functions that were once performed electromechanically or by human efforts.

The year 2000 problem is unique in that it has at least the potential ability to affect more computer systems at the same time than any other known event except the electromagnetic pulse from a nuclear explosion.

Potential Year 2000 Problems that Affect Executives

The year 2000 problem is unique in the business history. Although the problem is technical in nature, it poses very serious personal threats to more corporate and government executives than any other business issue in human history. The year 2000 problem may possibly exceed the great stock market crash of 1929 and the following depression as an issue that can damage the careers and finances of corporate executives and elected officials.

Because computers and software now drive modern businesses and government operations, failure to solve the year 2000 problem can cause very expensive damages that could lead to major lawsuits against both corporations and government agencies. In addition in every major industrialized country, corporate directors and corporate executives have legal obligations to act in the best interests of the shareholders of the corporations that employ them. Government officials also have an obligation to act in the public interest. Therefore, personal lawsuits for violation of fiduciary duty are very likely to occur for the following corporate and government executives:

- Boards of directors
- Chief executive officers (CEOs)
- Chief financial officers (CFOs)
- Chief information officers (CIOs)
- Chief technology officers
- Chief legal officers
- Corporate controllers
- Vice presidents of engineering
- Vice presidents of software engineering
- Vice presidents of manufacturing
- Vice presidents of human resources
- Vice presidents of quality assurance
- Government officials of agencies that disburse funds
- Government officials of taxation agencies
- Mayors and city managers

Every executive and board member should consider the consequences of the kinds of lawsuits that might occur if the following year 2000 problems occur for the organizations for which they have a legal responsibility to manage well:

- Income tax withholding amounts are miscalculated.
- Employee paychecks are miscalculated.
- Pension checks are miscalculated.
- Invoices are not paid in time or are paid incorrectly.
- Accounts receivable all become delinquent simultaneously.
- Customer orders are lost or canceled.
- Deliveries to customers are canceled or lost.
- Manufacturing lines are shut down.
- Injuries or deaths occur due to equipment malfunctions.

If these year 2000 problems occur, there will be a cascade of major lawsuits that might end the careers and damage the personal finances of many senior executives, even if they know little or nothing about software. Clients, suppliers, and employees may sue the organization for damages if they have been harmed by year 2000 problems. Tax and government agencies will certainly take legal action if tax information is miscalculated. In turn, shareholders may well sue the corporation, its board of directors, and top executives because the year 2000 problem has reduced the value of their shares. Unfortunately, it will be hard to mount an effective defense against year 2000 damage suits because the problem is clearly visible, highly publicized, and technically solvable. The only apparent reason for *not* solving the year 2000 problem is because executives and top officials did not perform their duties in a conscientious and capable manner, and would seem to have violated their fiduciary duty to their corporations.

Since a reasonable time line for making year 2000 repairs would have started in calendar year 1995, and included steady repair and renovation work during 1996, 1997, 1998, and 1999, even executives who change jobs or retire before the year 2000 problems occur may still be liable. Even criminal charges may be filed if unsolved year 2000 problems cause injuries or tax miscalculations. The only effective way to avoid damage lawsuits is to mount a thorough and comprehensive year 2000 repair program. Unfortunately, other kinds of lawsuits may occur because year 2000 repairs are very expensive and hence may reduce profits for several consecutive years. However, the consequences of *not* solving the year 2000 problem are enormously more hazardous to executives than the costs of *solving* them. Diligence and thoroughness are the best preventive measures that an executive can take.

The costs of year 2000 repairs will probably be equivalent to at least 30% of typical annual software budgets, but the damages from unrepaired year 2000 problems can top 100% of software budgets, while litigation costs and damages can top several hundred percent.

Time Line for Enterprises Starting Year 2000 Repairs in 1998

Unfortunately a significant percentage of US companies have still not started their year 2000 repairs. Based on recent surveys, I estimate that about 30% of US software companies with year 2000 problems have not yet actually started repairs, but are still in the assessment and awareness phases, or perhaps the triage phase.

Because of the conflict with the European currency conversion work, Western Europe has lagged behind the United States in year 2000 repair work, and a number of companies did not begin even exploratory assessment work or triage until 1997, and some have not yet started. From personal conversations with European consultants who have performed local surveys, and from visits to European conferences, I estimate that about 50% of Western European companies are lagging in year 2000 repairs and will begin serious work only in 1998 (if then).

For companies that don't begin their year 2000 repair efforts until 1998 or later, the probability of a successful completion is low—less than 50% if the year 2000 repair work is treated as a "business as usual" kind of activity. From the time lines of companies that began their year 2000 repairs in 1995, it appears that achieving full year 2000 compliance would normally take about three calendar years, with continued lower levels of work running well into the fourth year. Assuming a late start of January 1998, the only way of raising the probability of completing the year 2000 repair work by the end of 1999 is to deploy all available resources as rapidly as possible. This statement means that a number of unpalatable decisions must be made by top corporate and top software executives:

- There will not be time for date field expansions, so windowing, encapsulation, bridging, or other "masking" approaches will probably be used for most applications and database repairs.
- Year 2000 repairs must be regarded as having higher priority than any other current or planned software project.
- Other software projects must be put on hold, except for emergency updates and statutory repairs.
- The European currency conversion must be suspended until after year 2000 repairs are completed and probably not restarted until about 2005.

As discussed in several places in this book, my analysis of year 2000 repair effort indicates roughly four months of effort for every software professional in most industries, although some enterprises may top nine months of effort. The independent survey done by Dr. Leon Kappelman and his colleagues[1] at the Society of Information Management (SIM) reached a similar conclusion: Year 2000 repairs will cost roughly 30% of the annual budget for a typical information systems organization. These two studies are in general agreement, since four months of effort is roughly equivalent to 33% of a software budget. Because the early and proactive year 2000 repair groups started in 1995 or 1996, they were able to spread their repair efforts over 36 to 48 months without too much disruption of normal software projects, although some have discovered a need to add more people in the final year. For organizations that wait until 1998 to begin, they will need at least the same quantity of total resources, and probably even more since rushed repairs will elevate bad-fix injection rates.

Table 1.2 illustrates the differences in the staffing patterns for year 2000 repairs for a proactive company that started their year 2000 repair work in 1995 versus the staffing pattern for laggards that will begin their repairs in calendar year 1998.

As you can see, year 2000 repairs are likely to absorb all available software personnel except for a small number held in reserve for emergency and statutory repairs. For a 1998 year 2000 repair start time, this

Table 1.2: Staffing Profiles for Early and Late Year 2000 Repairs

Month	Year 2000 Staff for Repairs Starting in 1995	Year 2000 Staff for Repairs Starting in 1998	Difference per Month 1995 vs. 1998
January	5.00%	5.00%	0.00%
February	7.00%	10.00%	3.00%
March	10.00%	15.00%	5.00%
April	12.00%	15.00%	3.00%
May	15.00%	15.00%	0.00%
June	15.00%	25.00%	10.00%
July	15.00%	30.00%	15.00%
August	15.00%	35.00%	20.00%
September	15.00%	40.00%	25.00%
October	15.00%	50.00%	35.00%
November	15.00%	55.00%	40.00%
December	15.00%	60.00%	45.00%
January	15.00%	65.00%	50.00%
February	15.00%	70.00%	55.00%
March	15.00%	80.00%	65.00%
April	15.00%	85.00%	70.00%
May	15.00%	85.00%	70.00%
June	15.00%	85.00%	70.00%
July	20.00%	85.00%	65.00%
August	20.00%	85.00%	65.00%
September	25.00%	85.00%	60.00%
October	25.00%	85.00%	60.00%
November	25.00%	85.00%	60.00%
December	25.00%	85.00%	60.00%
Average	16.00%	55.63%	39.63%

cannot be a "business as usual" kind of project with any hope at all of finishing before the end of the century, because the "normal" year 2000 repair interval is greater than 36 calendar months if staffing averages only about 15% of the available software personnel working within an enterprise.

A Two-Year Calendar for Millennium Software Repairs Starting in 1998

It may be helpful for late starters in year 2000 repairs to glimpse a rough calendar of what needs to be accomplished beginning approximately January 1998. More complete discussions of various activities such as *triage* (dividing applications into sets needing immediate repairs, later repairs, or none at all) are discussed later in the book.

January 1998: Awareness

- Executive year 2000 project manager appointed.
- Year 2000 legal counsel selected.
- Year 2000 project office created and staffed.
- Year 2000 associations joined.
- Year 2000 insurance offerings evaluated.
- Year 2000 tool vendors surveyed.
- Year 2000 World Wide Web links surveyed.

February through March 1998: Triage

- Dormant applications identified.
- Active application repair priorities established.
- Year 2000 damage insurance acquired if needed.
- Director and officer insurance acquired if needed.
- Active application sizing performed.
  - Function point volumes
  - Source code volumes
  - Identification of applications with missing source code
  - Test library volumes
  - Database volumes
- Repair strategies selected for key applications.
  - Already compliant: no repairs necessary
  - Replacement
  - Date field expansion
  - Windowing
  - Bridging

- Encapsulation
- Object code repairs
- Formal year 2000 cost estimate prepared.
- Year 2000 staffing plan prepared.
- Year 2000 tool acquisitions started.
  - Search engines
  - Repair engines
  - Change control
  - Complexity analysis
  - Performance monitoring
- Year 2000 outsource needs evaluated.
- Year 2000 physical system inventory taken (faxes, security, elevators, and so on).
- Preliminary financial disclosure information collected.
- Preliminary legal liability assessment started.

April 1998 through March 1999: Year 2000 Repairs and Replacements

- Software windowing, encapsulation, bridging, and so on performed.
- Software source code date field expanded.
- Software object code date field trapped.
- Test library repaired or replaced.
- New test cases created and tested.
- Databases repaired or replaced.
- All year 2000 repairs unit and component tested.
- Physical system repaired or replaced.
- Bad-fix secondary repairs performed.
- Bad-fix repairs retested.
- Performance monitoring and tuning executed.
- Supplier surveys completed.
- Year 2000 resource and cost data collected.
- Year 2000 tax information collected.
- Second year 2000 financial disclosure data assembled.
- Legal and litigation status evaluated.

April through September 1999: Integration and Regression Testing

- Late repairs continue.
- Bad-fix repairs continue.
- Performance tuning continues.
- New applications with compliant applications are integrated.
- Hardware upgrades and performance tuning are executed.

- New applications undergo regression testing.
- Software integration and regression testing are performed.
- Object code repair regression testing is performed.
- Database integration and regression testing are performed.
- Multicompany regression testing is performed.
- International regression testing is performed.
- Quality assurance report of year 2000 status is prepared.
- Physical equipment replacements are installed.
- Third round of year 2000 financial disclosure data is assembled.
- Legal and liability status is evaluated.
- Post-2000 damage cost estimate is prepared.
- Post-2000 recovery plan is prepared.
- Public announcements of year 2000 compliance are prepared.

October through December 1999: Buffer and Contingencies

- Public announcements of year 2000 status are made.
- Financial disclosure of year 2000 repair costs is presented.
- Tax report on year 2000 costs is prepared.
- Legal and liability assessment of year 2000 status is performed.
- Late repairs continue.
- Bad-fix repairs continue.
- Performance tuning continues.
- Regression testing continues.
- Multicompany testing continues.
- Physical equipment final check is executed.
- Infrastructure final status check is executed.
  - Security systems
  - Telephone companies
  - Electric power companies
  - Manufacturing and assembly plants
  - Transportation systems
- Post-2000 damage teams are identified.
- Post-2000 recovery plans are reviewed.
- Year 2000 damage contact points are published.
  - Mailing address contacts
  - Telephone contacts
  - Email contacts
  - Web site contacts
- External year 2000 contact points are placed on final alert.
  - Clients
  - Suppliers

- Public utilities
- Competitors if applications connect
- Year 2000 damage control team is put on final alert status.

This two-year calendar includes a three-month buffer, which is only prudent. It is very unlikely that an enterprise that does not start its repairs until January 1998 will complete them by the end of 1999, since they are obviously slow moving. It would be irresponsible to plan actual repairs and testing right up to the wire at the end of 1999.

Note that this two-year plan includes very important milestones for financial disclosure of year 2000 costs, and for legal and liability status. Note also that the plan does not stop cold at the end of 1999, but assumes that year 2000 damage control parties will be fully staffed, equipped, and available for around-the-clock deployment if necessary. It would be a serious mistake to assume that 100% of year 2000 problems will be found, and to disband the year 2000 project office and release all year 2000 repair teams until well into the next century.

A One-Year Calendar of Post-2000 Damage Repair and Litigation

Although some enterprises may achieve 100% year 2000 compliance and fix every known instance of the year 2000 problem, the pervasiveness of the year 2000 problem means that there is a strong probability that some latent year 2000 hits will remain unrepaired as of January 1, 2000. This 12-month planning calendar for the aftermath of the year 2000 problem is built on that assumption. Another assumption is that the year 2000 project office will remain fully staffed in January 2000, and that year 2000 damage control parties will be identified and ready to move instantly.

January 2000: Immediate Damage Control

- All critical software systems are monitored for year 2000 compliance.
- All critical database queries are monitored for year 2000 compliance.
- All suppliers and contractors are monitored for year 2000 compliance.
- Physical problems are corrected (elevators, security systems, phones, faxes, and so on).
- Manual backup methods are deployed if needed (check writing, invoices, and so on).
- Emergency year 2000 repairs are executed for undetected problems.
- Year 2000 client-reported problems are corrected.
- Year 2000 subcontractor problems are reported and corrected.

- Year 2000 repair vendors are notified of problems they missed.
- Legal and liability status (your enterprise's own hazards) is analyzed.
- Legal and liability status (damages to your enterprise) is analyzed.
- An analysis of possible tax errors is performed.
- An analysis of billing and accounting errors is performed.
- Post-2000 repair cost estimate is updated.
- Post-2000 insurance claims are analyzed.
- Directors' and officers' liability status is analyzed.

February through July 2000: Damage Assessment and Litigation Filing

- Initial claims are made for damages under year 2000 insurance.
- Possible lawsuits are filed by clients for year 2000 problems.
- Possible lawsuits by shareholders are filed for year 2000 problems.
- Possible lawsuits by employees are filed for year 2000 problems.
- Possible lawsuits by tax authorities are filed for year 2000 problems.
- Possible lawsuits by your company are filed for botched year 2000 repairs.
- Overall liabilities for enterprise, directors, and officers are analyzed.
- Performance monitoring and tuning of applications are performed.
- Temporary repairs (such as encapsulation) are replaced by date field expansion.
- Manual backup methods are phased out if possible.

August through December 2000: Recovery and Replacement

- Litigation disclosures and depositions begin.
- Some companies begin bankruptcy filings.
- Hardware upgrades are deployed to restore lost performance.
- Replacement of "masked" year 2000 repairs with date field expansions continues.
- Overall year 2000 costs are accumulated, with estimates for remaining costs.
- Overall year 2000 costs are disclosed in financial reports to shareholders.
- Some year 2000 repair teams return to other work.
- Some suspended software projects are resumed.

As you can see by the year 2000 planning calendars for 1998, 1999, and 2000, the problem has severe business and legal repercussions as well as being a messy technical problem. The year 2000 repair and damage expenses are likely to be high enough so that many companies will report financial losses during calendar years 1998, 1999, and 2000. This in turn can depress share values, reduce tax revenues, and have other serious implications.

Rules of Thumb for Year 2000 Resource Planning

Accurate cost estimating for year 2000 repairs is extremely complicated since it involves software repairs, database repairs, test library repairs, tool purchases, hardware upgrades, contracts, and a host of other factors. The following *rough* rules of thumb are derived from our clients and from other year 2000 resource reports, and are merely starting points that year 2000 managers can use until they begin to substitute their own data.

- Assume that 50% of the applications in your portfolio are dormant and do not need repairs, and 50% are active applications and do need repairs. (Source: Kendall's[2] studies of dormant applications in eight IBM data centers)
- Assume that the source code is missing or uncompilable for about 15% of the applications in your active portfolio, so either replacement or object code repairs will be necessary. (Source: reports from SPR clients)
- Assume that "dead code," comments and blank lines in your applications for which you should not have to pay repair costs, totals 30% of the total volume of physical lines. (Source: reports from SPR clients)
- Assume that the amount of code in your active applications that needs repair is about 5% of the total code measured in physical lines. (Source: numerous year 2000 code studies such as those of Robbins and Rubin[3])
- Assume that your initial software year 2000 repairs based on the number of lines of code needing repair (5% of the total) will proceed at a rate of 1,500 lines of code per month, or 15 function points per month. (Source: US maintenance productivity rates in *Applied Software Measurement*[4])
- Assume that you will need at least one full time year 2000 repair specialist for every 5,000 function points (roughly 500,000 source code statements) in your active portfolio if you had 36 months in which to accomplish year 2000 repairs.[4] As the elapsed time passes, your staffing needs will rise accordingly. If you start year 2000 repairs in 1998 you will need one full-time repair specialist for approximately every 3,000 function points (roughly 300,000 source code statements) in your active portfolio.
- In the absence of "data point" metrics, assume that your database repairs and your source code repairs will take roughly the same amount of effort—in other words, one month of database repair work for every month of software repair work. (Source: reports from SPR clients)

- Assume that true date field expansion for databases is so complex that alternatives such as data duplexing or bridging are the most common strategies for year 2000 database repairs. (Source: numerous reports such as Kendall's[5] analysis)
- Assume that testing and regression testing your year 2000 repairs will each take about 60% as much effort as the repairs themselves, and more than half of the calendar time. (Source: Lefkon's[6] testing analysis)
- Assume that bad fixes will approximate 10% of your initial defect repairs, and hence the repairs will have to be redone. (Source: analysis of bad-fix injection rates during maintenance[7])
- Assume that 10% of your year 2000 test cases are incorrect and will need to be repaired. (Source: analysis of test case and test library errors reported by SPR clients[7])
- Assume that your year 2000 repairs will be about 95% efficient, but that 5% of the total possible number of year 2000 "hits" will be missed before the end of the century, and will not be discovered until *after* the year 2000. (Source: analysis of defect removal patterns among SPR clients[7])
- Assume that year 2000 repairs will degrade application performance and throughput by 10% to 20% unless performance monitoring, careful tuning, and extensive testing are used to regain performance. (Source: independent studies by Programart, Rubin Systems, and Software Productivity Research [SPR][8])
- If your enterprise average for software compensation levels is about $60,000 per year, expect your year 2000 repair costs to run from $0.25 to $1.00 per physical line of code. This is equivalent to $25 to $100 per function point. (Source: numerous year 2000 cost reports such as ViaSoft's[9])
- If you outsource your year 2000 repairs to a contractor, expect your year 2000 repair costs to run from $1.00 to $2.50 per physical line of code. This is equivalent to $100 to $250 per function point. (Source: numerous year 2000 cost reports such as Viasoft's[9] or Gartner Group's[10])
- Assume that year 2000 repairs will require about four months of effort on the part of every software professional in your enterprise. Expressed another way, assume that year 2000 repairs will cost about 30% of your annual software budget. (Source: independent studies by SPR and SIM[1])
- Assume that the damages, litigation, and recovery costs from unrepaired year 2000 problems in software and databases will cost about $3.00 to more than $20.00 per physical line of code. (Source: SPR and Giga Group[11] year 2000 aftermath and litigation estimates)

- Do *not* assume that any cost data about year 2000 repair costs will be accurate for your enterprise unless the data uses the same compensation rates, burden rates, and work pattern assumptions that your enterprise uses. This is an obvious fact and does not require a specific source of information.

Once again, these rules of thumb are not safe for serious year 2000 estimating purposes, but are included for the benefit of year 2000 project managers and enterprise executives who are seeking some kind of general guidance about potential resources for dealing with year 2000 issues.

References

1. Kappelman, Leon A., et al. *How Much Will Year 2000 Compliance Cost?* Version 2.12. Denton, TX: College of Business Administration, University of North Texas, May 30, 1997.
2. Kendall, Robert C. "Management Perspectives on Programs, Programming, and Productivity." In *Programming Productivity—Issues for the Eighties,* edited by Capers Jones, 201–211. Los Angeles: IEEE Computer Society, 1981.
3. Robbins, Brian, and Howard Rubin. *The Year 2000 Planning Guide.* Pound Ridge, NY: Rubin Systems, Inc., 1997.
4. Jones, Capers. *Applied Software Measurement.* 2nd ed. New York: McGraw-Hill, 1996.
5. Kendall, Robert C. "Year 2000: How to Make the Problem Smaller; How to Make it Bigger." *American Programmer* 10 (June 1997): 25–28.
6. Lefkon, Dick, ed. *Year 2000: Best Practices for Y2K Millennium Computing.* New York: Association of Information Processing Professionals (AITP)—SIG Mainframe, 1997.
7. Jones, Capers. *Software Quality—Analysis and Guidelines for Success.* Boston: International Thomson Computer Press (ITCP), 1997.
8. Shea, Brian. "Report on the Performance Impact of the Year 2000 Problem." *IBM Enterprise Systems Journal* (December 1996): 31.
9. Viasoft, Inc. *Viasoft Year 2000 Cost Analysis.* Phoenix: Viasoft, Inc., 1996.
10. Hall, B., and K. Schick. *The Year 2000 Crisis—Estimating the Cost.* Stamford, CT: Gartner Group, 1997.
11. Testimony of Ann Coffou, Managing Director of Giga Information Group, before the US House of Representatives Science Committee. March 20, 1997. Testimony available at http://www.policy.gsa.gov/mks/yr2000/hearing.htm.

2 Origins of the Year 2000 Problem

I N POPULAR detective-story fiction, it is well known that poisons such as arsenic accumulate slowly in the body. Tiny doses, each harmless in itself, can slowly accumulate until the victim perishes. In some ways, the year 2000 software problem resembles the slow accumulation of arsenic. For many years, software applications have been built with two-digit fields for year dates. Year by year these two-digit fields have been accumulating in software packages all over the world. The time is rapidly approaching when the slow and steady accumulation of these date fields will cause the applications containing them to perish, and it may be that some companies will perish with them! Unfortunately this is not harmless fiction but the real world.

Since fiscal years are often decoupled from calendar years, even before the end of calendar year 1999 many applications will stop or will begin to produce incorrect results. Already in 1996 some credit card companies with cards that are valid for five years have encountered the year 2000 problem.

The year 2000 problem will not stop abruptly in the year 2000 either. Continuing costs can be anticipated at least through 2005 and some will probably run even further. The postyear 2000 expenses will consist of (1) fixing obscure year 2000 instances that were missed prior to the end of the century, (2) repairing bad fixes that accidentally introduced new errors, (3) frantically completing new applications that were intended to replace aging legacy software but were not finished prior to the end of the century, (4) performing hardware upgrades and retuning of applications with performance that was degraded by hasty repairs, and assessing (5) litigation expenses for the host of anticipated year 2000 lawsuits.

Computers and hardware devices will be affected by the year 2000 problem since their internal clocks contain built-in calendar functions.

Computers and software now drive the main operating components of every major company, government, and military organization in the world. Therefore the year 2000 problem is very likely to be one of the most expensive single problems in human history. There are four major aspects of the costs of the year 2000 problem that need to be considered.

1. The costs of finding and fixing the year 2000 problem in millions of aging software applications. These costs can be apportioned into the costs for finding the myriad locations of the date fields, the costs of fixing or masking the date fields, and the costs of testing the fixes to ensure that no other damage has occurred during the repairs.

2. The costs of the litigation that will result when the problem is not fixed. This second year 2000 cost component will run well into the twenty-first century and will probably far exceed the direct costs of repairing the problem itself.

3. The continuing costs for running applications that halt frequently, no longer execute efficiently, and degrade data center operations. These are likely to be long-term continuing problems that can degrade data center throughput and software execution speed by 20% or more. This problem may exist well into the twenty-first century since many companies may be careless about testing applications after year 2000 repairs are made and even more lax about monitoring performance or reoptimizing the applications.

4. The costs associated with business failures, bankruptcies, and damages to national economies as a direct result of the year 2000 impact on the computers and software that contain vital business information.

One surprising aspect of the year 2000 problem is that some benefits can be envisioned as well as costs. Once the problem is fixed, enterprises will have far better data dictionaries than ever before. They will also have a much better understanding of the size, age, and complexity of their software portfolios and databases. In particular, organizations will begin to know how much of the contents of their portfolios are active applications, and how many applications are dormant or have stopped being used altogether.

Another benefit is that enterprises will learn much more about their future software needs and the costs of both building and maintaining software than they know today. An unexpected byproduct of the year 2000 problem is that software may finally become a commodity with tangible economic aspects.

Recall that major disasters such as the San Francisco fire and the Tokyo earthquake led to significant improvements in architecture and construction so that buildings are now much safer than they were prior to these disasters. It is likely that software applications constructed after the year 2000 crisis will be much safer and more stable than those built in the past. Just as earthquakes and other natural disasters tend to destroy unsafe structures, the year 2000 problem will probably destroy or eliminate a host of poorly structured and poorly maintained applications because it is impossible to change them.

Root Cause of the Year 2000 Problem: Conservation of Storage Space

Many articles have been written on why the year 2000 problem will occur, so it is only necessary to include a brief background discussion here. The root cause can be traced back to the early days of computers, when information was stored on punch cards. Data storage was so limited and so expensive that any method that could save storage was readily adopted. Since no one in the 1950s or 1960s had any idea how long software would last, it seemed natural to store dates in two-digit form. This method was convenient and seemingly effective.

Indeed, during the era of punch cards, paper tape, low-density magnetic tape, and direct access devices with limited storage, the two-digit date formats saved surprisingly large amounts of money. The costs of storage were so high in that era and the use of dates is so common that Dr. Leon Kappelman[1] has calculated that the accrued savings of the past 30 years and the current year 2000 repair costs are roughly commensurate. His calculations indicate that four-digit rather than two-digit dates might have raised the total volume of tape and disk space required by perhaps 3% during an era when this kind of storage was extremely costly.

It is unfair to blame computer programmers for the year 2000 problem, even though it is the presence of the problem in computer programs that is troublesome. The year 2000 problem actually originated as an explicit requirement by clients of custom software applications and the executives responsible for data centers as a proved and seemingly effective way of saving money. Many programmers knew that the clock would run out on the two-digit format at the end of the century, but when the two-digit format became a standard that situation was more than 30 years in the future. Even the proposed four-digit standards for date formats are not fully adequate, since the International

Standards Organization (ISO) format and the Microsoft date standard are incompatible, and neither recognizes the other's date format as a valid alternative.

Here too, unconscious attempts to conserve storage are causing problems. By adding an extra digit to both the ISO and Microsoft date formats, both could be accommodated by using the extra digit as a key (shown as "x" in the examples) to identify whether the ISO date format (x-yyyy-mm-dd) or the Microsoft date format (x-mm-dd-yyyy) was intended. The key could also identify other alternatives, such as the normal European date format (x-dd-mm-yyyy).

Using an extra digit as a key with, for example, these three meanings would make identifying which date format is intended a lot less messy than the current situation, in which any of the date formats might be used with no easy way of knowing which format is intended. The proposed date format key is:

1 = ISO date format
2 = Microsoft date format
3 = normal European date format

With the emergence of optical storage, the number of digits used for dates (or anything else) is becoming a trivial matter, yet most of us in the software world learned our trades when conservation of storage mattered a great deal, so we have unconsciously caused long-range problems for the software industry simply by not assigning enough space for information.

As another example of field size causing date problems, on January 18, 2038, yet another date crisis will occur when the UNIX operating system and the C programming language internal date representations expire. UNIX stores dates in terms of the number of seconds accrued after January 1, 1970. Four bytes of storage are used, and in January 2038 the number of seconds will hit the maximal value and hence the UNIX second counter will start over again at 0. Here, too, the root cause of the problem is conservation of storage by using only four digits. Using six digits instead of four would have extended the useful UNIX and C date life for many thousands of years, but the use of four digits will cause another mass migration of dates in less than 40 years. Unfortunately, in 1997, almost no one is paying any attention to this problem because it is more than 40 years away, even though it will be a problem of the same magnitude as the current year 2000 problem.

When the current two-digit date requirement actually became a US military and government standard, even programmers who knew that problems might occur were constrained by the standards to use the two-digit form. It is plainly not very effective to raise concerns about problems that won't occur until long after all of the executives and clients who might repair the situation have retired.

When magnetic storage was first introduced, the cost of data storage declined slightly but the early tape- and disk-based systems still were limited in capacity. Also, many card-based systems were transferred to tape or disk. The original versions of the source code and the two-digit date logic continued to be used since there was no immediate reason to change it.

By the late 1970s and early 1980s it started to be noted that software applications were sometimes having remarkably long lives. For example, IBM's MVS operating system was approaching 20 years of age, as were a number of other widely used applications. Some tremors of alarm about date limits began to show up, but there was still no immediate serious alarm since the end of the century was 20 years away. (However, a few far-sighted organizations recognized that the two-digit date format would necessitate such massive changes that they began to phase in conversion to the four-digit form as early as 1984.)

It was not until the early 1990s and the advent of optical storage that data storage costs declined to such a level as to be almost irrelevant. The early 1990s would have been the best time for addressing the year 2000 problem, but for sociological reasons the human species is not very effective in disaster prevention. Unfortunately, by the 1990s, quite a significant amount of the damage had long been done. Millions of applications with two-digit date fields had already been written and many of them were in daily use throughout the world. Many other kinds of fields are also artificially limited, such as fields for salaries, tax rates, inflation, or any other kind of information that attempts to model real-world phenomena.

Hazardous Implications of the Year 2000 Problem

Quite a bit has already been written about the kinds of applications that are going to be affected by the year 2000 problem. Suffice it to say the problem is not restricted to aging legacy applications. The year 2000 problem is also common in modern personal computer applications, and even embedded in the hardware of both mainframes and personal computers themselves! Any software package that uses dates or has calendar routines as embedded functions is likely to be affected by the year 2000 problem. Some common applications that will have to be modified include:

- Software with long-range calculations such as mortgages, life insurance premiums, interest compounding, pension payments, and social security benefit calculations
- Software calendar utility functions in commercial spreadsheets such as Lotus, Excel, Quattro, and many others (Some spreadsheets can move past the year 2000 problem, but their calendars cannot handle dates past 2075.)
- Calendar applications embedded in personal information managers and hand-held devices as well as those in personal computers
- Software on board commercial and military aircraft, weapons systems, and satellites
- Computer operating systems that use calendar and clock routines
- Software that controls telephone switching systems
- Much of the embedded software in physical devices such as software that affects badge-lock security systems, computerized personal identity security systems, aircraft navigation devices, computer-controlled medical instruments, computer-controlled manufacturing lines, and computer-controlled traffic systems.

The most serious implications are the litigation consequences of the failure of calendar routines. Many important financial applications will be affected. Worse, some of the consequences may even threaten human lives and safety. At least six kinds of potential litigation can be envisioned as a byproduct of the year 2000 problem:

1. Litigation filed by clients whose finances or investments have been damaged
2. Litigation filed by shareholders of companies whose software does not safely make the year 2000 transition
3. Litigation associated with any deaths or injuries derived from the year 2000 problem
4. Class-action litigation filed by various affected customers of computers or software packages
5. Litigation filed by companies who used outsource vendors, contractors, consultants, or commercial year 2000 tools but year 2000 problems still slipped through and caused damage
6. Litigation against hardware manufacturers, such as computer companies and defense contractors, if the year 2000 problem resides in hardware or embedded microcode and software

The end of the twentieth century is likely to be a very hazardous time for many executives, and for almost all software executives. Any executive who is in a position of fiduciary responsibility should by now be taking energetic actions to solve the year 2000 problem. These same executives should also be in discussion with their legal counsel regarding the probable liabilities that they and their companies will be facing from now until well into the twenty-first century.

Governments are not immune from the year 2000 problem. All government agencies associated with revenues such as state and federal tax agencies are probably going to have major year 2000 problems. This is also true of agencies such as social security that deal with benefits. (Governments can be sued, as can individual government executives.)

While the national government will be the most greatly affected by the year 2000 problem in terms of the volume of changes needed, the host of state, provincial, and local government bodies that use computers are likely to be damaged also. It can be anticipated that major errors are likely to occur in a variety of governmental applications dealing with welfare, unemployment, taxation, and even mundane accounts payable and receivable. A very likely byproduct of the year 2000 problem will be sharp increases in local taxes to defray some of the year 2000 expenses.

Although the military implications of the year 2000 problem are not widely discussed in the software press, the on-board computers in many weapons systems, ships, tanks, and military aircraft are going to be affected by the year 2000 problem. Logistics systems and various command, control, and communication (C^3) systems will also be affected. A very serious concern on the part of military computer systems experts is that the year 2000 problem will create so many surface problems with C^3 software that terrorist or foreign intelligence organizations could use the year 2000 chaos as a cover to penetrate sensitive systems while some of their protective methods are out of service or behaving erratically. Since the US military services are far and away the most automated and computerized armed forces in the world, the US Department of Defense will be facing one of the largest military expenses in human history.

Beneficial Implications of the Year 2000 Problem

Since the magnitude of the year 2000 hazards are so enormous, most of the software literature has focused on the negative side of the problem.

Surprisingly there will be some significant benefits associated with solving the year 2000 problem.

Most companies do not really know how much software they currently own and do not even have a clue as to how much software they truly need. Even worse, most companies do not know how many of the applications they own are active and still being used, or dormant and simply taking up space because there is no effective mechanism for retiring unused applications. These statements are true of databases and information owned by enterprises. Also, both databases and legacy applications tend to be added in a patchwork fashion in response to random but urgent needs. In addition, very few enterprises have really effective data dictionaries and some do not even know how many databases they own. As a result, two of the most vital and expensive business commodities of world history—software and data—have no solid economic understanding.

To solve the year 2000 problem and minimize the hazards, enterprises will be forced to develop a very detailed inventory of their software applications and databases. In addition, it will be necessary to develop a very detailed, enterprisewide data dictionary. Therefore, as companies begin to solve the year 2000 problem, they will find that they have much better knowledge and control over their software than they have ever had before. Within a few years after the end of the century, the companies that have solved their year 2000 problems will be in a very strong position to plan new applications and align their software and data assets with their business strategies.

Other Problems that Have the Same Origin as the Year 2000 Problem

Unfortunately the year 2000 problem is really only the tip of the iceberg. Date fields are not the only kinds of fields that were arbitrarily truncated to save space. Many applications also have trouble with financial calculations, name fields, and other kinds of information because not enough space was allocated when the applications were built. Although the situation is not recognized as an immediate problem, the historical attempts to save on computer tape and disk storage have created very weak and imperfect architectures for databases and data warehouses.

As stated, it is primarily due to storage costs during the 1960s that data transactions destroy the past value of a record when updates are made. For example, if your salary jumps from $7,500 a month to

$8,000 a month the new value will replace the old value in your company's salary database. The past value is either destroyed or removed from the active portion of the database to a remote archive facility. This method of destructive updating is embedded in database architectures, and means that analytical processes involving changes over long time periods are remarkably hard to do using computers and databases, because so many of the past values are not easily accessible. With optical storage it would be much better to keep the past data and simply add the new data to the same file, so that a continuous stream of changing values would be available.

This approach of nondestructive data updates would use large amounts of storage, but with storage costs dropping so low and volumes of storage becoming so large, this is no longer a topic of major concern. Nondestructive updates of data records would open up entirely new forms of data warehousing and on-line analytical processing (OLAP) dealing with rates at which data changes over various time periods.

Much of the difficulty in finding year 2000 instances in software is due to the fact that programming language designers were seeking to minimize storage size of both source and executable software. The next generation of compilers should be designed to create maps of data elements used within programs. Further, both programming languages and database tools could be designed so that expanding the field sizes allotted to various kinds of data, such as dates or names, could be accomplished at will.

It would also be useful for programming environments to include *dead code maps,* since leaving old code in applications after changes is a common practice. Also, programming language environments should include the same kind of search-and-replace logic capabilities now offered in word processing tools.

Another useful feature would be to include a *run history catalog* for every program and system owned by an enterprise. This catalog would record basic facts about every application such as the date of first deployment, dates of updates, features added, run frequency, date of last execution, hardware platforms and versions, applications that provide data, applications that detail where data is sent, security, languages and compiler versions used for creation, and so forth.

Even more useful information, which is very hard to find today, would be to include a *service history catalog* for every software application. This catalog would record the numbers and severity of defects found and repaired in the application. (Since this kind of repair information is kept by many automobile owners for their cars, you can see how useful it would be to have a complete service record.)

Since software is also a taxable asset from the point of view of the Internal Revenue Service (IRS) and many other tax agencies, these catalogs of basic application information could also record the acquisition or development costs as well as subsequent modification costs. In addition, the size of software applications in terms of both function points and various forms of code counts (for example, executable statements, data declarations, comments, blank lines, dead code, and so on) should become standard information items associated with every software package in the world. (Note that in the United States the Internal Revenue Code [IRC] may even make year 2000 repairs taxable if they are shared among the divisions of large corporations. Refer to Chapter 5 for additional information.)

Another kind of useful information that could be kept with every major software application is the numbers and kinds of test cases created and used. It would be very useful to correlate the service histories of software applications with the test case histories. Indeed, this data could lead quickly to much more efficient testing than has been the norm to date.

Software and databases are actually among the most expensive assets that corporations own. It is now time to recognize that fact and provide the same kind of asset protection methods to software and data that enterprises use for other expensive assets such as machine tools, fleets of vehicles, test instruments, and the like. In fact, software and databases are currently the only corporate assets for which basic information such as date of acquisition, service histories, and other significant facts are not recorded! The root cause of this failure to record basic asset information can be assigned to the historical need to conserve storage space when software was first entering the business domain.

It is possible that when the immediate crisis of the year 2000 problem is past, both software and databases created after the end of the twentieth century should be far better structured and more robust than software typically created before the end of the twentieth century.

Fallacies Associated with the Year 2000 Problem

Problems of the magnitude and seriousness of the year 2000 problem are difficult to encompass mentally, and hence many executives are in what psychologists call the *denial phase*—asserting that the problem is not really going to occur. The software trade press has alternated between denial and exaggeration of the problem, with some articles asserting that the year 2000 problem will blow over, while others assert that the problem is severe enough to trigger a business depression and cause bankruptcy of a significant percentage of US corporations.

One major fallacy is that there is no particular hurry associated with seeking out and fixing the year 2000 problem. Unfortunately, the year 1996 was the last year in which "average" programmers working without sophisticated automation could have had a reasonable chance of finding and fixing the year 2000 problem in a typical mid-size corporate portfolio of 500,000 function points. Roughly, October 1997 is the last time at which even specialists with automated search engines have a high probability of finding, fixing, and testing the year 2000 problem in a typical 500,000-function point corporate portfolio and finishing prior to midnight on December 31, 1999. This statement assumes a "business as usual" approach with year 2000 staffing rising no higher than 15% of total software employment.

If a company lags in starting their year 2000 repairs until calendar year 1998, the only real but slender hope of finishing in time is to adopt unusual methods such as suspending almost all other work and deploying about 85% of available resources, bringing in contractors, moving to 24-hour-a-day repair work, or abandoning date field expansions and using only various masking approaches as temporary repairs.

The year 2000 problem is very serious and will certainly affect many businesses that depend on computers and software. Some business failures will probably occur, especially among mid-size financial and insurance companies that have lagged in beginning their year 2000 repairs.

The US software industry is also likely to suffer, and the year 2000 problem may be advantageous for countries such as India and the Ukraine, which have a large surplus of software talent that could be applied to either fixing the year 2000 problem or to outsourcing other kinds of work while US software personnel are mired down in year 2000 repairs.

The most dangerous fallacy has been assertions made by the press that the year 2000 problem will be solved primarily by scrapping aging legacy applications that embody the year 2000 problem and replacing them with modern applications that are year 2000 compliant, such as moving from conventional mainframe software to more modern client-server replacement applications.

A quick look at average software development schedules illustrates why these assertions are sheer folly (Table 2.1). As this book is written

Table 2.1: *Average Software Development Schedules in Terms of Calendar Months*[a]

Size (function points)	End User	MIS	Outsource	Commercial	System	Military	Average
1	0.05	0.10	0.10	0.20	0.20	0.30	0.16
10	0.50	0.75	0.90	1.00	1.25	2.00	1.07
100	3.50	9.00	9.50	11.00	12.00	15.00	10.00
1,000	0.00	24.00	22.00	24.00	28.00	38.00	27.20
10,000	0.00	48.00	44.00	46.00	47.00	64.00	49.80
100,000	0.00	72.00	68.00	66.00	78.00	85.00	73.80
Average	0.68	25.64	24.08	24.70	27.74	34.05	27.00

[a]Table 2.1 is from the second edition of my recent book *Applied Software Measurement*.[2] It shows the US averages for six software subindustries for six size plateaus, each of which is an order of magnitude apart. Size is expressed in terms of function points and ranges from 1 function point to 100,000 function points.

MIS = management information system.

it is now mid 1997. The only applications that could be built and deployed between now and the end of 1999 are those that are less than about 2,000 function points in size, and this size margin is reduced at a rate of about 50 function points with every month that passes, starting in January 1997. Thus, by June 1997 the maximal probable replacement size will be down to about 1,700 function points.

Note that any software development project larger than about 2,000 function points that starts in the late summer or early autumn 1997 will probably not be completed until sometime after the year 2000 problem has already occurred. Indeed, for every day that passes the maximal size of software applications that could be completed by the end of 1999 goes down. By the end of 1997, for example, the maximal size would be only 1,000 function points rather than 2,000 function points.

Numerically, software applications less than 2,000 function points in size comprise about 65% of the applications with year 2000 problems, while the other 45% are larger than 2,000 function points. However, in terms of the work effort needed, the situation is reversed. About 65% of the effort for year 2000 repairs will be expended on larger systems in excess of 2,000 function points. Indeed, some applications with year 2000 problems are in the size range of 100,000 function points and would take more than 10 years to redevelop. (A simple rule of thumb for determining approximate software development schedules is to raise the size of the application in function points to the 0.40 power. This gives the number of calendar months from the start of deployment until delivery.) In other words, none of the major software applications in either the United States or the rest of the world can be replaced between now and the end of the century. You have to fix the year 2000 problem in your current applications, like it or not.

Another fallacy associated with the year 2000 problem is that it can be solved by simply buying software that is already compliant or by merging with another company that has software that is year 2000 compliant. This approach may work in a few rare cases, but it is not an effective overall solution to the year 2000 problem. Further, there are many kinds of software for which neither packages nor mergers are possible, such as weapons systems, defense applications, municipal and provincial government software, embedded software in physical devices such as medical instruments, and a host of other kinds of software for which there is no alternative but to fix the year 2000 problem.

The year 2000 problem is an interesting example of a problem that exerts a strong psychological and sociological impact as well as having a technical impact. No doubt the year 2000 software problem will serve as the basis for many masters and doctoral theses in psychology and sociology in the twenty-first century.

References

1. Kappelman, Leon, and Phil Scott. "Accrued Savings of the Year 2000 Computer Problem." In *Year 2000 Best Practices for Y2K Millennium Computing,* edited by Dick Lefkon, 103–104. New York: AITP—SIG Mainframe, 1997.
2. Jones, Capers. *Applied Software Measurement.* 2nd ed. New York: McGraw-Hill, 1996.

3 | Terms and Concepts Associated with the Year 2000 Problem

*T*O EVALUATE THE magnitude of the year 2000 problem it is necessary to start with some basic terms and definitions, of which seven terms are critical to the understanding of what follows. (See also the glossary for definitions of supplemental and specialized terms associated with the year 2000 problem.)

1. Application
2. Software portfolio
3. Database
4. Software staff
5. Enterprise
6. Software sites
7. Test libraries

These terms will be used often as the year 2000 problem is discussed, so it is well to begin with an understanding of what they mean.

Application

In the context of the year 2000 problem the term *application* is the general term for both individual computer programs and also the term for linked sets of programs that comprise larger entities termed *systems*. Software applications range in size from less than 10 function points at the low end to more than 100,000 function points for large systems such as defense applications.

Software applications that deal with calendar data can have a few to many hundreds of specific calendar calculation routines that will require modification and repair. Examples of applications that might be affected by the year 2000 problem include payroll applications, banking and financial applications dealing with interest calculations, and government applications dealing with taxes or social security. However, since modern software applications share data with other applications, the year 2000 problem must also be considered at the level of *all* software owned by an enterprise.

In the context of the year 2000 problem, two factors are beginning to emerge that were not well understood in the past: (1) dormant applications and (2) dead code. The phrase *dormant applications* refers to applications that reside in an enterprise's production library, but that are no longer run or executed. A study by Kendall[1] of eight IBM data centers found that roughly 50% of IBM's software consisted of dormant applications. Obviously these applications do not need immediate year 2000 repairs.

The phrase *dead code* refers to code segments left in software after changes are made. For example, sometimes repairs are made such as eliminating "go to" statements in software. The programmers are not sure that their updates will work correctly, so they routinely leave in the old code in case the new changes fail. However, the old code is cut off from the rest of the application in the sense that there are no longer entry points into the dead segments. This phenomenon is very important in a year 2000 context because many year 2000 vendors are charging on a "cost per line of code" basis, and it is folly to spend money fixing year 2000 hits in dead code that is no longer part of the current application's logic.

Software Portfolio

In general use the term *portfolio*, when applied to software, is defined as the total volume of software owned by an enterprise regardless of whether the software was purchased, leased, or built by the enterprise itself. In the context of the year 2000 problem, this basic concept has some implications that need to be considered.

First, the software that enterprises built for their own use is assumed to be where the bulk of their work will be performed for fixing the year 2000 problem. Presumably the vendors of software packages will be responsible for fixing the year 2000 problem in their commercial offerings. Therefore the portfolio sizes discussed here are the estimated sizes of the applications built and owned by the enterprises themselves. Thus a software portfolio for a bank or financial institution would consist of the specialized front office, back office, and automatic teller software that the bank has constructed or contracted for its own use. Other software used by the bank, such as commercial products like Microsoft Excel or Lotus Notes, is assumed to be the responsibility of the vendor for making year 2000 repairs.

Another aspect of software portfolios is that they should be segmented into "active" and "dormant" portions. As enterprises grow and business needs change, it often happens that software applications stop being used. However, these applications are usually not removed from the enterprise portfolio. Over time, a surprising number of these dormant applications can accumulate. In a year 2000 context, it is quite important to try and separate the dormant applications from the active applications before commencing year 2000 repairs. Obviously there is no need to make year 2000 repairs to dormant applications that may never be used again.

Unfortunately most companies do not keep very good records of active versus dormant status, so an early part of the year 2000 analysis is to try and identify these dormant applications. This is particularly important if a year 2000 outsource vendor will be doing the year 2000 repairs, because otherwise your enterprise may be charged for repairing dormant applications, which is such an obvious waste of money that it may well cause negative audit reports.

One assumes that the year 2000 problem will be fixed in a single master copy of an application, regardless of how many additional copies exist. For example, this book was written using Microsoft Word for Windows version 6.0. The Microsoft word product is approximately 5,000 function points in size. A large corporation might own a thousand copies of such a product. However, for studying the year 2000 problem it can be assumed that if the problem is fixed once, the fix will be valid for all copies of the product. Therefore in this book the phrase *portfolio size* is defined as the volume of a single copy of each application owned by the enterprise.

Under the single-copy definition most large corporations will own between 250,000 and 1,000,000 function points per site as the sum of one copy of each of their software applications. If each duplicate or all copies were considered, then the volume of software might be 500 to 2,500 times larger. However, for dealing with aspects of the year 2000 problem such as finding the affected areas and repairing them, I assume that the work will take place on only one master version of each application.

An invisible component of software portfolios are applications built by end users such as accountants or engineers. These applications are usually kept on personal computers and, except for the developers, they may not be visible to the professional software organizations of the enterprise. However, some of these end-user applications are used for business purposes and are affected by the year 2000 problem.

The end-user aspect of the year 2000 problem is going to be difficult to accommodate. Fortunately, end-user applications are almost always less than 100 function points in size and even large corporations seldom have more than a few hundred of them. This means that as a percentage of corporate portfolios, end-user applications will probably not amount to much more than 1% of the total volume of software affected.

Database

In addition to software applications, modern enterprises own enormous quantities of information with about half of it stored in computerized database systems. To conserve expensive magnetic storage, many databases use two-digit date-recording fields and hence are subject to the year 2000 problem. Not only must repairs be made to software, but it will also be necessary to make repairs to many computerized databases. (Information stored on paper is more or less immune to the year 2000 problem.) However, database repairs are among the most complicated aspects of the entire year 2000 problem. First, there is no data point metric, so most companies have no idea how much data they own. Second, actually expanding date fields in databases can be prohibitively expensive. Therefore most of the database repairs will probably use some form of masking, such as developing date "windows" that will convert incoming and outgoing dates into values less than 1999.

Also affected under the general heading of databases are data warehouses, repositories, data mining, OLAP, and the transmission of data back and forth between companies, and between companies and governmental groups. The data implications of the year 2000 problem are quite severe, and unless they are resolved the worst-case scenario could be to shut down or damage some critical databases and, for practical purposes, to put an end to things like data mining and OLAP for an indefinite period.

As can be seen from the fact that there are no current data point metrics, the fundamental technologies associated with large-scale collections of on-line data are still fairly primitive. Indeed, one of the unexpected benefits of the year 2000 problem may well be to create entirely new forms of data representation, new data point metrics, and other technological improvements. Ever since the use of computers for information storage began, database methods have striven to conserve storage space more than any other goal. As a result, database records are usually truncated and stripped to the bare essentials. For example, the entire method of updating records is destructive, since each time a value changes the old value is destroyed. This form of destructive updating was developed to conserve storage space, but imposes severe limits on the usefulness of data itself. There is no convenient way to look at trends over time, because all past values are either missing or relegated to archival storage, where access is inconvenient.

Kendall, whose work is often cited in this book, has long recommended a concept called *extended records,* which not only eliminates destructive updating but includes additional information with stored data, such as the identity of the program that created the data, the date of last update, the programs authorized to use the data, and other relevant factors.[2] The rationale for Kendall's view is that using computerized storage merely to record the current values of changing data is an arbitrary limitation developed to conserve expensive storage and is no longer necessary now that optical storage methods are reducing storage costs toward zero.

Hopefully, when the immediate trauma of the year 2000 problem is behind us, database architects and vendors will examine the fundamental issues associated with on-line storage of information, and will develop new forms of databases and data warehouses based on preserving changes rather than destroying them, thus opening up important new kinds of data analysis.

Furthermore, the lack of any kind of size metric for database volumes, and the lack of any way of normalizing the numbers and severities of data errors, indicates that there is an urgent need for developing data point metrics similar in structure and usefulness to the software function point metrics.

Software Staff

Large, modern software development organizations can have more than 100 specialized occupations in their total software employment: programmers, analysts, quality assurance administrators, database administrators, testing specialists, technical writers, and so on. (For additional information on software specialization, refer to *Patterns of Software Systems Failure and Success.*[3]) Since the year 2000 problem is more than just a programming problem, the data shown in this book is based on the total complement of the technical workers employed by software producers. Of the professional software personnel employed by major corporations, the occupations that will be most greatly affected by the year 2000 problem are:

- Attorneys
- Data center managers
- CIOs
- Computer operations personnel
- Configuration control specialists
- Cost-estimating specialists
- Customer support specialists
- End users who use software
- End users who program their own software
- Database administrators
- Maintenance specialists
- Network managers
- Programmers
- Programmers/analysts
- Quality assurance personnel
- Systems programmers
- Systems administrators
- Systems analysts
- Testing specialists
- Year 2000 consultants
- Year 2000 project managers
- Year 2000 specialists

My SPR colleagues and myself estimate that the total number of professional software personnel in the United States is about 1,920,000, but the number of nonprofessional personnel who can write end-user applications is about 8,000,000. These "invisible" end-user applications are going to be very troublesome for the year 2000 problem even though they may be small in size.

Enterprise

In this book the general term *enterprise* is preferred over the more restricted terms *company* and *corporation* because many of the groups that are affected by the year 2000 problem are government agencies, nonprofit associations, and even religious groups. In the context of the year 2000 problem, an enterprise is an organization that is assumed to own software. Examples of enterprises can include corporations such as IBM, government agencies such as the IRS (at the federal level), or the State of Florida's Bureau of Motor Vehicles. An enterprise can also be a military unit such as the Navy's Surface Weapons centers, or even a religious organization such as the Genealogical Division of the Church of Latter Day Saints.

Since software often resides on computers at each site, there is an assumption that some repair work will be necessary at each site. Of course there are also networked applications on a single host that operate at multiple sites. This is one of the reasons why a careful inventory of portfolios is necessary. One major technical challenge of the year 2000 problem is the fact that enterprises are now linked together electronically. For example, an automobile manufacturer may have direct computer communications with more than 500 subsidiaries and suppliers. Thus the year 2000 problem will extend horizontally across more than individual enterprises. Entire industries are going to be affected.

Software Sites

Most large enterprises such as corporations and government agencies are geographically dispersed. For example, during the time that I worked for IBM there were 26 major IBM programming laboratories scattered around the world. During the time that I worked for ITT, that multinational conglomerate had software development groups in no less than 50 cities. In the context of the year 2000 problem, it can be assumed that repairs will take place at every major site owned by an enterprise. Therefore it is necessary to make assumptions as to how many sites exist for typical enterprises.

It can be assumed that large corporations in the Fortune 500 class will typically average about 15 sites or locations where software is developed and maintained. However, really large enterprises such as IBM, Andersen, Electronic Data Systems, Lucent, Siemens-Nixdorf, and the like, can approach 30 or more discrete sites where year 2000 repairs might occur.

Test Libraries

Since the year 2000 problem originated as an explicit requirement rather than as an accidental coding problem, it was not detectable during ordinary testing. Indeed, test cases usually *enforced* the incorrect two-digit date format if they did anything at all to date fields! The implications of having huge libraries of regression test cases, all of which seek to enforce a two-digit year 2000 date field, has not been reported in the year 2000 literature. Indeed, this phenomenon was not added to this manuscript until the fifth iteration in January 1997.

Regression test libraries throughout the world probably contain an average of three test cases for every function point in major software applications. While not all of the test cases deal with dates, I estimate that about 20% of them do. This means that the effort devoted to repairing and upgrading test libraries will not be trivial, and the overall effort might approximate 15% of the effort fixing the code itself.

Not only do existing test libraries need to be repaired, but an additional suite of year 2000 test cases must also be produced. The function point metric has started to be used as a tool for predicting test case volumes, since each of the five main elements of function point metrics require testing (inputs, outputs, inquiries, logical files, and interfaces). Although the data is still evolving and uncertain, a preliminary value for using function point metrics for sizing year 2000 test cases can be hypothesized. Assume that it will take one year 2000 test case for every 25 function points in your corporate portfolio. Thus if your company owns 100,000 function points you might need about 4,000 year 2000 test cases. (More detailed estimates for testing various kinds of year 2000 repairs are discussed later in Chapter 6.) This ratio of year 2000 test cases is only a working hypothesis and will need to be refined as more empirical data becomes available. However, the fact that function points can be used for predicting test case volumes is well established— it is the number of test cases for the year 2000 problem that is uncertain.

Another issue of year 2000 testing has not yet surfaced in the literature: errors in year 2000 test cases themselves. Studies of the error density of test libraries by IBM, and queries among SPR's clients, indicate a surprising finding. Test cases often have more errors or defects than the software that is being tested! The implications of this discovery can have a significant impact on year 2000 testing, which will probably be the most expensive activity of the year 2000 repair work. If 5% to 10% of the newly created year 2000 test cases are themselves in error, the impact will have two results: (1) testing costs will be raised and (2) some year 2000 problems may escape due to test case errors.

References

1. Kendall, Robert C. "Management Perspectives on Programs, Programming, and Productivity." In *Programming Productivity—Issues for the Eighties,* edited by Capers Jones, 201–211. Los Angeles: IEEE Computer Society, 1981.
2. Kendall, Robert C. Unpublished communication from Robert Kendall to the author. August, 1983.
3. Jones, Capers. *Patterns of Software Systems Failure and Success.* Boston: International Thomson Computer Press, 1996.

Function Points versus Lines of Code Metrics for the Year 2000 Problem

THE FIRST STEP in exploring the economic consequences of the year 2000 problem is to construct an approximate inventory of the total volume of software installed and operational in the United States and then use the US data as a jumping off place for evaluating the hazards of other countries. This is not an easy task and probably cannot be done with high precision, but by making some reasonable assumptions it is possible to accomplish.

Although some research organizations such as the Gartner Group have attempted to enumerate the costs of the year 2000 problem using the lines of code or LOC metric,[1] this metric is not accurate enough for serious economic analysis of software problems. It is surprising that so many organizations would attempt large-scale economic analyses using a metric known to be flawed and hazardous. It is even more surprising that all major software benchmark studies now use function point metrics.

In fact neither the function point metric nor the LOC metric is capable of dealing with all economic manifestations of the year 2000 problem. Neither LOC nor function points work for normalizing problems in databases or dealing with hardware upgrades, nor are they good metrics for dealing with the repairs needed to regression test libraries. Also, neither LOC nor function points can be used for the many aging legacy applications for which the source code is missing and no longer available. Indeed, for active applications with missing source code it can only be suggested that the applications be replaced, or that one or more methods of solving the year 2000 problem in object code will be perfected in time to be used, although this is not a safe assumption.

While LOC-based measuring and estimating methods served the software community well for many years, they are rapidly dropping from use because software technologies have changed so much that it is difficult and even dangerous to apply them under some conditions. For example, many legacy applications have substantial volumes of dead code left over from past repairs. Year 2000 service vendors who base their charges on cost per line of code are reaping windfall profits from things like dead code and dormant applications.

Further, the usage of the LOC metric obviously assumes the existence of some kind of procedural programming language where programmers develop code using some combination of alphanumeric information, which is the way languages such as COBOL, C, FORTRAN, and hundreds of others operate. However, the development of Visual Basic, and its many competitors such as Realizer, has changed the way many modern programs are developed. Although these visual languages do have a procedural source code portion, quite a bit of the more complex kinds of "programming" are done using button controls, pull-down menus, visual worksheets, and reusable components. In other words, programming is being done without anything that can be identified as a line of code for measurement or estimation purposes. Also, the object-oriented programming languages and methods such as Objective C, SMALL-TALK, Eiffel, and the like, with their class libraries, inheritance, and polymorphism, have also entered a domain in which attempting to do year 2000 estimates using conventional LOC is not a very effective approach.

As the twentieth century ends, the volume of programming done using languages for which the LOC metric no longer works well for estimating purposes is increasing rapidly. By the end of the century perhaps 30% of the new software applications will be developed using either object-oriented languages, visual languages, or both. Hopefully these new applications in languages in which the LOC metric does not work will be year 2000 compliant. However, it would not be too surprising to see entirely new software applications that still include two-digit date logic.

Over and above the fact that the LOC metric is difficult to apply to many modern programming languages, there are far-reaching and serious economic problems with attempting to use LOC metrics for measurement and estimation purposes. Most of the important kinds of software that have year 2000 problems, such as operating systems, billing systems, aircraft navigation systems, word processors, spreadsheets, and the like, are quite large compared with the size of applications built

20 years ago. Twenty years ago a programming application of 100,000 LOC was viewed as rather large. Even IBM's main operating system, OS/360, was only about 1,000,000 LOC in size during its first year of release, although the modern incarnation (MVS) now tops 10,000,000 LOC. Today, a size of 100,000 lines of code is more or less an entry-level size for a modern Windows 95 application. Many software packages can top 250,000 LOC, while things like major operating systems are in the 10,000,000 LOC and greater domain. For large applications, coding costs are not the major driver.

For large systems, programming itself is only the fourth most expensive activity.[2] The three higher cost activities cannot really be measured or estimated effectively using the LOC metric. Also, the fifth major cost element, project management, cannot be estimated or measured easily using the LOC metric. The rank order of large-system software cost elements is:

1. Defect removal (inspections, testing, finding and fixing bugs)
2. Paper document production (plans, specifications, user manuals)
3. Meetings and communication (clients, team members, managers)
4. Programming
5. Project management

As you can see, the usefulness of a metric such as LOC, which can only measure and estimate one out of the five major software cost elements, is a significant barrier to economic understanding. Because of the many requests for correlating SPR year 2000 data based on function points and Gartner Group year 2000 data based on LOC, an example of both forms is provided later in this book. However, the example is valid only for a selected set of programming languages. There is no convenient way of using LOC across all programming languages in a way that creates valid economic conclusions.

Function Points and Programming Languages

As of 1996, the SP Research catalog of programming languages[3] identifies almost 500 programming languages in current use. For some of the languages that are affected by the year 2000 problem, there is not an accurate definition of what a line of code is in that language. For example, it is very difficult to enumerate LOC for languages such as query-by-example, the control functions of Visual Basic, spreadsheets such as Lotus and Excel, database languages, and a host of others. Even for procedural languages such as COBOL and FORTRAN there are wide variations in how LOC are counted. A survey of software journals that I carried out found that about one third of the software literature used physical lines as the basis for determining LOC, one third used logical statements, and the remaining third did not identify which method was used. Since the difference between the number of physical lines and logical statements in a COBOL program can amount to more than 300%, you can see that the ambiguity associated with using LOC is far too great for serious economic study.

For the data in this book the well-known function point metric is used. Function point metrics originated in the 1970s within IBM and have become the most widely used metric in the software world. The International Function Point Users Group (IFPUG) is the largest software measurement association in the United States, and there are affiliated associations in some 20 countries.

The function point count of a software application is based on enumerating five external attributes of the application:

1. Inputs
2. Outputs
3. Inquiries
4. Logical files
5. Interfaces

These five attributes are assigned various weighting factors, and there are also adjustments for complexity. The actual counting rules assumed here are based on the version 4.0 counting practices manual published by the IFPUG[4] in 1995. Because some readers may be unfamiliar with the function point metric, it is useful to show the relationship between function points and LOC for various languages using the rules for logical statement counts defined in *Applied Software Measurement*.[2] Table 4.1 illustrates why LOC metrics are difficult to apply to general software economic issues that span multiple programming languages. There are hundreds of programming languages and they vary in power over an enormous range. (See Appendix D for a more complete list of languages involved in the year 2000 problem.)

Computer literacy is very common in the United States, and end-user applications constitute a large but invisible component of the year 2000 problem. For software that was done by professional software personnel the software usually resides in a formal corporate portfolio, often under formal configuration control. End-user applications, on the other hand, typically reside on the hard drives of personal computers in

Table 4.1: Ratios of Logical Source Code Statements to Function Points for Selected Programming Languages

Language	Nominal Level	Source Statements per Function Point		
		Low	Mean	High
Basic assembly	1.00	200	320	450
Macro assembly	1.50	130	213	300
C	2.50	60	128	170
BASIC (interpreted)	2.50	70	128	165
FORTRAN	3.00	75	107	160
ALGOL	3.00	68	107	165
COBOL	3.00	65	107	150
CMS2	3.00	70	107	135
JOVIAL	3.00	70	107	165
PASCAL	3.50	50	91	125
PL/I	4.00	65	80	95
MODULA 2	4.00	70	80	90
ADA 83	4.50	60	71	80
LISP	5.00	25	64	80
FORTH	5.00	27	64	85
QUICK BASIC	5.50	38	58	90
C++	6.00	30	53	125
Ada 95	6.50	28	49	110
Database	8.00	25	40	75
Visual Basic (Windows)	10.00	20	32	37
APL (default value)	10.00	10	32	45
SMALLTALK	15.00	15	21	40
Generators	20.00	10	16	20
Screen painters	20.00	8	16	30
SQL	27.00	7	12	15
Spreadsheets	50.00	3	6	9

someone's office and are under no configuration control at all. Other than the originator of the application, it may be that no one in the company even knows of the existence of the software. Yet some of these privately developed end-user applications are used for important business purposes within the enterprise.

Support for finding and fixing the year 2000 problem will be much tougher for some languages than for others. Assembly language applications will probably be the toughest, because many date calculations are hard to find since they are performed using register manipulation. Another language that may be difficult in year 2000 terms is PL/I. IBM was pushing the PL/I language very hard as a business tool in the early

1970s, and several industries such as oil and energy began to adopt PL/I. As of 1996, however, there is a shortage of tools for analyzing PL/I programs and a shortage of trained PL/I programmers. But as this book was being written several vendors announced expanded year 2000 support that includes PL/I among other languages. This support is welcome, but of course still does not compensate for the lack of experienced PL/I programmers on a global basis.

Other programming languages that manifest the year 2000 problem but have a current shortage of available tools or trained programmers available include ALGOL, APL, BASIC, CHILL, CMS2, CORAL, FORTH, LISP, MODULA, MUMPS, PASCAL, Prolog, Ratfor, RPG, and a host of proprietary languages that companies have built for their own use, such as ITT's ESPL/I and IBM's PLS. The language that probably has the highest incidence of year 2000 calculations is COBOL, since this is a very old language (dating back to the 1960s) and it is widely used for business applications. Although COBOL accounts for about 60% of management information systems software, the COBOL language is seldom or never used for systems software, weapons systems, embedded software, and many other technical applications. As a result, while COBOL is, numerically, the language with the greatest year 2000 exposure, COBOL applications may only comprise 30% or so of the entire universe of applications needing year 2000 repairs. The C and C++ languages are at almost the same level as COBOL, and in third place is the Assembly language. However, COBOL has the most plentiful supply of year 2000 tools and services of any language. Indeed, from a scan of the advertisements in software journals it appears that COBOL may have more year 2000 support than all the other languages put together.

The Volume of US Software Expressed in Terms of Function Points

By interesting coincidence each reference to a calendar date in a software application seems to require approximately one function point to encode in quite a large variety of programming languages. This coincidence makes expressing the effort and costs in terms of work hours per function point, function points per staff month, and cost per function point comparatively straightforward.

In terms of languages that are affected by the year 2000 problem, these languages are probably the top of the heap in year 2000 impact, and are listed in Table 4.2 in order of the numbers of applications in US software portfolios as of 1996.

Table 4.2: Impact of the Year 2000 Problem for Selected Languages

Language	Programmers	Applications	Function Points
COBOL	550,000	12,100,000	605,000,000
Spreadsheets	600,000	3,600,000	54,000,000
C	200,000	2,600,000	156,000,000
Basic	250,000	2,250,000	45,000,000
Query	150,000	1,950,000	29,250,000
Database	200,000	1,600,000	120,000,000
C++	175,000	1,400,000	105,000,000
PASCAL	90,000	1,080,000	54,000,000
Assembly	50,000	750,000	93,750,000
Ada83	90,000	720,000	54,000,000
FORTRAN	50,000	575,000	28,750,000
PL/I	30,000	270,000	13,500,000
Jovial	15,000	105,000	7,875,000
Other	1,000,000	7,000,000	336,000,000
Total	3,450,000	36,000,000	1,702,125,000

Note that Table 4.2 reveals a hidden aspect of the year 2000 problem. There are only about 1,920,000 professional software personnel in the United States, but Table 4.2 shows a total of 3,450,000 programmers. The reason that the total for programmers is so large is that it includes applications developed by nonprofessional programmers such as accountants, managers, and engineers.

Mixed-Language Applications and the Year 2000 Problem

One other aspect of the year 2000 problem that has not yet received adequate attention is that of dealing with applications that contain multiple programming languages. Among SPR's database of information covering about 7,000 software projects, roughly 2,000 of them contain more than one programming language. Mixed-language applications are very common among all classes of software: systems, military, information systems, and commercial. Some of the more common programming language combinations include:

- Ada and CMS2
- Ada and Jovial
- Basic and Assembly
- C and Assembly

- C and C++
- C++ and Assembly
- COBOL and database languages
- COBOL and PL/I
- COBOL and RPG
- COBOL and SQL
- COBOL and SQL and database languages

About 30% of US software applications contain at least two languages, based on our clients' portfolios. The maximal number of programming languages that we have observed in a single system is 12. It is hard enough to find and fix year 2000 problems for applications containing only one language; those containing multiple languages will be even harder.

When multiple programming languages are used for an application, many of the year 2000 search engines come to a halt. These engines are keyed to a specific language such as COBOL, but may not be able to deal with applications where COBOL, RPG, and perhaps other languages are all part of the same package. Thus for these mixed-language applications, the search for year 2000 hits may have to drop back to very labor-intensive manual approaches rather than high-speed automated approaches.

Although the data is preliminary (Table 4.3), rough rules of thumb can be hypothesized for the additional effort of finding and fixing year 2000 problems in mixed-language applications. Hopefully the vendors and service bureaus that are now gearing up to perform year 2000 repairs will be able to handle mixed-language applications for at least the more common combinations such as COBOL and SQL.

Table 4.3: Impact of Multiple Programming Languages on Year 2000 Repair Efforts

No. of Languages in Application	Percent Increase in Year 2000 Repair Efforts
1	0%
2	15%
3	20%
4	25%
5	30%
6	35%

A Year 2000 Repair Case Study

Because of the enormous shortage of empirical data on year 2000 repairs, it is of interest to step through a case study to clarify some of the cost elements of year 2000 repairs at the activity level. Let us assume that we have a COBOL application of 1,000 active logical source code statements in the data and procedure divisions, using round numbers. This example is exaggerated somewhat to highlight a few of the common size variations that can occur.

Let us assume that our programming staff earn an average of $5,500 per month or $66,000 per year. To this we will add a monthly burden rate of $2,900 per month or $34,800 per year. Thus our total burdened compensation rate is $8,400 per month or $100,800 per year. (These amounts are not uncommon, but they were selected because they yield an even $50 per hour and hence simplify the example.) The nominal number of work hours in a typical month is roughly 168. (However in real life, coffee breaks, meetings, classes, and other factors reduce the number of effective work hours per month to about 132.) Using this value and a nominal monthly burdened compensation rate of $8,400, our hourly costs are exactly $50 per hour.

Table 4.4 illustrates some of the possible size differences between counting logical statements and physical lines.

The first troublesome aspect of this case study from a year 2000 cost point of view is the fact that the size of the application using physical LOC is more than twice as large as the size of the application using logical statements, if you deal only with the data and procedure divisions. The number of gross physical LOC totals 2,500, while the number of active logical statements in the active portion of the application is only 1,000. Note that there are 100 logical statements of dead code that no doubt also reside in the procedure division, but dead code should not be counted for productivity or economic purposes.

Although COBOL averages about 106.7 source code statements in the procedure and data divisions per function point, in this example let us assume an even 100 source code statements per function point. Therefore this example is assumed to be exactly 10 function points in size. However, when the ratio of function points to physical LOC is calculated, our 10 function points are equivalent to 2,400 lines, or a ratio of 240 physical lines per function point. This, of course, is more than twice the ratio based on logical statements, and illustrates why *back-firing* (converting source code values into function point values) is not

Table 4.4: Sample COBOL Application Showing Sizes of Code Divisions

Division	Logical Statements	Physical Lines
Identification division	25	25
Environment division	75	75
Data division	300[a]	350
Procedure division	700[a]	950
Dead code	100	300
Comments	200	700
Blank lines	100	100
Total	1,500	2,500
Date References		
Identification division	2	2
Environment division	0	0
Data division	30	30
Procedure division	30	50
Comments	0	0
Total	62	82

[a]SPR's code-counting rules for COBOL enumerate only logical statements in the procedure and data divisions for productivity purposes. These rules are specified in Appendix A of *Applied Software Measurement.*[2]

recommended when physical LOC are the starting point. The portion of the code containing date references comprises only 62 logical statements, so the total function point size associated with date logic is only a fraction of a function point, or 0.62 function points.

Let us now consider in this sample application the amount of work, in hours, that your in-house programming staff might devote to year 2000 repairs (Table 4.5). Note that the cost per function point and cost per logical statement columns are based on the entire application. However, if you count only the 62 source code statements that actually contain year 2000 date references, the costs would be $645 per function point, or $6.45 per logical statement. This practice is rare, and most year 2000 repair costs are normalized to the entire application rather than only to the affected portions. This is because two of the three cost elements—searching and testing—involve all active code. Only the repairs themselves involve just the affected code.

Assuming personnel who are conversant with the application (such as the programmer who originally wrote the code), if you were to do this year 2000 repair project internally the total costs might be $400,

Table 4.5: Internal Year 2000 Search, Repair, and Test Effort and Activity Cost

Activity	Hours	Costs	Costs per Function Point	Costs per Logical Statement
Searching for year 2000 hits	2.00	$100	$10	$0.10
Recoding date fields to four digits	2.00	$100	$10	$0.10
Testing year 2000 repairs	4.00	$200	$20	$0.20
Total	8.00	$400	$40	$0.40

which as you can see is equivalent to about $40 per function point or $0.40 per logical statement. If you were to submit this project to a year 2000 service provider or outsourcer, their normal pricing structure is based on gross physical LOC in the entire application. Since the case study contains 2,400 physical LOC, you are in for a fairly large bill, as noted by year 2000 cost reports such as those of the Gartner Group,[1] Viasoft,[5] Robbins and Rubin,[6] Kappelman and colleagues,[7] as well as this book. Assuming that their charges were a more or less average $1.50 per gross physical LOC, your bill would amount to $3,600 or roughly nine times higher than your costs if you do the work yourself.

In recent months a number of year 2000 service providers have stated in software magazines that their business has not grown as fast as they planned, although the vendors tend to place the blame on clients and assert that the clients are lagging in their year 2000 repairs. It is true that many companies are slow in getting started on year 2000 repairs, and hence will probably miss the deadline. However there is another problem that year 2000 outsourcers have caused for themselves. What many of our leading clients are actually doing are keeping the year 2000 repairs in house, because the typical year 2000 outsource vendor price structure based on the gross total physical LOC is deemed unfair and unjustified by the more astute year 2000 project managers. Adding to the dismay of year 2000 project managers, the portions of the application that have nothing whatsoever to do with the year 2000 problem (such as comments and dead code) are included in the vendor pricing structure.

In this small and admittedly somewhat exaggerated example, the dead code amounted to 300 physical lines and the comments to 700 physical lines. This means that a total of 1,000 physical lines will be included in the vendor's charge scheme at a rate of $1.50 per line, or $1,500 in all. It is no wonder that year 2000 service providers are not finding their business growing as fast as they anticipated. With this kind of questionable pricing practice, they may not have any business at all for much longer. This kind of situation is very troubling to those who are examining the year 2000 problem.

The situation will become even more troublesome when it is scaled up to the full portfolio level. Many corporations own in excess of 500,000 function points or more than 50,000,000 logical source code statements. When a portfolio of this magnitude is viewed in terms of gross physical lines, it can total more than 125,000,000. At a typical rate of $1.50 per gross physical LOC, the total costs for year 2000 repairs using external contractors could exceed $187,500,000, while doing the same work in house might be accomplished for perhaps $35,000,000.

As stated several times, this case study tends to exaggerate the situation to illustrate why year 2000 cost estimating is a complex task. For example, if your in-house personnel are novices or unfamiliar with the application, then the search-and-repair effort could easily be twice what is shown here. On the other hand, if you have acquired year 2000 search engines and year 2000 repair engines, then the search activity might take only a few minutes, and the manual repairs, over and above the repairs done automatically, may take less than an hour. Testing is still going to be expensive however.

Further, if your year 2000 problems reside in languages such as Assembly or C, which are more difficult to scan than COBOL, then your search time could be longer. This is also true for applications with mixed languages, on which automated search engines may not work. Conversely, if you are dealing with an offshore outsourcer with low labor costs, or with an outsourcer that excludes comments and dead code, the outsource costs could also be much lower than shown here. However, the published rates for in-house year 2000 repairs generally run from about $0.25 to $1.00 per logical source code statement (roughly $25 to $100 per function point), while the external outsource repairs for the year 2000 problem generally run from about $1.00 up to $2.50 per source code statement (roughly $100 to $250 per function point). The pricing differentials between in-house year 2000 work and contracted year 2000 work are so unbalanced that many sophisticated corporations are avoiding the domestic outsource vendors for year 2000 repairs and are either doing the work themselves or making business arrangements with offshore vendors in India, the Ukraine, the Czech Republic, or some other country where labor costs and overhead costs are low.

Correlating the Gartner Group LOC Data and the SPR Function Point Data

Because the two primary sources of year 2000 cost data use different metrics and were developed using different assumptions, many organizations have requested information about how the data published by the Gartner Group[1] in terms of cost per line of source code correlates with the data published here in terms of cost per function point. Neither the LOC metric nor the function point metric can handle every aspect of the year 2000 problem, such as database repairs. Therefore both the Gartner Group data and the SPR data must be viewed as having large margins of error. Further, since the initial reports on year 2000 costs, both the Gartner Group and SPR have revised their original cost figures. Interestingly, the revisions of both companies are in an upward direction overall, with the Gartner Group noting increased difficulties among their clients, while SPR is beginning to include post-2000 damages and recovery costs.

For an interesting analysis that attempts a detailed correlation of both the Gartner Group report and the data shown in this book, Keith Jones' recent book, *Year 2000 Crisis Solutions*,[8] shows points of similarity and points of difference. For topics where the Gartner Group and SPR deal with the same cost elements, such as source code date field expansions, these two independent studies are often in close agreement. They differ in the activities that are included in the bottom-line costs.

It is possible to convert data based on logical source code statements into an equivalent amount of function points by means of a mathematical conversion approach called *backfiring*. Indeed, both SPR and one of the Gartner Group subsidiaries, Real Decisions, perform backfiring from LOC data to function point data as normal parts of their software assessment and benchmark service offerings. Allan Albrecht, the inventor of function point metrics, is actually one of the pioneers of the backfiring method, which originated in the mid 1970s. Although backfiring from a starting point of physical LOC is sometimes used, it is not as reliable as backfiring from the starting point of logical statements. There are too many random patterns associated with physical lines for that method to generate repeatable results.

In addition to different interpretations of code volume, the year 2000 problem will also require many different kinds of repair activities.

The topic of activity-based costing is very relevant to the year 2000 problem. The year 2000 problem has a number of unique and complicated aspects, and only if cost estimates and cost measurements drop down to the level of specific activities will the data be accurate enough for serious economic analysis purposes.

As stated, the year 2000 problem is likely to be the most expensive set of software changes and updates in human history, and accurate cost collection is mandatory for dealing with this problem. The problem is far too complex a topic for manual cost-estimating methods if it is viewed in its entirety. For example, the full set of year 2000 repairs can include all of the following activities at both the corporate and individual project levels:

Corporate-level Year 2000 Activities

- Overall software portfolio analysis
- Overall database analysis
- Overall hardware and microcode analysis
- Subcontractor year 2000 compliance effort
- Executive involvement in year 2000 status
- Taxes paid for reusable year 2000 solutions
- Legal preparation for possible year 2000 lawsuits

Application- or Project-level Year 2000 Activities

- Year 2000 software repairs for specific applications
- Year 2000 software replacements for specific applications
- Retuning software to recover lost performance
- Year 2000 database repairs
- Year 2000 test library repairs
- Year 2000 test case creation
- Year 2000 test case execution
- Year 2000 bad-fix repairs

The economic analysis of the year 2000 problem is made even more complex by the fact that for two of the three main components that need repairs, there is no standard metric for determining size. There is no data point metric or any test point metric for dealing with sizes of databases and test libraries. In this book, the phrase *equivalent function points* is used simply to provide a very rough indicator of the relative volumes of these three artifacts:

1. Software—function points
2. Databases—equivalent function points
3. Test libraries—equivalent function points

The chart of accounts for dealing with the year 2000 problem is very complex, since some of the work takes place against the entire portfolio, while other activities take place only against the portions of the portfolio that are affected by the year 2000 problem.

A *Case Study of Year 2000 Repair Activities*

Rather than merely point out differences and similarities between the Gartner Group LOC and SPR function point approaches, it is better to illustrate both LOC costs and function point costs in a case study. The case study selected is for a mid-size manufacturing organization with a portfolio of 100,000 function points or more than 11,000,000 source code statements in a variety of programming languages. (COBOL, Assembly, Natural, RPG II, SMALLTALK, and SAS are representative of the mix of languages that organizations may have in their software portfolios.) The company in question is assumed to have a total software population of about 250 managers and technical workers, a total employment of about 2,500 managers and workers, and is assumed to support a community of about 25,000 clients. As you can see, these numbers are merely an order of magnitude apart, although the ranges are not uncommon.

Let us first analyze the expense pattern prior to the year 2000 itself, using the concept of activity-based costing. Knowing only the overall costs of year 2000 repairs is not granular enough for serious budgeting or economic analysis. It is necessary to consider the actual work steps that must be performed. Table 4.6 illustrates a very hypothetical year 2000 chart of accounts and rough repair data for dealing with a 100,000-function point software portfolio, plus a collection of databases that might approximate 110,000 equivalent function points. In addition, Table 4.6 assumes that 10,000 regression test cases will need to be updated and about 24,000 new test cases will need to be created to deal with the overall year 2000 repair effort. Table 4.6 has too high a margin of error to be used for any purpose other than ensuring that topics such as test case repairs, bad fixes, and database repairs are not accidentally omitted. Some of the overall assumptions for Tables 4.6 and 4.7 are that the enterprise in question has a total employment of about 2,500 people and a software employment of about 250 personnel.

Table 4.6 presents a very complex chart of accounts because it includes four different kinds of work and combines five general occupational groups.

Table 4.6: Activity-Based Chart of Accounts for Year 2000 Repairs

Assumptions	Overall Portfolio[a]	Year 2000 Repairs[a]	Language	FP	LOC per FP	LOC
Burdened monthly compensation level	$10,000	$10,000	COBOL	57,000	107	6,099,000
Burdened hourly compensation level	$76	$76	Assembly	20,000	213	4,260,000
Size in FPs	100,000	8,000	Natural	9,000	53	477,000
Source statements per FP	114	114	RPG II	7,500	58	435,000
Size in source code statements (LOC)	11,440,500	915,240	SMALLTALK	3,500	21	73,500
Database size (equivalent FPs)	110,000	11,000	SAS	3,000	32	96,000
Year 2000 test cases (equivalent FPs)	10,000	24,000	—	100,000	114	11,440,500

Activities	Year 2000 Staff	Effort (mo)	Schedule (mo)	Burdened Costs	Net Cost per FP	Net Cost per LOC
Year 2000 insurance	—	—	—	$2,000,000	$20.00	$0.17
Corporate portfolio analysis	10.00	66.67	6.67	$666,667	$6.67	$0.06
Corporate database analysis	11.00	73.33	6.67	$733,333	$7.33	$0.06
Year 2000 executive involvement	6.67	50.00	7.50	$500,000	$5.00	$0.04
Subtotal	16.67	116.67	7.00	$1,900,000	$19.00	$0.17

Continued on next page

Table 4.6: Activity-Based Chart of Accounts for Year 2000 Repairs, continued

Activities	Year 2000 Staff	Effort (mo)	Schedule (mo)	Burdened Costs	Net Cost per FP	Net Cost per LOC
Repairing year 2000 problems in software	20.00	266.67	13.33	$2,666,667	$26.67	$0.23
Masking year 2000 problems in software	16.00	53.33	3.33	$533,333	$5.33	$0.05
Creating new year 2000 test cases	16.00	80.00	5.00	$800,000	$8.00	$0.07
Testing year 2000 repairs in software	20.00	177.78	8.89	$1,777,778	$17.78	$0.16
Retuning software to regain performance	16.00	106.67	6.67	$1,066,667	$10.67	$0.09
Repairing year 2000 bad fixes in software	20.00	26.67	1.33	$266,667	$2.67	$0.02
Year 2000 software project management	2.67	35.56	13.33	$355,556	$3.56	$0.03
Subtotal	20.67	746.67	36.13	$7,466,667	$74.67	$0.65
Regression test library year 2000 analysis	5.00	13.33	2.67	$133,333	$1.33	$0.01
Repairing year 2000 problems in test cases	5.00	33.33	6.67	$333,333	$3.33	$0.03
Testing year 2000 repairs to test libraries	5.00	20.00	4.00	$200,000	$2.00	$0.02
Repairing year 2000 bad fixes in test cases	5.00	6.67	1.33	$66,667	$0.67	$0.01
Year 2000 test library project management	1.00	10.00	10.00	$100,000	$1.00	$0.01
Subtotal	6.00	83.33	13.89	$833,333	$8.33	$0.07

Continued on next page

Table 4.6: Activity-Based Chart of Accounts for Year 2000 Repairs, continued

Activities	Year 2000 Staff	Effort (mo)	Schedule (mo)	Burdened Costs	Net Cost per FP	Net Cost per LOC
Repairing year 2000 problems in databases	16.92	366.67	21.67	$3,666,667	$36.67	$0.32
Testing year 2000 repairs in databases	14.67	183.33	12.50	$1,833,333	$18.33	$0.16
Repairing year 2000 bad fixes in databases	14.67	27.50	1.88	$275,000	$2.75	$0.05
Year 2000 database project management	2.20	55.00	25.00	$550,000	$5.50	$0.05
Subtotal	17.62	632.50	35.90	$6,325,000	$63.25	$0.58
Total year 2000 repairs	43.28	1,579.17	36.49	$18,525,000	$185.25	$1.64

[a]Assume 132 work hours per staff-month at an average monthly salary of $5,000 and a burden rate of 100%.

FP = function point; LOC = lines of code.

Work Categories in Table 4.6

1. The work of corporate portfolio analysis
2. The work of repairing software applications
3. The work of repairing test libraries
4. The work of repairing databases

Occupational Groups in Table 4.6

1. Executive effort
2. Year 2000 project management effort
3. Technical staff programming effort
4. Test personnel effort
5. Database administration effort

To create this table at all, some simplifying assumptions had to be made. For example, the sizes of the database and test library parameters are expressed in terms of a synthetic metric called *equivalent function points* because there are no standard metrics for sizing either databases or test case volumes. In addition Table 4.6 also includes one activity, year 2000 insurance, that has a rather high cost but no staff effort assigned, since purchasing insurance is a financial transaction rather than a development activity. However, given the fact that year 2000 insurance is not inexpensive, it is appropriate to include the cost. Table 4.6 is merely an example of the preyear 2000 cost elements and does not cover all possible postyear 2000 expenses such as hardware upgrades, legal expenses, or the direct costs of reissuing materials such as paychecks, bonds, and annuities that were calculated incorrectly.

After the dawn of January 1, 2000, quite a number of other year 2000 expenses will continue for several years. Table 4.7 illustrates an expense pattern for the same enterprise, but takes the view that these expenses will occur in the aftermath of the year 2000 problem to deal with the latent errors and recovery processes. Table 4.7 is highly speculative and obviously has a large margin of error. However, some of the underlying assumptions (Table 4.7) are valid even if the quantification of those assumptions is suspect or in error.

Table 4.7: Post-2000 Recovery and Litigation Expenses

Assumptions	Overall Portfolio	Post-1999 Repairs
Software portfolio (FPs)	100,000	800
Software portfolio (source code)	11,440,500	91,524
Database (equivalent FPs)	110,000	1,100
Regression tests (equivalent FPs)	10,000	3,400
Legal staff	5	5
Suppliers/subcontractors	75	25
Total software personnel	250	0
Internal users affected	2,500	375
External users affected	37,500	5,625

Activities	Year 2000 Staff	Effort (mo.)	Schedule (mo.)	Burdened Costs	Net Cost per FP	Net Cost per LOC
Executive involvement	6.67	66.67	10.00	$666,667	$6.67	$0.06
Computer/hardware upgrades	0.00	0.00	0.00	$1,000,000	$10.00	$0.09
Subtotal	6.67	66.67	10.00	$1,666,667	$16.67	$0.15
Internal damage recovery	126.67	126.67	1.00	$1,266,667	$12.67	$0.11
Subcontractor damage recovery	126.67	126.67	1.00	$1,266,667	$12.67	$0.11
Subtotal	253.33	253.33	1.00	$2,533,333	$25.33	$0.22

Continued on next page

Table 4.7: Post-2000 Recovery and Litigation Expenses, continued

Activities	Year 2000 Staff	Effort (mo.)	Schedule (mo.)	Burdened Costs	Net Cost per FP	Net Cost per LOC
Post-1999 "hot line" customer service	6.25	75.00	12.00	$750,000	$7.50	$0.07
Post-1999 year 2000 repairs	2.67	32.00	12.00	$320,000	$3.20	$0.03
Post-1999 year 2000 masking	1.60	5.33	3.33	$53,333	$0.53	$0.00
Year 2000 recalls/ recovery	22.50	160.71	7.14	$1,607,143	$16.07	$0.14
Warranty and goodwill activities	11.25	112.50	10.00	$1,125,000	$11.25	$0.10
Subtotal	17.71	385.55	21.77	$3,855,476	$38.55	$0.34
Litigation preparation	7.50	75.00	10.00	$750,000	$7.50	$0.07
Litigation	11.25	281.25	25.00	$2,812,500	$28.13	$0.25
Actual damages	—	—	—	$56,250,000	$562.50	$4.92
Punitive damages	—	—	—	$112,500,000	$1,125.00	$9.83
Awards from countersuits	—	—	—	–$135,000,000	–$1,350.00	–$11.80
Insurance payments	—	—	—	–$3,855,476	–$38.55	–$0.34
Subtotal	13.13	356.25	27.14	$33,457,024	$334.57	$2.92
Total post-2000 expenses	28.43	1,061.80	35.00	$41,512,500	$415.13	$3.63
Total year 2000 repairs	43.28	1,579.17	36.49	$18,169,444	$181.69	$1.61
Total pre/postyear 2000 repairs	71.71	2,640.96	71.49	$59,681,944	$596.82	$5.24

FP = function points; LOC = lines of code.

The expenses illustrated in Table 4.7 are assumed to start early in the year 2000 and will continue until perhaps several years have gone by. These assumptions are unproved, but are probably realistic. It is obviously alarming that the year 2000 expenses in Table 4.7 that occur *after* the end of 1999 may actually be larger than that the year 2000 expenses shown in Table 4.6 which occurred *before* the end of the century. The major assumptions made in producing the data used in Table 4.7 are the following:

- Not all year 2000 repairs will be made by January 1, 2000.
- Some year 2000 repairs will inject fresh bugs or will be classified as bad fixes.

- Some year 2000 repairs will degrade software performance and throughput.
- Some retuning of applications must occur to recover performance.
- Some new computers must be acquired to recover performance.
- Some internal operations will be damaged by missed year 2000 problems.
- Some customer relations will be damaged by missed year 2000 problems.
- The company illustrated in Table 4.7 will be sued by at least one client.
- The company illustrated in Table 4.7 will sue at least one subcontractor.
- The company illustrated in Table 4.7 will have taken out year 2000 insurance.

The largest costs and the most questionable assumptions are those involving litigation. If the company in question is not sued, and does not sue any other company, then the postyear 2000 expenses will drop below the preyear 2000 expenses. Regardless of the high margin of error in Table 4.7, it does contain a strong warning that year 2000 expenses will not stop abruptly with the turn of the century and may well continue into the next century for a period of some years.

As you can see from these tables, detailed charts of accounts that reach the levels of activity-based cost analysis provide the most useful method for dealing with complex software economic issues such as the year 2000 problem. The data in Table 4.7 is alarming enough so that it might be appropriate to consider the best-case scenario for the year 2000 situation. The best-case scenario for resolving the year 2000 problem would be as follows:

- One hundred percent of year 2000 repairs are made on time or early.
- The bad-fix rate for year 2000 repairs is 0%.
- The performance degradation from year 2000 repairs is 0%.
- One hundred percent of subcontract or package year 2000 problems are repaired.
- One hundred percent of database problems are masked or repaired.
- One hundred percent of regression test problems are repaired.
- The overall year 2000 costs are less than planned.
- Some aging legacy systems are replaced by modern, superior equivalents.
- There is no litigation either as plaintiff or defendant.
- As a result of year 2000 repairs software portfolios are known precisely.
- As a result of year 2000 repairs dormant applications are retired.

- As a result of year 2000 repairs dead code is removed.
- As a result of year 2000 repairs maintenance productivity improves.
- As a result of year 2000 repairs maintenance quality improves.
- As a result of year 2000 repairs user satisfaction improves.

These best-case results are improbable, but illustrate goals or targets that year 2000 project managers and service vendors might strive to achieve. Chapters 14 and 15 deal with some of the many post-2000 damage and recovery costs in a more detailed fashion.

A Checklist of Year 2000 Repair and Recovery Costs

The year 2000 problem is remarkably extensive and will involve many kinds of costs that are outside the scope of standard software cost estimating tools. This is because the year 2000 problem will involve software, databases, test libraries, hardware upgrades, new personnel and consultant hiring, and legal fees. There are estimating tools that can handle the year 2000 software repairs, and some that can deal with other individual aspects of the year 2000 problem. However, there are no known commercial software cost-estimating tools that can deal with all aspects of the year 2000 problem simultaneously.

As an alternative, standard spreadsheets provide at least the ability to accumulate costs and effort, even if they do not provide any guidance or rules for how large some of the expense categories may be. Table 4.8 is a general checklist (generated on spreadsheet form) of all of the major year 2000 costs that have been identified to date. Note that this is a generic checklist; it applies to all industries, government organizations, and military groups. Also note that Table 4.8 is only a skeleton of the factors that should be evaluated when costing year 2000 repairs. Expenses may very well run far into the twenty-first century.

It is a somewhat alarming indication of the complexity of the year 2000 problem that a simple listing of possible expense categories (Table 4.8) is so large. The many discrete kinds of activities associated with the year 2000 problem indicates, yet again, that simplistic estimating methods such as multiplying physical LOC by rates that run from $1.00 to about $2.00 will not be adequate. Indeed, very simplistic methods will lead to two unfortunate consequences: (1) severe overcharges for the year 2000 source code repairs and (2) severe undercharges or even accidentally omitting every other kind of year 2000 repair work such as

Table 4.8: Year 2000 Cost Analysis Worksheet (Version 1.1, July 8, 1997)

Year 2000 Tool Acquisition	1997	1998	1999	2000	2001	TOTAL
Year 2000 search engines						
Year 2000 repair engines						
Complexity analyzers						
Code-restructuring tools						
Performance-monitoring tools						
Change management tools						
Test library control tools						
Year 2000 test tools						
Defect-tracking tools						
Reverse-engineering tools						
Reengineering tools						
Database analysis tools						
Other						
Subtotal						

Year 2000 Staff Hiring Costs	1997	1998	1999	2000	2001	TOTAL
Number of personnel needed						
Personnel agency fees						
Interview expenses						
Moving and living expenses						
Signing bonus						
Other						
Subtotal						

Year 2000 Personnel Expenses	1997	1998	1999	2000	2001	TOTAL
Number of first-shift personnel						
Number of second-shift personnel						
Number of third-shift personnel						
Average first-shift compensation						
Second-shift overtime						
Third-shift overtime						
Weekend/holiday overtime						
Other						
Subtotal						

Continued on next page

Table 4.8: Year 2000 Cost Analysis Worksheet (Version 1.1, July 8, 1997), continued

Postyear 2000 Downsizing	1997	1998	1999	2000	2001	TOTAL
Number of surplus personnel						
Downsizing benefits packages						
Other						
Subtotal						

Year 2000 Consulting Fees	1997	1998	1999	2000	2001	TOTAL
Year 2000 awareness sessions						
Year 2000 executive briefings						
Year 2000 compliance audits						
Function point sizing						
Year 2000 source code sizing						
Year 2000 repair cost estimating						
Year 2000 software triage						
Year 2000 software repairs						
Year 2000 database repairs						
Year 2000 test case repairs						
Temporary personnel, manual						
Other						
Subtotal						

Year 2000 Software Triage	1997	1998	1999	2000	2001	TOTAL
Dormant applications, identification						
Dormant applications, archival						
Active applications, identification						
Critical applications, identification						
Other						
Subtotal						

Year 2000 Software Preliminaries	1997	1998	1999	2000	2001	TOTAL
Source code counting, physical						
Source code counting, logical						
Function point backfiring						
Complexity analysis						
Code restructuring						
Dead code removal						
Other						
Subtotal						

Continued on next page

Table 4.8: Year 2000 Cost Analysis Worksheet (Version 1.1, July 8, 1997), continued

Year 2000 Software Repair Costs	1997	1998	1999	2000	2001	TOTAL
Date expansion						
Windowing						
Encapsulation						
Compression						
Bridging						
Bad-fix secondary repairs						
Replacement, commercial						
Replacement, custom						
Withdrawal without replacement						
Developing manual backups						
Other						
Subtotal						

Year 2000 Software Performance	1997	1998	1999	2000	2001	TOTAL
Prerepair performance analysis						
Postrepair performance analysis						
Performance hardware monitors						
Performance software monitors						
Software retuning expenses						
Hardware upgrade expenses						
Network upgrade expenses						
Other						
Subtotal						

Software Year 2000 Test Expenses	1997	1998	1999	2000	2001	TOTAL
Test library analysis						
Regression test case repairs						
New year 2000 test creation						
Year 2000 test execution						
Year 2000 test case repairs						
Other						
Subtotal						

Continued on next page

Table 4.8: Year 2000 Cost Analysis Worksheet (Version 1.1, July 8, 1997), continued

Database Year 2000 Analysis	1997	1998	1999	2000	2001	TOTAL
Database year 2000 analysis						
Database date field expansions						
Database windowing						
Data duplexing						
Database bridging						
Database shutdowns						
Data encryption analysis						
Other						
Subtotal						

Database Year 2000 Testing	1997	1998	1999	2000	2001	TOTAL
Test library analysis						
Test case repairs						
Creating new database test cases						
Database test execution						
Database performance testing						
Year 2000 OLAP testing						
Year 2000 data warehouse testing						
Other						
Subtotal						

Physical Equipment Reviews	1997	1998	1999	2000	2001	TOTAL
Security systems						
Telephone systems, PBX						
Power supply systems						
Heating systems						
Water supplies						
Air-conditioning systems						
Elevators						
Vaults and time locks						
Fire control systems						
Personal computers						
Mini computers						
Mainframe computers						
Embedded computers						
Special-purpose computers						

Continued on next page

Table 4.8: Year 2000 Cost Analysis Worksheet (Version 1.1, July 8, 1997), continued

Physical Equipment Reviews, continued	1997	1998	1999	2000	2001	TOTAL
Manufacturing equipment						
Test equipment						
Scientific instruments						
Other						
Subtotal						

Physical Equipment Repairs	1997	1998	1999	2000	2001	TOTAL
Security systems						
Telephone systems, PBX						
Power supply systems						
Heating systems						
Water supplies						
Air-conditioning systems						
Elevators						
Vaults and time locks						
Fire control systems						
Personal computers						
Mini computers						
Mainframe computers						
Embedded computers						
Special-purpose computers						
Manufacturing equipment						
Test equipment						
Scientific instruments						
Other						
Subtotal						

Military Equipment Reviews	1997	1998	1999	2000	2001	TOTAL
Weapons systems						
Satellites						
Command and control						
Communications						
Other						
Subtotal						

Continued on next page

Table 4.8: Year 2000 Cost Analysis Worksheet (Version 1.1, July 8, 1997), continued

Military Equipment Repairs	1997	1998	1999	2000	2001	TOTAL
Weapons systems						
Satellites						
Command and control						
Communications						
Redeployment of personnel						
Redeployment of equipment						
Other						
Subtotal						

Special Year 2000 Expenses	1997	1998	1999	2000	2001	TOTAL
Year 2000 insurance premiums						
Additional work to amortize costs						
US taxes on year 2000 repairs						
Supplier year 2000 surveys						
Client year 2000 surveys						
Competitor year 2000 surveys						
Offshore government year 2000 liaison						
Federal government year 2000 liaison						
State government year 2000 liaison						
Local government year 2000 liaison						
Advertising year 2000 progress						
Membership in year 2000 groups						
Year 2000 travel expenses						
Year 2000 conference fees						
Year 2000 training expenses						
Layoffs due to year 2000 damages						
Unit closings due to year 2000						
Other						
Subtotal						

Anticipated Year 2000 Damages	1997	1998	1999	2000	2001	TOTAL
Internal damages for missed repairs						
Client damages for missed repairs						
Bad publicity for missed repairs						
Recovery costs for missed repairs						

Continued on next page

Table 4.8: Year 2000 Cost Analysis Worksheet (Version 1.1, July 8, 1997), continued

Anticipated Year 2000 Damages, continued	1997	1998	1999	2000	2001	TOTAL
Goodwill costs for missed repairs						
Funds in escrow for missed repairs						
Lost-opportunity costs						
Fines and penalties						
Tax consequences of year 2000						
Other						
Subtotal						

Year 2000 Legal Expenses	1997	1998	1999	2000	2001	TOTAL
Year 2000 attorney fees						
Year 2000 litigation expenses						
Year 2000 damages						
Year 2000 punitive damages						
Year 2000 settlement costs						
Year 2000 funds in escrow						
Other						
Subtotal						

Year 2000 Disclosure Expenses	1997	1998	1999	2000	2001	TOTAL
Year 2000 cost accumulation						
Year 2000 reporting costs						
Year 2000 audit expenses						
Other						
Subtotal						

Year 2000 Revenues	1997	1998	1999	2000	2001	TOTAL
Year 2000 consulting						
Year 2000 tool revenues						
Year 2000 insurance payments						
Year 2000 litigation, damages paid						
Year 2000 tax credits						
Other						
Subtotal						

Year 2000 Inflation Assumptions	0	10%	15%	10%	10%	

Total Year 2000 Expenses

database repairs, hardware upgrades, test library repairs, and many other noncoding activities.

As large and complex as this checklist is in its current form, there are many other kinds of year 2000 costs that are not included, since the checklist would be too large for convenient use or publication. For example, one possible line of defense for the year 2000 problem is to close a business unit or acquire a competitor with software that is already year 2000 compliant. Neither of these rather extreme situations is listed, and if either should occur it would involve a host of supplemental costs.

Relative Costs of Year 2000 Damages and Repair Activities

As the year 2000 problem approaches, an increasing variety of year 2000 repair strategies are starting to occur. For example, in the past year new methods such as bridging, date windowing, data duplexing, compression, and encapsulation have been added to the "standard" method of date field expansion. Still newer methods are under development but have not yet surfaced or become available, such as object code repair tools for applications in which the source code is missing, and automated year 2000 test case generators. These alternative methods are discussed in later chapters, but it is useful to consider the relative costs of various year 2000 repair strategies, and also the relative costs of the damages and litigious expenses that might occur from not fixing the year 2000 problem.

Table 4.9 uses preliminary data and has a high margin of error, but it attempts to establish ratios of possible costs using in-house date field expansion as the basis of comparison. The phrase *in-house date field expansion* means that the work of the year 2000 repairs will be done by employees of the company rather than by contractors or outsource vendors. The repair strategy selected is to convert the date fields from two-digit to four-digit formats. (This strategy is the basis for costs shown later in the book.)

Table 4.9 assumes a constant value of $50 per staff-hour, or $8,400 per staff-month, or $100,800 per staff-year as the basis of the costs illustrated. Since actual salaries and burden rates can vary from these nominal values by more than 50% in either direction, it is obvious that the costs must be adjusted for local conditions. Further, the Cost per

Table 4.9: Provisional Rankings of Potential Year 2000 Cost Elements

Expense Category	Percent[a]	Cost per LOC[a]	Cost per FP[a]
Litigation, year 2000 deaths or injuries	10,000%	$50.00	$5,000.00
Litigation, year 2000 damages	5,000%	$25.00	$2,500.00
Litigation, shareholder	2,500%	$12.50	$1,250.00
Litigation, professional malpractice	750%	$3.75	$375.00
Litigation, tax errors	600%	$3.00	$300.00
Post-2000 recovery costs	325%	$1.95	$195.00
Database date field expansion (outsourced)	300%	$1.35	$135.00
Post-2000 damages (missed year 2000 hits)	275%	$1.65	$165.00
Database date field expansion (in-house)	250%	$1.13	$112.50
Software date field expansion (outsourced)	250%	$1.25	$125.00
Date field compression	120%	$0.60	$60.00
Software date field expansion (in-house)[a]	100%	$0.50	$50.00
Software date field expansion (offshore)	90%	$0.45	$45.00
Bridging (database applications)	65%	$0.33	$32.50
Data duplexing (batch applications)	40%	$0.20	$20.00
Encapsulation (date shifting)	35%	$0.18	$17.50
Regression test library repairs (outsourced)	35%	$0.18	$17.50
Year 2000 regression testing	35%	$0.18	$17.50
Windowing (sliding)	30%	$0.15	$15.00
Year 2000 performance restoration	25%	$0.13	$12.50
Year 2000 insurance	25%	$0.13	$12.50

Continued on next page

Table 4.9: Provisional Rankings of Potential Year 2000 Cost Elements, continued

Expense Category	Percent[a]	Cost per LOC[a]	Cost per FP[a]
Windowing (fixed)	20%	$0.10	$10.00
Regression test library repairs (in-house)	20%	$0.10	$10.00
Year 2000 date searching (manual)	20%	$0.10	$10.00
Triage of applications	10%	$0.05	$5.00
Year 2000 date searching (automated)	5%	$0.03	$2.50
Year 2000 awareness briefings	2%	$0.01	$1.00

[a]Percentages and costs are relative to in-house date field expansions.

LOC = lines of source code; FP = function point.

LOC column is particularly troublesome because these costs will vary from language to language, and there are close to 500 programming languages that might contain year 2000 problems.

The results presented are based on a simple multiple of 100 logical source code statements for every function point. This is a representative value for many procedural languages, such as COBOL or FORTRAN, but in this context it is merely used to illustrate a rough range of relative costs.

The purpose of Table 4.9 is not to provide exact data on year 2000 cost elements, but to indicate the relative magnitude of various year 2000 cost elements. However, when the data in Table 4.9 is sorted in descending order, it provides a strong caution to executives and boards of directors: The postyear 2000 costs for litigation, damages, and recovery are more than an order of magnitude more expensive than any of the year 2000 repair cost elements themselves. The obvious lesson that can be gained from the data in Table 4.9, even with a high margin of error, is that the only prudent course of action is to attack the year

2000 problem with diligence and competence, since the consequences of failure are much more severe than the costs of the repairs themselves, even though these costs are alarmingly high and may be unbudgeted.

Obviously the data in Table 4.9 should not be used for serious business purposes such as estimating year 2000 repair costs for specific companies. The table is only a way of illustrating how many different kinds of year 2000 cost elements need to be considered. The sum total of more than $100 per line of code or more than $10,000 per function point is merely the arithmetic sum of the respective columns. However, to repeat a warning to executives, a strong lesson can be drawn from the alarming size of these totals. No matter how expensive it may be to fix the year 2000 problem, it will be much more expensive to deal with the litigation and damages that might occur from *not* fixing the year 2000 problem.

Checklist of Critical Application Types

There is a widespread misconception in the press and sometimes in news coverage that the year 2000 software problem affects, primarily, financial applications. Unfortunately the year 2000 problem affects an almost astonishingly wide range of software applications. For example, few people who ride elevators in modern office buildings realize that the elevators are controlled by software, and that this software has built-in protection algorithms that will cause elevators to descend to the ground floor if the time for a safety inspection is past due.

At midnight on December 31, 1999, many elevator systems throughout the world will descend to ground level and stay there, because the switch from 99 to 00 will cause an apparent safety inspection violation. Of course sending out inspectors and resetting the inspection date can eliminate the problem, but in the first few days of January 2000 so many problems will be occurring so rapidly that some elevators may remain out of service for a week or more, simply because more pressing issues are at hand.

The following is a short checklist of some of the kinds of software applications in which year 2000 date problems are likely to be found and may cause trouble if they are not repaired.

Checklist of Critical Software Application Types

Accounts payable
Accounts receivable
Aircraft maintenance
Aircraft navigation
Air traffic control
Annuity calculations
Automated teller
    machines
Automotive
    registrations
Banking systems
Billing systems
Birth registrations
Building security
Capacity planning
Cash management
C^3
Computer security
Cost accounting
Cost estimating
Cost tracking
Credit card
    processing
Currency conversion
Customer order
    processing
Data acquisition
    systems
Death registrations
Debit card processing
Delinquent accounts
Divorce registrations
Drivers' license
    renewals
Early-payment
    discounts

Electricity billing
Electricity-generating
    controls
Elevator inspection
    software
Employee
    compensation
Encryption algorithms
Fuel oil delivery
    systems
Funds transfer
Freight tariffs
Futures trading
General ledgers
Global positioning
    systems
Hospital administration
Hotel reservations
Human resource
    management
Insurance premium
    payments
Interbank funds
    transfers
Interest calculations
Inventory
    management
Just-in-time inventory
    systems
Manufacturing
    automation
Medical instrument
    controls
Mortgage payments
Motor vehicle
    registrations

Navigation systems
Nuclear safety systems
Operating systems
Overtime calculations
Payroll calculations
Pension payments
Prescription expirations
Railroad freight
    scheduling
Railroad passenger
    reservations
Railroad routing
    systems
Records retention
    schedules
Reservation systems
Satellite positioning
    systems
Security systems
Stock market trading
Subscription systems
Tax calculations
Tax payment logging
Telephone billing
    systems
Telephone switching
    systems
Traffic light
    synchronization
Traffic ticket
    accounting
Weapons' control
    systems
Withholding
    calculations

As you can see, the year 2000 problem will affect a wide range of software applications. This list also illustrates how pervasive computers and software have become at the end of the twentieth century, with almost every human activity from birth to death now involving computers, software, databases, and other forms of automation.

References

1. Hall, B., and K. Schick, *The Year 2000 Crisis—Estimating the Cost.* Stamford, CT: Gartner Group, 1997.
2. Jones, Capers. *Applied Software Measurement.* 2nd ed. New York: McGraw-Hill, 1996.
3. Jones, Capers. *Table of Programming Languages and Levels.* Version 8.2. Burlington, MA: SPR, 1996.
4. IFPUG. *IFPUG Counting Practices Manual.* Release 4.0. Westerville OH: IFPUG, 1995.
5. Viasoft, Inc. *Viasoft Year 2000 Cost Analysis.* Phoenix: Viasoft, Inc., 1996.
6. Robbins, Brian, and Howard Rubin. *The Year 2000 Planning Guide.* Pound Ridge, NY: Rubin Systems, Inc., 1997.
7. Kappelman, Leon A., et al. *How Much Will Year 2000 Compliance Cost?* Version 2.12. Denton, TX: College of Business Administration, University of North Texas, May 30,1997.
8. Jones, Keith. *Year 2000 Crisis Solutions.* Boston: ITCP, 1997.

5 | The Size of the Year 2000 Problem for the United States

$\blacktriangleright$O FAR AS I can determine there has never been an accurate or even approximate inventory of the total volume of software deployed within any country. The data presented here is known to be imperfect and have a high margin of error. However, for studying problems such as the year 2000 issue, it is better to have partly speculative data with a high margin of error than no data at all. Hopefully future research can correct any errors and improve the accuracy of the results. But if the information were not published at all, there might be no incentive to carry out research that will eliminate any errors shown here.

Volume of Software Installed in the United States

Using the assumptions for portfolios, sites, and software staff discussed earlier, Table 5.1 shows the approximate size of the installed software portfolios in the United States. The data in Table 5.1 is derived from multiple sources and can be assumed to have a large and unknown margin of error. The immediate source of the data in Tables 5.1 and 5.2 was a 10-year demographic survey of US and global software populations originally derived from market research performed by the ITT corporation and updated semiannually by myself.[1]

Regardless of the margin of error in Table 5.1, one fact is painfully obvious. The United States is the world's largest producer and largest consumer of software, so the costs of the year 2000 problem will be greater in the United States than in any other country. The year 2000 problem is one of those comparatively rare problems that affects industrialized and computerized nations much more severely than those that are not yet fully automated. This same statement is true of industries and governments, as well as countries. Industries such as banking and insurance, which are highly automated, will have much higher costs

Table 5.1: US Software Applications, Sites, Staff, and Software Portfolios

Industry	Applications	Software Sites	Software Staff	Portfolio Size (FP)
Military	6,000,000	1,000	200,000	300,000,000
Manufacturing	4,444,444	8,500	250,000	200,000,000
Finance	2,454,545	2,500	150,000	135,000,000
Services	2,222,222	1,500	125,000	100,000,000
Communications	1,800,000	1,000	100,000	90,000,000
Insurance	1,800,000	1,500	90,000	81,000,000
Wholesale	1,777,778	1,500	100,000	80,000,000
Defense	1,600,000	2,000	100,000	80,000,000
Federal	1,333,333	500	75,000	60,000,000
Retail	1,200,000	3,500	75,000	60,000,000
Software	1,050,000	1,000	75,000	52,500,000
Health care	510,000	1,500	30,000	25,500,000
Municipal	533,333	1,500	30,000	24,000,000
Energy	500,000	1,000	25,000	20,000,000
Transportation	416,667	1,000	25,000	18,750,000
States	355,556	150	20,000	16,000,000
Other	8,002,668	15,000	450,000	360,000,000
Total	36,000,546	44,650	1,920,000	1,702,750,000

FP = function point.

associated with the year 2000 problem than less automated groups such as publishing.

Also, the potential liabilities associated with litigation also seem to correlate with the volumes of software used by an industry. However, the litigation potential is also affected by the probability that not fixing the year 2000 problem will cause economic damage, or even injury or loss of life, which may occur if the year 2000 problem affects air traffic control, railroad switching controls, or nuclear power plants.

In considering the impact of the year 2000 problem, it is obvious that the expenses will be large primarily because the problem is found throughout the entire portfolio of legacy applications. Changing any single application might not be too difficult, but when *every* application, or at least a high percentage of applications, owned by a large company is affected, the cumulative effort will be enormous. Table 5.2 provides rough approximations of the percentage of portfolios that are likely to be modified, and the anticipated productivity rates for finding and repairing the year 2000 problem.

Table 5.2: Productivity Assumptions for Year 2000 Repairs

Industry	Portfolio Size (FP)	Year 2000 Impact	Portfolio Changes	Productivity (FP/PM)	Effort (PM)
Military	300,000,000	7.00%	21,000,000	11.00	1,909,091
Finance	135,000,000	6.00%	8,100,000	18.00	450,000
Manufacturing	200,000,000	5.00%	10,000,000	18.00	555,556
Communications	90,000,000	8.00%	7,200,000	17.00	423,529
Services	100,000,000	10.00%	10,000,000	18.00	555,556
Insurance	81,000,000	10.00%	8,100,000	18.00	450,000
Wholesale	80,000,000	11.00%	8,800,000	17.00	517,647
Federal	60,000,000	10.00%	6,000,000	15.00	400,000
Defense	80,000,000	4.00%	3,200,000	12.00	266,667
Retail	60,000,000	11.00%	6,600,000	16.00	412,500
Software	52,500,000	7.00%	3,675,000	19.00	193,421
Municipal	24,000,000	10.00%	2,400,000	16.00	150,000
Health care	25,500,000	7.00%	1,785,000	16.00	111,563
States	16,000,000	10.00%	1,600,000	16.00	100,000
Energy	20,000,000	7.00%	1,400,000	16.00	87,500
Transportation	18,750,000	7.00%	1,312,500	16.00	82,031
Other	360,000,000	8.00%	128,800,000	16.00	1,800,000
Total(T)/Average(A)	1,702,750,000(T)	8.12%(A)	129,972,500(T)	16.18(A)	8,465,060(T)

FP = function point; PM = person-month.

The data in Table 5.2 regarding the percentage of software needing modification has been generally duplicated by other researchers, such as the analysis performed by Robbins and Rubin.[2]

The technical work associated with finding and fixing the year 2000 problem can be broken down into four discrete activities:

1. Finding and isolating the year 2000 sections of applications
2. Modifying the applications to repair the problem
3. Testing the repairs to ensure that they work
4. Regression testing the application to ensure no secondary damage has occurred

Table 5.2 assumes that all four of these activities will be performed. However, from preliminary observations of companies that have already begun their year 2000 work, steps 3 and 4 (testing and regression testing) are sometimes performed in a very careless fashion. Carelessness in regression testing and validating year 2000 repairs will have three damaging impacts later that can run well into the twenty-first century.

1. Missed year 2000 instances will be plentiful and troublesome.
2. Bad fixes or fresh bugs accidentally injected will be common and troublesome.
3. The performance or execution speeds of applications will be seriously degraded.

The approximate distribution of effort over the four aspects of the year 2000 problem will vary significantly by language, due to the presence or absence of available tools (Table 5.3).

Table 5.3: Distribution of Year 2000 Repair Efforts

Year 2000 Activities	Range of Total Costs
Finding the year 2000 instances	10% to 50%
Fixing the year 2000 instances	15% to 30%
Testing the year 2000 repairs	10% to 30%
Regression testing the portfolio	20% to 50%

Finding and isolating the year 2000 problem should be easiest for object-oriented languages (for example, Objective C and SMALLTALK) in which dates are handled in well-formed class libraries. Next would be COBOL, since there are several specialized tools that can seek out date references in COBOL applications. Such tools also exist for other common languages such as C and FORTRAN. The toughest language will probably be Assembly, followed by languages that have tool shortages such as PL/I, LISP, FORTH, and the like.

The next aspect of the study of the year 2000 problem is to assign approximate costs for the overall repairs that must be performed. Here there is quite a bit of uncertainty, since there are large variances in cost structure by industry and by geography. For example, the costs of updating financial applications in New York City or San Francisco will be much greater than the costs of updating retail applications in the rural South because urban areas have higher compensation rates than rural areas and because financial institutions have higher compensation rates than retail.

Table 5.4 shows the approximate US costs for finding and fixing the year 2000 problem. Note that these costs assume actual date expansions from two to four digits in affected software applications. Alternative

Table 5.4: US Repair Costs for the Year 2000 Problem

Industry	Effort (PM)	Burdened Cost/PM	Costs	Costs per Changed FP	Costs per Total FP
Military	1,909,091	$7,500	$14,318,181,818	$682	$48
Finance	450,000	$11,000	$4,950,000,000	$611	$37
Manufacturing	555,556	$8,400	$4,666,666,667	$467	$23
Communications	423,529	$10,000	$4,235,294,118	$588	$47
Services	555,556	$8,000	$4,444,444,444	$444	$44
Insurance	450,000	$9,200	$4,140,000,000	$511	$51
Wholesale	517,647	$7,500	$3,882,352,941	$441	$49
Federal	400,000	$7,900	$3,160,000,000	$527	$53
Defense	266,667	$11,000	$2,933,333,333	$917	$37
Retail	412,500	$7,500	$3,093,750,000	$469	$52
Software	193,421	$9,000	$1,740,789,474	$474	$33
Municipal	150,000	$7,000	$1,050,000,000	$438	$44
Health care	111,563	$8,000	$892,500,000	$500	$35
States	100,000	$7,700	$770,000,000	$481	$48
Energy	87,500	$8,000	$700,000,000	$500	$35
Transportation	82,031	$8,000	$656,250,000	$500	$35
Other	1,800,000	$8,400	$15,120,000,000	$525	$42
Total(T)/Average(A)	8,465,060(T)	$8,476(A)	$70,753,562,795(T)	$534(A)	$42(A)

PM = person-month; FP = function point.

repair strategies, under the general term *masking*, include windowing, bridging, encapsulation, and other methods with costs that may be higher or lower than the expansions of date fields themselves.

The platform on which the application resides will also affect the costs. Common platforms such as IBM mainframes and AS400 machines will be comparatively straightforward, as will standard IBM compatible personal computers.

UNIX, OS/2, DOS, Macintosh, and various Windows versions will need repairs, but all are marketed by vendors that are actively moving toward year 2000 compliance. Tougher will be software that runs on "orphan" platforms or on specialized computers such as military on-board ANYUK computers.

Hardware and Performance Implications of the Year 2000 Problem

Fixing the year 2000 problem in software will have some possible implications for the performance of the applications, which may necessitate hardware upgrades to more powerful computers, or at least retuning of the applications to regain former performance levels. The performance and hardware implications of the year 2000 problem are under-reported in the literature and at conferences. Many mainframe software applications have been optimized to reduce machine use and maximize throughput. This kind of performance optimization is very important for selected applications with very high transaction rates, such as credit card processing, automated gasoline pump authorization, rental car computer systems, and airline reservation systems.

Any year 2000 repairs that are made in a hasty or perfunctory manner without adequate testing and reoptimization can result in several major problems:

- Introduction of bad fixes or new bugs as a byproduct of year 2000 repairs
- Major degradation of application throughput and data center efficiency levels
- Use of masking logic rather than actual repairs, which may degrade performance

The topic of *masking logic* is fairly new to the year 2000 scene. The concept is based on creating an external software tool that converts dates into a format with which the original application can deal, rather than by actually going into the application and fixing the problem itself. Several types of masking logic exist, such as windowing, encapsulation, bridging, and so forth. Any of the forms of masking that add processing steps to applications with high transaction rates are likely to degrade performance to unacceptable levels. This means that great caution is needed for applications such as credit card processing or real-time data acquisition when using windowing, bridging, encapsulation, or other masking approaches that depend on external manipulation of dates prior to presenting them to the affected application. Although masking logic is effective for overt, surface-level year 2000 repairs, it is not completely effective for hidden or secondary instances of the year 2000 problem. Also, the time required to perform the masking logic (in both input and output directions) tends to degrade the overall throughput of the applications.

I estimate that sloppy year 2000 repairs are likely to affect mainframe data centers the most, since the bulk of aging US legacy applications were originally built for IBM mainframe computers. It is difficult to estimate precisely, but I suspect that the minimal degradation from the year 2000 problem will be a de facto 10% loss in data center through-put. This is the most conservative estimate. The most probable estimate is about 20% or higher. The worst-case scenario might cause a 30% slowdown in data center efficiency and throughput, which could trigger a set of catastrophic secondary problems in things like delayed billings, slow processing of tax returns, and a host of other speed-related issues.

An independent model of performance degradation in response to sloppy year 2000 repairs has also been reported by Robbins and Rubin.[2] Their model reaches a similar conclusion and places the performance loss at something more than 20%.

A second independent analysis of hardware performance degradation was performed by the Programart Corporation[3] and documented in the December 1966 issue of the *Enterprise Systems Journal*. The Programart study found about a 25% degradation in throughput on IBM mainframes running MVS when year 2000 repairs were rushed and testing and performance tuning were marginal.

The normal response to a major degradation of throughput is installation of performance monitors followed by either expensive optimization of software applications, major increases in hardware capacity, or both. I would predict that performance tuning of applications degraded by careless year 2000 testing might add $5,000,000,000 to the US year 2000 costs, while hardware upgrades to service the demand could add $10,000,000,000 to $20,000,000,000 to US year 2000 costs in the years 1999 through about 2005. Note that hardware and data center costs are not measured using function points or LOC, so these costs are over and above the software costs discussed later in this book.

One recent topic dealing with performance issues is the fact that some companies may want to migrate from noncompliant hardware platforms to compliant ones. In addition, some companies are leasing or purchasing new computer systems primarily for making year 2000 repairs and testing out possible year 2000 repairs. Certain aspects of year 2000 testing, such as the need to test across corporate barriers for factors such as electronic data interchange (EDI), are very likely to cause major problems that will necessitate extra time and probably extra computing capacities as well. Another aspect of making hasty repairs to the year 2000 problem is that of bad fixes or secondary defects accidentally created while fixing prior defects. Ordinary maintenance or defect repairs in the United States are accompanied by about a

7% bad-fix injection rate. That is, about 7% of defect repairs accidentally inject a new defect as a byproduct of the repair itself.

The year 2000 problem is an especially tricky kind of defect to repair, and many of the applications that contain this problem are old and poorly documented, and some are in antique or proprietary languages supported by only a few current, expert programmers. It may be easy to fix year 2000 problems in COBOL or C applications, but many applications are written in languages for which both year 2000 search tools and experienced programmers are not readily available, such as:

- APL
- Assembly
- CHILL
- CORAL66
- CMS2
- Electronic Switching PL/I
- FORTH
- Machine languages
- RPG I

Do not assume that because a programming language is not as well known as COBOL that only a few minor applications may be written using it. The CHILL and CORAL programming languages are specialized languages developed for telephone switching systems. Indeed, because of the high sales volumes of the Alcatel (formerly ITT) System 12 switching system, it is probable that almost 20% of international telephone calls initiated throughout the world pass through switching systems controlled by the CHILL programming language. Yet the world's total number of experienced CHILL programmers is perhaps only a few thousand, while there are millions of COBOL programmers.

In general terms, about 70% of the world's software applications are written in fairly common programming languages with an adequate supply of trained programming personnel. The other 30%, however, are written in hundreds of proprietary or obscure programming languages for which there are very few trained programmers. Even worse, for some of these languages there are not even any courses or tutorial materials available, so there is no easy way of creating trained personnel. Even the well-known story on the year 2000 problem in *Newsweek* in June 1997[4] assumed, incorrectly, that COBOL was the primary language affected by the year 2000 problem. For those unfamiliar with the enormous number and diversity of programming languages, refer to Appendix D for a list of almost 500 programming languages in current use.

If there are few programmers for an obscure language, it is highly unlikely that any of the commercial year 2000 search-and-repair engines will be able to seek out year 2000 problems. Even the major year 2000 outsource vendors may have trouble, since they may not have programmers experienced in proprietary languages. The factors associated with obscure and proprietary languages are very likely to elevate the year 2000 bad-fix potential above US norms of 7%. I estimate that about 10% of year 2000 repairs will trigger the accidental injection of a new bug or defect. This means that year 2000 repairs may string out for months after the first wave of initial repairs, as fresh bugs brought on by bad fixes begin to surface. Unfortunately, bad fixes are usually left out of year 2000 budgets and may also be omitted from outsource and maintenance agreements with contractors. The result of bad fixes is that many year 2000 repair budgets will probably be overrun by at least 10%.

In round numbers, preliminary analysis suggests that about $40 will be expended for every function point in existing portfolios, with perhaps another $5.00 per function point for bad-fix repairs. Since most corporations own more than 100,000 function points and major corporations own more than 1,000,000 function points, the cumulative costs will be major indeed.

Year 2000 Repairs by Industry

Another interesting aspect of the year 2000 problem is to consider how much effort must be expended between now and the year 2000 by the software community. It appears that the problem is large enough so that essentially every technical worker in the software domain will be engaged on the problem for more than four months between now and 1999! Table 5.5 shows the approximate effort in terms of expended person-months and costs between now and the end of the century on a per capita basis. That is, the effort and costs are expressed in terms of the impact on every software technical worker in the United States, ranked in descending order.

An independent study of year 2000 repairs carried out by Dr. Leon Kappelman and his colleagues[5] in the SIM year 2000 working group reached conclusions that were surprisingly close to the results shown in Table 5.5 although there was no apparent duplication of the samples used in either the SIM study or the table. The SIM analysis indicated that year 2000 repair costs were averaging about 30% of annual soft-

Table 5.5: Per Capita Effort and Costs for the Year 2000 Problem

Industry	Months per Staff Member	Costs per Capita
Military	9.55	$71,591
Insurance	5.00	$46,000
Communications	4.24	$42,353
Federal	5.33	$42,133
Retail	5.50	$41,250
Wholesale	5.18	$38,824
States	5.00	$38,500
Services	4.44	$35,556
Municipal	5.00	$35,000
Other	4.00	$33,600
Finance	3.00	$33,000
Health care	3.72	$29,750
Defense	2.67	$29,333
Energy	3.50	$28,000
Transportation	3.28	$26,250
Software	2.58	$23,211
Manufacturing	2.22	$18,667
Average	4.37	$36,060

ware budgets. Since 30% of annual budgets and 4 months of programming effort are roughly equivalent, it is encouraging that the results from these two independent studies are similar. Of course, it is possible for both studies to be wrong and the similarity is merely an accident.

In general, the human race is not very good in preventing disasters and tends to wait until the last minute before taking action. That tendency is already visible in the context of the year 2000 problem. At some point sociologists and psychologists will have many interesting research opportunities centering around the year 2000 problem. This is an obvious problem that will occur at a fixed point in time, yet the problem remained ignored and underreported until it is almost too late to deal with it. Indeed, although software journals have been running articles about the year 2000 situation for several years, the major journals such as *Newsweek* did not start full year 2000 coverage until June 1997. One of the editors at *Forbes* was quoted in 1996 as saying they would not begin coverage until 1999, although now that *Newsweek* has broken the ice[4] the other major journals will surely accelerate their own year 2000 stories. Book publishers have also lagged, with only one or two books appearing prior to 1997, but more than 20 year 2000 books planned for release during late 1997 and early 1998.

The optimal time to start fixing this problem was 1995 or earlier. It is now 1997 as this book is being written, and time is already beginning to run short. Approximately October 1997 is the last year that a mid-size corporation can commence their year 2000 repairs with any hope of finishing before the end of the century assuming a "business as usual" repair strategy with less than 15% of software resources used for the year 2000 problem. This statement is based on date field expansion using manual methods as the primary repair strategy. However, if automated search-and-repair tools are used, and if bridging, windowing, encapsulation, and some of the other masking approaches are used, then the year 2000 repairs might begin as late as June 1998 and may possibly be completed, although it will be a tight race.

There are also several unusual and controversial methods that can be used to accelerate year 2000 repairs discussed later in this book, but it is well to introduce them now.

- Cancel all other software projects except emergency maintenance and statutory updates, and elevate the year 2000 resources from less than 15% of available software personnel to more than 85% of available software personnel.
- Suspend European currency conversion efforts until 2005, on the grounds that the year 2000 problem is a far more urgent issue.
- Switch year 2000 repairs from a one-shift activity to 24-hour around-the-clock repairs. This might be done by establishing a global network of year 2000 repair factories, with three year 2000 repair facilities located eight time zones apart.
- Suspend antitrust legislation for a five-year period in the context of year 2000 repairs and encourage key industries to pool their year 2000 resources. For example, airlines, banks, automobile manufacturers, telecommunications, medical facilities, and defense contractors are "key industries" in the sense that year 2000 failures can trigger devastating economic problems.
- Suspend enforcement of IRC regulation 482, which might cause reusable year 2000 repairs to be treated as taxable income in the United States.

Table 5.6 shows the approximate schedule implications of several year 2000 repair strategies.

Table 5.6: Percentage of Year 2000 Repairs Completed Based on Start Year and Use of Manual or Automated Search Procedures

Year When 2000 Repairs Start	Applications Corrected by 1999 (manual search)	Applications Corrected by 1999 (search engines)	Applications Corrected by 1999 (24-hour repairs)
1994	100%	100%	100%
1995	100%	100%	100%
1996	99%	100%	100%
1997	85%	100%	100%
1998	75%	90%	100%
1999	40%	65%	85%

The good news about Table 5.6 is that the year 2000 search-and-repair teams are becoming quicker and more thorough as time passes. The early attempts at year 2000 search and repair work were trial-and-error affairs that were not particularly cost-effective. By the time a year 2000 repair team has worked on half a dozen or so major systems, they tend to become much more efficient than they were earlier. This means that top-gun year 2000 teams can achieve much faster rates and much higher removal efficiency levels than novices.

It should be noted that the year 2000 problem is one for which automated search engines are going to be highly beneficial. However, the accuracy of these search engines is still something of an unknown value. Right now no one is sure if automated year 2000 search engines will find 100% of the year 2000 instances. On the other hand, no one is sure if manual searches will find 100% of the year 2000 instances either. (There is also an opposite problem—reporting false year 2000 instances—but this is less serious than missing real year 2000 hits.)

For fixing other kinds of software bugs, a standard metric used is *defect removal efficiency*. This metric is calculated by keeping track of defects found by developers during inspection and test stages, and then accumulating bugs found by clients or users in the first six months of usage. If the developers found 90 bugs during testing and the clients found 10 bugs, then the defect removal efficiency is 90% because 9 out of every 10 bugs were removed before clients used the software. The US average for defect removal efficiency, taken from *Software Quality—Analysis and Guidelines for Success,*[6] is only about 85%. But the best-in-class results can top 97% in terms of defect removal efficiency. From very preliminary assumptions based on early year 2000 repairs in common languages such as COBOL and C, I've assigned a tentative defect removal efficiency level of about 95% for the year 2000 problem. That is, 95 out of every 100 year 2000 date references will perhaps be found and fixed, assuming a competent year 2000 search team.

It would be wonderful to assume that the best-in-class year 2000 repairs could achieve 100% in terms of defect removal efficiency, but in the past 30 years of measuring software development I've never seen more than one or two cases when software projects achieved zero-defect status after release and hence achieved 100% defect removal efficiency levels. This same kind of defect removal efficiency metric is very appropriate for the year 2000 problem. However, no one actually knows at present what kind of efficiency can be expected. In spite of the lack of solid empirical data to back them up, my tentative projections for selected programming languages based on the efficiencies noted for other kinds of software defects are presented in Table 5.7.

Two interesting questions as this report is written in 1997 are: What percent of year 2000 repairs have already been accomplished and what percent remain to be done? These are hard questions to answer. Unfortunately, the majority of companies and government groups are still in preliminary fact-finding mode and have not yet begun the tougher work of actually seeking out the year 2000 hits and making corrections. For unknown reasons, starting repairs in calendar year 1998 seems to be a popular goal, although in fact a 1998 start date is too late to guarantee a successful completion by January 1, 2000.

The result of this lag time in getting started means that a significant number of companies will still be working on year 2000 repairs when the clock runs out at midnight on December 31, 1999. Further, repairs made during calendar year 1999 and especially during the last half of 1999 are probably going to be rushed and careless, so there will be a

Table 5.7: Probable Year 2000 Removal Efficiency for Selected Languages

Language	Average Year 2000 Removal Efficiency Levels	Maximal Year 2000 Removal Efficiency Levels
COBOL	95%	99.99%
PL/I	94%	99.00%
FORTRAN	94%	99.00%
C++	93%	99.00%
C	92%	98.00%
Macro Assembly	85%	90.00%
Basic Assembly	85%	90.00%

Table 5.8: Trail of Year 2000 Expenses for Software, Hardware, and Litigation from 1994 through 2005

Year When 2000 Repairs Start	Software Expense	Hardware Expense	Litigation Expense	Damages From Unrepaired Year 2000 Hits
1994	1%	0%	0%	0%
1995	3%	0%	0%	0%
1996	10%	1%	1%	0%
1997	15%	1%	2%	2%
1998	20%	5%	5%	3%
1999	27%	20%	10%	5%
2000	15%	25%	17%	50%
2001	7%	20%	24%	22%
2002	4%	15%	25%	10%
2003	0%	10%	10%	5%
2004	0%	2%	5%	2%
2005	0%	1%	2%	1%

high probability of missed year 2000 hits, performance degradation, bad fixes, and the other problems associated with excessive haste and poor quality control. From queries and surveys among our clients, the expenditure pattern presented in Table 5.8 seems to be a rough approximation.

If the year 2000 problem follows the pattern illustrated in Table 5.8, software repairs will peak during calendar year 1999. Of course, many companies will miss the 1999 deadline so they will be working frantically during 2000. In addition, bad fixes or secondary bugs will continue to surface long after the original repairs are done. Missed year 2000 hits will peak in the year 2000. However, hardware upgrades and legal expenses will not peak until 2000 and 2001, respectively. In other words, the year 2000 problem will leave a trail of major expenses until well into the twenty-first century.

Year 2000 Repairs by Company Size

To CIOs, CEOs, and other managers concerned with enterprise software, the most important topic is not what the problem is going to cost the country or their industry, but rather what the problem is going to cost their particular enterprise. Unfortunately, it would require an on-site study of each enterprise to quantify the exact costs. Indeed, as this book is being written many enterprises have already commissioned site studies to begin to quantify the expenses of the year 2000 problem.

Table 5.9: Effort and Costs of the Year 2000 Problem by Size of Software Staff

Software Staff	No. of Sites	Portfolio Size (FP)	Effort (mo)	Total Costs	Cost per FP	Cost per LOC
5	1	6,000	23	$197,784	$33	$0.33
10	1	11,500	45	$379,087	$33	$0.33
25	1	27,500	107	$906,511	$33	$0.33
50	1	50,000	194	$1,648,203	$33	$0.33
100	1	95,000	416	$3,523,033	$37	$0.37
500	2	450,000	1,969	$16,688,051	$37	$0.37
1,000	3	900,000	4,200	$35,601,176	$40	$0.40
5,000	5	4,500,000	21,000	$178,005,882	$40	$0.40
10,000	10	9,000,000	42,000	$356,011,765	$40	$0.40
20,000	15	18,000,000	84,000	$712,023,529	$40	$0.40

FP = function point; LOC = lines of code.

However, by using some of the general assumptions presented earlier, it is possible to state the approximate overall costs of fixing the year 2000 problem for enterprises of various sizes.

Table 5.9 is based on the total number of technical software staff employed, and shows approximate costs for enterprises with as few as five technical personnel, up to enterprises with as many as 10,000 technical personnel. Some of the background assumptions of Table 5.9 include:

- A burdened cost per staff-month of $8,400, which yields $50 per hour
- Large, geographically dispersed enterprises, which raises repair costs
- The large enterprise has more large systems, and they are harder to fix

Table 5.9 has a significant margin of error and is not a substitute for a thorough on-site analysis of an enterprise's actual portfolio. The actual range of data in Table 5.9 is due to variations in the following contributing factors.

- Expansion or masking can cause variations of more than ±50%.
- Manual or automated tools can cause variance of more than ±50%.
- Employee compensation rates can vary by more than ±50%.
- Enterprise burden rates can vary by more than ±50%.
- The complexity of applications can vary by more than ±35%.
- Programming languages can cause variations of more than ±25%.
- Use of an outsource vendor can cause variations of more than 100%.

All of these are independent variables, and any combination can move in any direction based on local conditions.

To refine the information shown in Table 5.9, readers are urged to carry out the following analysis either on their own or aided by consultants who specialize in the year 2000 problem.

Year 2000 Repair Sizing and Estimating Sequence

1. Quantify the size of your portfolio of legacy applications.
2. Subtract dormant applications, which do not need year 2000 repairs.
3. Subtract applications to be replaced by new year 2000-compliant applications.
4. Quantify the size of your software databases and repositories using function points, logical statements, and physical LOC.
5. Explore the incidence of year 2000 references in your legacy applications.
6. Explore the incidence of year 2000 references in your current databases.
7. Explore the incidence of year 2000 references in your regression test libraries.
8. Determine whether expansion, windowing, or encapsulation will be used.
9. Estimate the effort to repair each year 2000 reference.
10. Estimate the effort to test and validate each year 2000 reference.
11. Estimate the bad-fix injection potential of faulty year 2000 repairs.
12. Estimate the repairs or replacement for fax machines and hardware devices.
13. Estimate the costs of dealing with external vendor and client year 2000 problems.
14. Estimate hiring costs and relocation for hiring year 2000 specialists.
15. Estimate external consulting fees for year 2000 outsourcers or specialists.
16. Estimate litigation preparation expenses for unrepaired year 2000 hits.
17. Estimate potential damages for unrepaired year 2000 hits.
18. Estimate the damages from unrepaired year 2000 problems.
19. Estimate the recovery costs from unrepaired year 2000 problems.
20. Estimate the costs of year 2000 customer support, hot lines, and 24-hour teams.

It should be obvious, but unfortunately it is not, that a twenty-first step must also be included.

21. Stop using two-digit date fields in your new applications!

Surprisingly, some two-digit date fields are still being used in new software applications as late as 1997! This is true of both mainframe applications and shrink-wrapped personal computer software.

Triage of Software Applications

After train wrecks, earthquakes, and combat operations, physicians and caregivers practice an approach called *triage* that divides the wounded into three major categories: (1) those who need immediate care and may survive, (2) those whose care can be delayed without increasing the risks unduly, (3) those who will probably not survive whether they get care or not. Enterprise year 2000 managers are urged to try a form of triage on their portfolios of applications, although four categories might result rather than three.

1. Active applications that must be fixed prior to the end of 1999 (about 30% of total)
2. Active applications that must be replaced prior to 1999 (about 15% of total)
3. Active applications that may not need repair (about 5% of total)
4. Dormant applications with repairs or replacement that may never occur (50% of total)

Below the level of triage there lies another and more complex sorting process that does not have a general name, but involves sorting active applications into the following subcategories:

1. Applications that are year 2000 compliant (about 12% of actives)
2. Applications to be withdrawn without replacement (about 3% of actives)
3. Applications to be replaced by packages (about 5% of actives)
4. Applications to be replaced by custom software (about 10% of actives)
5. Applications to be repaired by date field expansion (about 20% of actives)
6. Applications to be masked temporarily by encapsulation (about 10% of actives)
7. Applications to be masked temporarily by windowing (about 20% of actives)
8. Applications to be masked temporarily by bridging, (about 20% of actives)

The percentages assigned to these various year 2000 repair strategies will vary from company to company and industry to industry, so the percentages shown here are merely to give rough approximations derived from our clients.

Robert Kendall, now an independent consultant, worked for the IBM corporation for many years. Kendall[7] performed a study involving eight IBM data centers running large mainframes that produced interesting results. Although Kendall's study was not about the year 2000 problem, some of his findings may provide a ray of hope for year 2000 project managers. He noted that a substantial portion of the software at all of IBM's data centers could be classified as dormant because it had not been run or executed for more than a year. Somewhere between 40% and 70% of the total number of applications owned and present in software program libraries were found to be no longer in use. Assuming that other corporations besides IBM also have large inventories of dormant applications mixed in with their active applications, there is a chance that the need for immediate year 2000 repairs prior to the end of 1999 can be reduced by simply archiving dormant applications and removing them, or at least by deferring repairs until a more convenient time in the twenty-first century. However, as Kendall points out, finding out which applications are truly dormant is not an easy task. Therefore a formal portfolio analysis is still a necessary stage in the year 2000 repair sequence of activities.

As stated earlier, by interesting coincidence each reference to a calendar date in a software application seems to require approximately one function point to encode in quite a large variety of programming languages. This coincidence makes expressing the effort and costs in terms of work hours per function point, function points per staff-month, and cost per function point comparatively straightforward.

Year 2000 Repairs by Programming Language

It is interesting to consider the approximate costs of the year 2000 problem for selected programming languages. Table 5.10 gives the cost per language, although with a high margin of error. It assumes date field expansion as the repair strategy, and a burdened personnel cost of $50 per hour, or $8,400 per month. Obviously if some other strategy is selected (such as windowing) or if compensation is higher or lower than $50 per hour, adjustments will be needed.

Although COBOL is the language with the greatest number of year 2000 "hits" it will probably be among the least expensive to modify due to the large numbers of specialized tools and consulting groups in the COBOL domain.

Dr. Tom Love,[8] an independent management consultant and a well-known expert on object-oriented topics, reports that object-oriented languages such as Objective C, SMALLTALK, Eiffel, and so on should be among the *least* expensive if the applications are well formed and the date calculations are handled by formal class libraries. Indeed, since object-oriented business applications are comparatively recent, many may already use adequate space for all date digits and hence the year 2000 problem may not be present in some object-oriented applications. On the other hand, the object-oriented paradigm has a steep learning curve and there may also be object-oriented applications with incorrect date calculations "hard coded" into the application just as they would be in procedural languages.

The most expensive of the widely known languages will probably be Assembly language and PL/I, both of which have shortages of tools and trained personnel. However, there are hundreds of proprietary languages and obscure languages that will be very difficult to repair, since there will be a shortage of both tools and available programming talent. For example, the CORAL66 and CHILL programming languages are both used for telecommunication software and not much else. The Electronic Switching PL/I (ESPL/I) is another example of a language with few current programmers. Table 5.10 shows the approximate overall expenses by language for a sample of some of the more commonly used programming languages.

Although this data has a high margin of error, it appears that the repair costs for the year 2000 problem may be one of the largest single technology expenses in human history.

It is of interest to consider the relative proportion of expense among the four major activities associated with the year 2000 problem for selected programming languages (Table 5.11).

Note that Table 5.11 includes CHILL, CMS2, and Algol, which are not in Table 5.10. Table 5.11 is only approximate and has a high margin of error. However, it is obvious that there will be significant differences from language to language based on the presence or absence of available year 2000 tools, and on the structure of the language itself.

Table 5.10: Approximate Costs for the Year 2000 Problem by Language

Language	Function Points	Cost per Function Point	Total Cost
COBOL	605,000,000	$28	$16,940,000,000
Spreadsheets	54,000,000	$35	$1,890,000,000
C	156,000,000	$35	$5,460,000,000
V-Basic	45,000,000	$30	$1,350,000,000
Query	29,250,000	$40	$1,170,000,000
Database	120,000,000	$45	$5,400,000,000
C++	105,000,000	$35	$3,675,000,000
PASCAL	54,000,000	$40	$2,160,000,000
Assembly	93,750,000	$80	$7,500,000,000
Ada 83	54,000,000	$35	$1,890,000,000
FORTRAN	28,750,000	$35	$1,006,250,000
PL/I	13,500,000	$65	$877,500,000
Jovial	7,875,000	$60	$472,500,000
Other	336,000,000	$60	$20,160,000,000
Total(T)/Average(A)	1,702,125,000(T)	$45(A)	$69,951,250,000(T)

Table 5.11: Distribution of Year 2000 Expenses by Programming Language[a]

Language	Finding Year 2000 Instances	Repairing Year 2000 Instances	Testing Year 2000 Instances	Portfolio Regression Test	Total
Assembly	$25	$20	$20	$15	$80
PL/I	$25	$10	$15	$15	$65
Jovial	$20	$12	$13	$15	$60
CMS2	$20	$12	$13	$15	$60
CHILL	$20	$15	$15	$10	$60
Algol	$15	$12	$13	$10	$50
Database	$7	$13	$15	$10	$45
Query	$10	$12	$12	$6	$40
PASCAL	$5	$10	$15	$10	$40
C++	$8	$6	$13	$8	$35
Spreadsheets	$5	$7	$20	$3	$35
C	$15	$7	$5	$8	$35
Ada 83	$5	$7	$8	$15	$35
FORTRAN	$5	$7	$13	$10	$35
4-GLs	$5	$10	$10	$10	$35
V-Basic	$5	$5	$15	$5	$30
COBOL	$5	$6	$7	$10	$28
SMALLTALK	$3	$3	$5	$7	$18
Average	$11	$10	$13	$10	$44

[a]Results shown in terms of cost per function point.

Year 2000 Software Repairs by State

For problems as large and complex as the year 2000 problem, showing the approximate effort and cost at the national level results in numbers that are so large that the human mind has trouble grasping their significance. Table 5.12 shows the approximate effort and costs for year 2000 repairs for all 50 states in the United States, plus the District of Columbia, in descending order.

Table 5.12: Year 2000 Software Repairs by State for the United States

State	No. of Software Personnel	Year 2000 Effort (mo)	Burdened Monthly Salary	Year 2000 Costs per State
California	214,000	1,061,440	$9,000	$9,552,960,000
New York	138,000	670,680	$9,000	$6,036,120,000
Texas	130,000	598,000	$8,600	$5,142,800,000
Illinois	98,000	450,800	$8,300	$3,741,640,000
Florida	92,000	447,120	$8,200	$3,666,384,000
Pennsylvania	94,000	432,400	$8,300	$3,588,920,000
Ohio	86,000	395,600	$8,300	$3,283,480,000
Michigan	70,000	322,000	$8,300	$2,672,600,000
New Jersey	60,000	291,600	$9,000	$2,624,400,000
Massachusetts	49,000	238,140	$9,000	$2,143,260,000
North Carolina	52,000	239,200	$8,400	$2,009,280,000
Virginia	46,000	218,960	$8,400	$1,839,264,000
Georgia	48,500	218,250	$8,300	$1,811,475,000
District of Columbia	41,500	205,840	$8,200	$1,687,888,000
Maryland	36,000	174,960	$8,400	$1,469,664,000
Indiana	40,000	176,000	$8,300	$1,460,800,000
Washington	35,000	170,100	$8,500	$1,445,850,000
Wisconsin	36,000	165,600	$8,300	$1,374,480,000
Tennessee	37,000	165,020	$8,300	$1,369,666,000
Minnesota	33,300	153,180	$8,300	$1,271,394,000
Missouri	34,500	150,420	$8,300	$1,248,486,000
Alabama	32,000	147,200	$8,200	$1,207,040,000
Louisiana	33,000	143,880	$8,200	$1,179,816,000
Connecticut	26,500	128,790	$8,500	$1,094,715,000
Kentucky	28,400	126,664	$8,200	$1,038,644,800
Oregon	24,000	116,640	$8,700	$1,014,768,000
Colorado	25,900	119,140	$8,500	$1,012,690,000
Arizona	26,500	121,900	$8,300	$1,011,770,000
South Carolina	24,000	110,400	$8,300	$916,320,000
Oklahoma	23,000	100,280	$8,300	$832,324,000

Continued on next page

Table 5.12: Year 2000 Software Repairs by State for the United States, continued

State	No. of Software Personnel	Year 2000 Effort (mo)	Burdened Monthly Salary	Year 2000 Costs per State
Iowa	20,500	89,380	$8,300	$741,854,000
Mississippi	19,500	85,020	$8,200	$697,164,000
Kansas	18,300	79,788	$8,300	$662,240,400
Arkansas	18,200	79,352	$8,200	$650,686,400
New Hampshire	12,500	57,500	$8,400	$483,000,000
West Virginia	12,750	55,590	$8,200	$455,838,000
Utah	11,500	52,900	$8,300	$439,070,000
Nebraska	11,500	50,140	$8,300	$416,162,000
New Mexico	11,000	47,960	$8,300	$398,068,000
Hawaii	8,600	37,496	$9,000	$337,464,000
Maine	8,700	37,932	$8,400	$318,628,800
Rhode Island	7,500	33,450	$8,500	$284,325,000
Idaho	7,500	32,700	$8,300	$271,410,000
Montana	5,750	25,070	$8,300	$208,081,000
Nevada	5,750	25,070	$8,300	$208,081,000
Delaware	5,150	23,690	$8,300	$196,627,000
South Dakota	5,000	21,800	$8,200	$178,760,000
Alaska	4,500	19,620	$8,700	$170,694,000
North Dakota	4,000	19,440	$8,200	$159,408,000
Vermont	4,000	18,400	$8,400	$154,560,000
Wyoming	3,700	16,280	$8,400	$136,752,000
US Total(T)/ Average(A)	1,920,000(T)	8,968,782(T)	$8,400(A)	$75,337,768,800(T)

Note that Table 5.12 uses simple ratios for dealing with compensation, so that the totals are slightly different from other tabular data in this report. Although Table 5.12 has a high margin of error, it can be hypothesized that the software-intensive industries in the top 10 states are likely to be severely affected by the work associated with the year 2000 problem. At the very least, there will be significant delays in starting new software projects because the year 2000 problem is likely to absorb almost all of the available software personnel for the next several years.

State government responses to the year 2000 problem vary as widely as do any other industry. Some state governments, such as Florida, have well-planned year 2000 containment strategies[9] while other states have not yet addressed the year 2000 problem. Incidentally, if state governments were ranked using the same income criteria as the Fortune 500 companies, some 46 states out of 50 would have incomes large enough to be classified in the Fortune 500 category. This means, of course, that state governments also have a great deal of software and, hence, major year 2000 problems.

Aggregate of All Year 2000 Software-Related Costs for the United States

At this point it is appropriate to attempt to consolidate some of the disparate cost elements of the year 2000 problem and see what the possible costs may be for the United States when all of the various cost elements are assembled into one total. Because hardware upgrades, database repairs, and litigation expenses are not normalized using function point metrics or LOC metrics, the only kind of convenient overall aggregation of year 2000 expenses is a simple summation of the various components. Table 5.13 gives a rough approximation of all major year 2000 cost elements.

It is an interesting "sanity check" to see how the year 2000 costs relate to the overall cost per capita for US citizens. Assuming a year 2000 population for the United States of about 280,000,000 citizens, then the per capita year 2000 cost for the United States amounts to about $989 for every citizen. Assuming a US working population at the end of the century of roughly 120,000,000 workers, then about $2,308 would be the cost for every working person in the United States. Assuming only software workers, with a century-end total of about 1,920,000 technical software staff plus managers, the overall costs would amount to about $144,270 for everyone in the US software business at the end of the century. This is a very significant expense that is likely to cause a number of software-intensive companies to file for bankruptcy prior to the end of the twentieth century.

Table 5.13: Overall Total of US Year 2000 Expense Elements

Year 2000 Topic	US Year 2000 Cost
Initial software repairs	$70,000,000,000
Secondary bad-fix software repairs	$7,000,000,000
Test library repairs	$10,000,000,000
Database repairs	$60,000,000,000
Hardware chip replacements	$10,000,000,000
Hardware performance upgrades	$20,000,000,000
Litigation and damages	$100,000,000,000
US Total	$277,000,000,000

If we back out litigation and hardware costs, of course, the per capita expenses drop by more than 50%. They are still a rather significant amount and may well have a disrupting affect on the US economy, and will certainly disrupt the cash flow and profitability of a large number of enterprises. Although function points are not normally used for dealing with hardware costs or litigation, it is a simple calculation to divide estimated total US expenses of $277,000,000,000 by the anticipated US software portfolio of 1,702,750,000 function points. This results in a per function point cost of about $162.67 for every function point deployed in the United States. Here, too, backing out litigation and hardware costs would lower the amount by more than 50%. Even with this reduction, the overall total is quite an alarming figure.

The overall year 2000 costs will, in reality, be comprised of the results of the independent year 2000 repairs being performed by thousands of corporations and government groups on literally millions of applications. There are far too many variables and far too much uncertainty to be sure of what the real costs are going to be.

Later in this book some of the many sources of cost variance will be discussed in a global context. At this point, however, let us continue to consider some of the factors that will affect overall costs. We turn next to the tools and technologies that can affect the year 2000 repair prognosis.

Tools and Technologies that Affect the Year 2000 Problem

From more than 10 years of software assessment and benchmark studies, myself and my colleagues at SPR have published information on the approximate value of a large number of software technologies and tool categories, such as formal inspections, complexity analysis tools, cost-estimating tools, and the like. For example, *Assessment and Control of Software Risks,*[10] *Patterns of Software Systems Failure and Success,*[11] and *Applied Software Measurement*[12] have all included provisional rankings of the return on investment (ROI) in various software-related tools and methods. These books deal with the value of various tools and methods to the software community. To explore the value of software itself to the business user community, which takes the ROI concept a stage higher, the work of Paul Strassmann[13], such as *The Squandered Computer,* is highly recommended. This new book, published in 1997, deals with the value of the overall software and computing complex, with some very interesting analyses of the value of outsourcing arrangements.

In the context of the year 2000 problem, it is interesting to use the lower level software ROI information as a background to show the kinds of tools and methods that have some relevance to the year 2000 problem. Every time this ROI data is published it is important to state that the data has a very high margin of error, and can vary significantly from the stated data points. The "value" of any given technology fluctuates in response to the size and complexity of the project, the number of users, and a host of other factors. Further, the actual empirical data supporting the ROI analysis is not perfect and, for many technologies, is known to be incomplete. However, in spite of the fact that the specific dollar amounts are questionable and should not be taken seriously, the overall rankings of value have some utility.

For some technologies, such as formal inspections, there is a continuous stream of data that dates back to the late 1970s. Thus many projects have been analyzed that (1) did not use inspections at all, (2) were starting to use inspections, and (3) had been using inspections for one or more years. When the results of 50 of each of these project types are compared, the value or ROI of inspections is clearly evident, since in this case the high-use-of-inspection group has shorter schedules, lower costs, and better quality than the no-inspections and inspection-novice groups. In repeated trials involving more than 50 companies and 500 projects of generally the same class, type, and size, the projects using inspections end up with higher quality, lower costs, and shorter schedules than identical projects that don't use inspections at all.

For newer technologies, such as Quality Function Deployment and the year 2000 technologies, there are no long-range studies since the technologies themselves are only a few years old. The results are therefore based partly on empirical observations and partly on modeling anticipated future value. Such hybrid studies, which mix historical data with mathematical modeling, are of course questionable, but if we wait until empirical data is complete and ample we will be waiting into the next century.

Once again, the actual ROI values shown here are only rough approximations, but the rank listings from high to low values are more substantial and can usually be supported, although technologies that are close together can easily swap places from trial to trial. However, it is highly unlikely for technologies near the top of the list to drop to the bottom or, conversely, for technologies near the bottom to rise to the top.

Example ROI Calculation

The following is a simplified example of the kind of analysis that comprises ROI calculations. Assume that the total development cost of a software project, Case A, that does not use inspections is $1,000 per function point. (The testing costs for a project without inspections amount to $400 per function point.) Assume that the development schedule for the project was 18 months. The maintenance costs for defect repairs and customer support total $2,000 per function point.

Next assume that the total development cost for a similar project, Case B, that *did* use inspections was $900 per function point. The inspections themselves cost $100 per function point, but testing costs were reduced to $200 per function point. The development schedule for the project was 12 months. The maintenance costs for defect repairs and support total $500 per function point.

When comparing Case A and Case B, it can be seen that an investment of $100 per function point for inspections generated savings of $200 per function point in testing costs. Further, the savings in maintenance costs were $1,500 per function point. Thus, in this simple example, an investment of $1 for inspections created a direct ROI of $17 in value for every $1 invested.

When the impact of shorter development schedules are considered, which might result in additional revenues or more savings, the ultimate value could obviously be even higher. This kind of ROI analysis is crude and imperfect, but at least it is now possible to carry out preliminary value studies of software tools, methods, and approaches. Of course, the class time for students learning inspections and the cost of an instructor should be factored in as well, but this is merely an example of how the ROI data is derived and not an in-depth ROI study of formal inspections.

There is no question that the technologies and methods at the top of the list are valuable to large numbers of our clients and to many corporations. Conversely, the technologies at the bottom of the list are often dangerous and harmful.

Table 5.14 shows more than 125 software-related technologies in descending order, based on the cumulative ROI after four years of deployment, for those that have more than four years of use behind them. The technologies that affect the year 2000 issue are highlighted using a "star" method, similar to the way restaurants and hotels are rated in Michelin guides. The number of stars does not indicate positive

Table 5.14: Approximate Return on Investment in Selected Software Technologies

Selected Software Technology	12 Months	24 Months	36 Months	48 Months	Year 2000 Impact
Reusability (all high-quality artifacts)	$3.75	$9.15	$21.75	$43.75	**
I-CASE (full integration)	$1.50	$5.50	$15.50	$23.00	**
Quality measurements (full life)	$1.15	$3.50	$12.00	$20.00	**
Cost estimation tools	$2.50	$5.00	$12.00	$17.50	***
Methodology management tools	$2.50	$5.00	$12.00	$17.50	**
Quality estimation tools	$4.00	$7.00	$10.00	$17.00	***
Baldrige Award (winning)	$4.50	$7.00	$12.00	$16.50	
Formal code inspections	$3.50	$7.00	$12.00	$16.00	*
Formal design inspections	$3.50	$6.00	$10.00	$15.50	
High-volume beta testing	$2.00	$4.00	$10.00	$15.00	*
Optimal staff hiring practices	$2.00	$4.00	$8.00	$14.00	**
Project management tools	$4.00	$8.00	$10.00	$13.50	***
Year 2000 reusable components	$0.90	$5.00	$9.00	$13.00	****
SEI CMM 5	$3.50	$4.75	$10.00	$12.75	
Activity-based costing	$1.50	$3.00	$6.00	$12.50	**
Year 2000 activity-based costing	$1.50	$3.00	$6.00	$12.00	***
Global change management tools	$3.00	$6.00	$8.00	$12.00	***
Joint application design	$3.00	$5.00	$8.00	$12.00	
Error-prone module removal	$4.00	$6.00	$8.00	$12.00	***
Year 2000 repair tools	$5.00	$6.00	$10.00	$12.00	****
Year 2000 search tools	$6.00	$8.00	$10.00	$12.00	*****
In-house year 2000 repairs	$4.00	$6.00	$8.00	$12.00	***
Defect removal efficiency metrics	$1.50	$4.00	$7.00	$11.50	**
Object-oriented programming	$2.00	$5.00	$9.00	$11.00	**
Data warehouses	$0.90	$1.50	$5.00	$10.50	***
Data warehouse development tools	$1.15	$3.00	$6.00	$10.50	**
Year 2000 removal efficiency metrics	$1.50	$3.00	$5.00	$10.00	***
Year 2000 date expansion	$0.60	$1.75	$6.00	$10.00	*****
Productivity measurements, activity	$1.75	$2.75	$6.00	$10.00	**
SPR assessments	$1.50	$4.50	$6.50	$10.00	
Year 2000 replacements	$1.50	$4.00	$8.00	$10.00	****
Quality function deployment	$1.75	$3.75	$6.00	$10.00	
Structured coding	$2.00	$4.00	$7.00	$10.00	**
Year 2000 masking	$4.00	$6.00	$6.50	$9.75	*****
Defect-tracking tools	$2.50	$5.00	$7.50	$9.75	***

Continued on next page

Table 5.14: Approximate Return on Investment in Selected Software Technologies, continued

Selected Software Technology	12 Months	24 Months	36 Months	48 Months	Year 2000 Impact
Requirements automation tools	$1.50	$3.75	$6.00	$9.50	
Design automation tools	$1.50	$3.50	$5.50	$9.50	
Database design tools	$1.50	$3.50	$5.50	$9.50	*
SEI CMM 4	$3.00	$4.00	$7.00	$9.50	
Document workflow tools	$1.00	$3.00	$6.00	$9.25	
User satisfaction surveys	$2.00	$4.00	$8.00	$9.00	
Intranet access	$2.50	$4.00	$7.00	$9.00	**
Benchmarking (quality)	$2.00	$3.50	$5.00	$9.00	*
Data quality analysis tools	$1.00	$3.00	$7.00	$9.00	**
SAP/R3	$0.40	$0.80	$3.00	$9.00	**
Structured design	$2.00	$3.50	$5.00	$9.00	**
Function point metrics (IFPUG)	$1.50	$2.50	$5.00	$9.00	***
SEI assessments	$1.75	$2.50	$5.00	$9.00	
Year 2000 reusable test cases	$4.00	$5.00	$6.00	$9.00	****
Function points from design tools	$1.75	$3.00	$4.50	$8.50	
Reverse-engineering tools	$1.25	$2.50	$4.50	$8.00	**
Restructuring tools	$2.50	$5.00	$6.00	$8.00	****
Information engineering	$1.00	$1.75	$5.00	$8.00	*
Internet access	$2.00	$3.00	$5.00	$8.00	*
Optimal office ergonomics	$2.00	$4.00	$6.00	$8.00	*
OLAP	$1.10	$2.00	$6.00	$8.00	*
Formal risk analysis programs	$3.00	$4.00	$6.00	$8.00	***
Year 2000 regression testing	$4.00	$4.50	$5.00	$8.00	*****
Client-server architectures	$0.50	$1.00	$5.00	$7.50	***
Function point metrics (Mark II)	$1.75	$3.00	$4.00	$7.50	*
Cyclomatic complexity metrics	$1.80	$3.00	$4.00	$7.50	****
Year 2000 estimating specialists	$1.50	$2.50	$3.50	$7.50	****
Low-volume beta testing	$2.00	$3.00	$5.00	$7.00	**
Annual management training	$2.75	$4.00	$5.50	$7.00	
Code reuse (high quality)	$1.00	$2.00	$5.00	$7.00	**
Year 2000 repair specialists	$2.00	$3.00	$5.00	$7.00	*****
Specialists (maintenance)	$1.70	$2.50	$4.00	$6.50	***
Database query languages	$1.50	$2.50	$3.50	$6.50	**
Reusable controls (commercial)	$1.10	$1.75	$3.00	$6.00	*
Regression testing	$3.50	$4.00	$4.50	$6.00	*
Reusable designs	$0.10	$0.50	$2.50	$6.00	
Staff morale surveys	$2.00	$2.50	$4.00	$6.00	
Specialists (estimating)	$1.75	$3.00	$4.00	$6.00	**
Specialists (Web masters)	$2.00	$3.00	$4.00	$6.00	
Test coverage analysis tools	$1.75	$2.75	$3.50	$6.00	***
Annual staff training (10 days)	$2.00	$3.00	$4.00	$6.00	

Continued on next page

Table 5.14: Approximate Return on Investment in Selected Software Technologies, continued

Selected Software Technology	12 Months	24 Months	36 Months	48 Months	Year 2000 Impact
Informal code reviews	$2.00	$3.00	$4.00	$5.50	**
Code change control tools	$1.90	$2.50	$4.25	$5.50	****
Universal Modeling Language	$0.90	$1.20	$3.00	$5.50	
Benchmarking (productivity)	$1.25	$1.75	$3.00	$5.50	
Code execution simulation tools	$2.50	$3.50	$4.50	$5.50	**
Year 2000 outsourcing (international)	$3.00	$4.00	$4.50	$5.50	****
Total quality management	$0.85	$1.50	$4.50	$5.25	
Informal design reviews	$2.00	$3.00	$4.00	$5.00	
Unit testing	$1.50	$2.50	$3.50	$5.00	***
System testing	$3.00	$3.50	$4.00	$5.00	***
Reengineering tools	$2.00	$3.00	$4.00	$5.00	**
Reusable requirements	$1.75	$3.00	$4.00	$5.00	
Specialists (technical writing)	$1.50	$2.50	$3.00	$5.00	
Specialists (database administration)	$1.50	$2.50	$3.50	$5.00	**
Reusable project plans	$2.00	$3.00	$4.00	$5.00	**
Reusable test cases	$1.50	$2.00	$4.00	$5.00	***
Backfiring (LOC to function point tools)	$1.25	$2.00	$4.00	$5.00	**
Data modeling tools	$1.00	$1.50	$2.00	$5.00	**
SEI CMM 3	$1.75	$2.50	$3.00	$5.00	
Feature point metrics	$1.50	$1.80	$2.00	$5.00	*
Outsourcing (domestic)	$0.75	$0.80	$1.50	$4.75	*
Object-oriented design	$0.50	$0.90	$2.50	$4.50	
Test library control tools	$1.00	$1.75	$3.00	$4.50	***
Reusable cost estimates	$1.50	$2.50	$3.00	$4.50	**
Reusable data	$1.50	$2.00	$3.00	$4.50	**
Year 2000 outsourcing (domestic)	$2.50	$3.00	$4.00	$4.50	****
Function point metrics (3D)	$1.20	$1.50	$2.75	$4.00	*
CASE tools (partial)	$1.75	$2.00	$2.50	$4.00	*
Outsourcing (international)	$3.50	$2.75	$3.00	$4.00	*
LOC counting tools (logical)	$1.25	$1.75	$3.50	$4.00	***
Time-box prototyping	$1.30	$1.60	$2.00	$3.75	
Reusable user documents	$0.75	$1.25	$2.50	$3.75	
ISO certification (international)	$1.20	$2.75	$3.00	$3.75	
Specialists (quality assurance)	$0.75	$1.50	$2.00	$3.75	*
Year 2000 date windowing	$5.00	$4.50	$4.00	$3.50	****
Change management tools (code only)	$1.00	$1.25	$1.50	$3.50	**

Continued on next page

Table 5.14: Approximate Return on Investment in Selected Software Technologies,
        continued

Selected Software Technology	12 Months	24 Months	36 Months	48 Months	Year 2000 Impact
Reusable interfaces	$1.00	$1.50	$2.00	$3.50	
Informal prototyping	$0.75	$1.50	$2.00	$3.00	*
Formal standards (IEEE, ISO, etc.)	$1.00	$1.50	$2.00	$3.00	
Logical statement LOC metrics	$1.10	$1.75	$2.00	$2.75	**
SEI CMM 2	$1.00	$1.15	$1.50	$2.50	
Reusable architectures	$1.00	$1.25	$1.75	$2.50	
Business process reengineering	$1.10	$1.80	$2.00	$2.25	
Year 2000 encapsulation	$5.00	$4.00	$3.00	$2.00	****
Clean room development	$1.10	$1.30	$1.30	$1.70	
Object-oriented metrics	$1.35	$1.55	$1.60	$1.70	
RAD	$2.50	$2.00	$1.75	$1.60	
End-user applications	$2.50	$2.00	$1.75	$1.50	***
Productivity measurements, project	$1.50	$1.40	$1.30	$1.20	*
LOC-based estimation tools	$1.50	$1.30	$1.20	$1.10	**
LOC counting tools (physical)	$1.25	$1.15	$1.05	$1.00	**
ISO certification (domestic)	$1.20	$1.10	$1.00	$0.95	
Year 2000 date compression	$2.00	$1.50	$1.25	$0.90	**
Defects per KLOC metrics	$1.05	$1.00	$0.95	$0.90	*
SEI core metrics	$1.10	$1.00	$0.90	$0.75	*
SEI CMM 1	$0.75	$0.75	$0.70	$0.70	
Good-enough quality methods	$0.90	$0.80	$0.75	$0.70	
Downsizing (layoffs)	$0.95	$0.90	$0.80	$0.70	
Shared offices (poor ergonomics)	$0.90	$0.80	$0.70	$0.60	*
Correctness proofs	$0.90	$0.80	$0.70	$0.60	
Software science metrics	$0.95	$0.85	$0.80	$0.60	
Manual cost-estimating methods	$1.10	$1.00	$0.90	$0.55	*
Cost-per-defect metrics	$0.90	$0.80	$0.70	$0.50	*
Physical LOC metrics	$0.90	$0.70	$0.60	$0.50	****
Manual year 2000 cost estimates	$1.00	$0.80	$0.70	$0.50	***
Year 2000 LOC charge metrics	$0.80	$0.70	$0.60	$0.45	*****
Code reuse (low quality)	$0.90	$0.80	$0.60	$0.40	*

LOC = lines of code.

No star means no impact on the year 2000 problem.

*Minor impact on the year 2000 problem.

**Some impact on the year 2000 problem.

***Significant impact on the year 2000 problem.

****Important impact on the year 2000 problem.

*****Major and critical impact on the year 2000 problem.

or negative directions for the impact—only the magnitude of the impact. To judge the positive and negative direction of impact, the final value column, which shows a cumulative value after 48 months of deployment, can give a rough approximation, although the actual dollar values are unreliable for many year 2000 tools since they have not been available long enough to accumulate 48 months of data. Note that the values shown are quite preliminary, and future data may indicate a need for modification. The data in Table 5.14 is cumulative over a 48-month period from the time of deployment.

In general business terms, the ROI data is intended to show the approximate cumulative return for every $1 invested. Since the entire field of quantifying ROI for software technologies is both new and uncertain, there is not yet any definitive data on what constitutes a "good" or a "bad" investment. The preliminary data suggests that a six-level classification may be useful:

Excellent ROI	>$15 returned for every $1 invested
Very good ROI	>$10 returned for every $1 invested
Good ROI	>$5 returned for every $1 invested
Fair ROI	>$2.50 returned for every $1 invested
Marginal ROI	>$1 returned for every $1 invested
Poor ROI	<$1 returned for every $1 invested

To summarize the net results of Table 5.14, the set of tools and technologies that I believe will have the greatest impact on the year 2000 problem include the following four-star and five-star set:

- Year 2000 reusable components
- Year 2000 masking of all forms
- Year 2000 search tools
- Year 2000 repair tools
- Year 2000 replacement applications
- Activity-based year 2000 pricing methods
- In-house year 2000 repairs
- Year 2000 date expansion logic
- Year 2000 encapsulation logic
- Year 2000 windowing logic
- Year 2000 bridging logic
- Year 2000 reusable test cases
- Year 2000 regression testing
- Change control tools
- Cyclomatic complexity metrics
- Code restructuring tools (COBOL)

- Logical statement metrics
- Function point metrics
- Year 2000 estimating specialists
- Year 2000 repair specialists
- Physical LOC metrics
- International year 2000 outsourcing
- Domestic year 2000 outsourcing
- LOC year 2000 pricing methods

This set of year 2000 tools and technologies can serve as a convenient checklist for year 2000 project managers. Hopefully you have evaluated everything on this list, and have already reached the final selection of tools and technologies that are appropriate for your particular situation.

The year 2000 problem is a very pervasive issue that will probably engage many of the normal software tools in special ways. For example, change control and version management technologies have been on the commercial market for many years, but will assume major roles in the year 2000 issue. In addition, a number of new kinds of tools are being rushed into the market in direct response to the needs of the year 2000 problem. Year 2000 search engines and automated year 2000 repair tools are examples.

Yet another word of caution is indicated about some of the year 2000 technologies that are harmful or hazardous. The most troubling of these is the simplistic usage of physical LOC as a charge mechanism for year 2000 repairs. Many contractors and outsource vendors are charging (or at least attempting to) from $1 to more than $2 per physical line of code. As already discussed in previous sections, quite a lot of code does not need to be repaired, and vendors should not attempt to charge for physical LOC that consist of (1) blank lines, (2) comments, and (3) dead code.

Even worse, concentrating on simple metrics such as physical LOC often blinds even year 2000 project managers to the other things that need repair and that can't be measured with either LOC or function point metrics:

- Enterprise analysis of year 2000 exposures
- Hiring and signing bonuses of year 2000 specialists
- Databases and data warehouse repairs
- Physical devices such as fax machines, elevators, and security systems
- Regression test libraries
- Litigation preparations

Estimating year 2000 costs is a very complex issue, and it needs to be done across both software and nonsoftware activities. Simplistic estimates based on LOC are insufficient to deal with all year 2000 cost issues.

Unusual Methods for Speeding Up Year 2000 Repairs

To fit year 2000 repair work into normal software routines without disruption and confusion, the work should have started before 1995. Obviously for many companies this did not happen, and some have still not begun! To raise the probability that year 2000 repairs can be substantially accomplished by the end of the century, some nonstandard business practices may be needed. (Incidentally, as this book is being written, not one year 2000 specialist believes any longer that the year 2000 problem will be solved by more than a handful of leading corporations.) However, these unusual approaches can elevate the probability of fixing most of the more serious problems before the end of the century.

Around-the-Clock Year 2000 Repair Centers

There are not enough hours and weeks left between now and the year 2000 to continue to work on the problem for only one eight-hour shift out of every 24 hours. What would be highly efficient would be for one or more of the larger companies (for example, companies the size of IBM, EDS, or Andersen) to establish three year 2000 repair factories located roughly eight hours apart, such as having a lab in the western part of the United States, one in Spain, and one in India. These linked year 2000 repair facilities could be set up to move work from one location to another at the end of the normal working day, so that year 2000 repairs proceeded around the clock on a 24-hour cycle. In 1998 each of these locations would probably work one shift. However, during 1999, it would be even more effective if these three locations worked on two- or three-shift schedules.

The reason that three separate facilities might be needed, rather than running year 2000 repairs around the clock in one building in one country, is due to a number of factors. For example, in the United States there is such a severe shortage of software personnel that it is unlikely that teams could be assembled for the third shift, and probably there would be trouble filling up even the first and second shifts!

There is also a significant problem of physical facilities. The normal custom for software work in the United States and indeed much of the world is to assign a specific office or cubicle to each software professional. If three-shift work commenced, obviously the work space would need to be shared by multiple workers, or additional space would be needed.

Also, the usual premium pay for second- and third-shift work in the United States is expensive, while locating year 2000 repair centers in locations where the work could be concentrated during the first shift, and where labor costs may be lower than in the United States, would offer some attractive savings.

Suspension of Antitrust Regulations for Year 2000 Repairs

Many large corporations in the same industry use almost identical kinds of software for identical purposes. The year 2000 problem is too vast and too expensive to have thousands of disconnected year 2000 repair groups when it is obvious that significant economies of scale would result from vertical year 2000 repairs within industries such as banks, insurance companies, airlines, retail chains, hospitals, and the like.

While it is unlikely that the Department of Justice would view joint year 2000 work by competitors as being anticompetitive or even falling under antitrust regulations, it would facilitate the process if the Department of Justice made a public statement to this effect. (Incidentally, as discussed later in this section, the Department of Justice itself is far behind schedule on its own year 2000 repairs. That being the case, they should hardly fault other organizations for wanting to move faster and more efficiently.)

The most cost- and time-effective year 2000 strategy would be the establishment of jointly funded year 2000 repair facilities for key industries such as banks, airlines, insurance companies, and so forth. These joint repair facilities could also make use of the previous suggestion of running 24 hours a day.

Suspension of IRC 482 for Year 2000 Reuse

In the United States the federal income tax rules may be interpreted by the IRS in a way that treats reusable year 2000 materials (such as bridging tools and windowing tools) as taxable income for the locations that use these tools, even though the developing location did not actually charge for the tool. On the surface, IRC 482 appears to be hazardous to any form of reuse. Expert tax guidance by an attorney, tax accountant, or both should be part of every large corporation's year 2000 project team. IRC 482 transcends the year 2000 problem and can raise troublesome issues for object-oriented class libraries, component-based development, shared test materials, and all other forms of software-related reusability.

Suspension of Nonyear 2000 Projects

If there were a software Richter scale similar to the scale used for measuring earthquakes, the year 2000 problem rates about an eight. Basically it will destroy everything in its path. There are no other software projects that can be envisioned with positive value that is as great as the negative impact of the year 2000 problem. Therefore it seems prudent to terminate every other software project other than "emergency repairs" and deploy 100% of available software resources on the year 2000 problem until it is resolved.

Since most of our clients are currently running below 15% of their software staff assigned to the year 2000 problem, the suspension of all other work except emergency repairs and statutory updates should raise the year 2000 resource pool by about 4:1, and compress year 2000 repair cycles by a smaller but still significant amount—perhaps 2.5:1. Moving from 15% resource software staff use to about 85% software staff use should accelerate year 2000 repairs and allow companies starting late to have a chance of finishing in time. However, to be successful, this strategy needs to be implemented almost at once, and certainly no later than the first quarter of 1998. Incidentally, unless year 2000 repairs are the highest priority item of an enterprise and have all available resources dedicated to them, it will be very difficult for executives and boards of directors to defend themselves against year 2000 damage suits.

Imagine you are a corporate executive on the witness stand in a lawsuit (or even a class-action lawsuit) brought by clients or employees because year 2000 problems did some serious harm. How would you answer questions such as:

- Did you assign all of your available staff to year 2000 repairs?
- What percentage of your staff did other work and not year 2000 repairs?
- What priority did you give to year 2000 repairs?
- What percentage of your budget in 1996 through 1999 went to year 2000 repairs?

It is fairly obvious that unless software and corporate executives take the year 2000 problem as a serious business issue, they themselves may face unpleasant legal and financial consequences, and criminal charges are not beyond the realm of possibility.

Suspension of European Currency Conversion

Using the hypothetical software Richter scale, as discussed earlier, the year 2000 problem rates about an eight and the European currency conversion rates about a 6.5, which is still very serious. It would be prudent to suspend the European currency conversion work until after the year 2000 crisis, which probably means deferring it until about 2005.

Acquisition of Year 2000 Service Companies

I formerly worked for the ITT Corporation, which was a conglomerate that acquired companies rather frequently. Since it is difficult to hire software personnel right now, large corporations might find that it is quicker and more cost effective to buy entire year 2000 service companies than it is to negotiate service contracts with these same enterprises.

Using a similar chain of reasoning, corporate mergers and acquisitions of competitors with year 2000-compliant applications may also be an interesting but unusual strategy. Given the high costs of software personnel and the overall national shortage of software personnel, acquiring small software companies and local programming "body shops" simply to gain access to their personnel may become common as the year 2000 approaches.

Year 2000 Schedules versus Resources

Since December 31, 1999, is a fixed point in time, it is not possible to use safely the "standard" software methodology for dealing with projects for which there is too much work for the available staff—namely, slipping the schedule. The only available alternative is to increase the number of people who work on the year 2000 problem. This alternative will come face to face with one of the derivative problems brought on by the year 2000 crisis. There are no longer any surplus software personnel in the major industrialized countries. Even outsourcing companies are turning away year 2000 repair business for lack of available personnel. Even retired software employees are coming back into the workforce on a temporary basis, as bonuses and compensation make returning to work a lucrative proposition.

Given these stringent conditions, the only viable alternative for many corporations is to use their own software staff (assuming they can keep them). When this book was started in 1996, the "average" year 2000 repair team among my clients comprised less than 5% of the total software employees. Mid 1997, the average year 2000 complement is now approaching 15% of available software personnel, and is continuing to rise. At this point, it is obvious that the year 2000 work will begin to compete for resources with normal development and maintenance projects, and also with other "crash" projects such as the European currency conversion work. At a nominal 15% of available resources, the year 2000 repair cycle will typically stretch out to more than three calendar years, and may reach four calendar years. Obviously this strategy is no longer applicable when only a little more than two calendar years remain.

Given the gravity and serious consequences of the year 2000 situation, there seems to be no other effective alternative than to accelerate a trend that is already in progress and move the majority of all available software personnel into the year 2000 repair arena until the year 2000 problem is satisfactorily resolved.

Assuming an enterprise has finished with triage but does not start year 2000 repairs in earnest until January 1, 1998, the following discussion shows the probability of completing the work in time, assuming various staffing alternatives:

If you adopt a "business as usual" approach and use no more than 15% of your software staff for single-shift year 2000 repairs, you have little or no hope of succeeding, and a high probability of both failing and being sued.

If you take the year 2000 problem as a serious risk, deploy all of your software personnel except those held back for emergency statutory work, so that at least 85% of your software staff is used for year 2000 repairs, you have a fair chance of succeeding. Of course, you will have to suspend all other planned development, enhancement, and maintenance work unless you need to add enhancements to amortize year 2000 costs over multiple years rather than expensing them for the current year.

If you attack the year 2000 problem with maximal vigor by using 85% of your own personnel, augmenting your personnel by contractors and outsourcers, and doing some year 2000 work off-shore so that your year 2000 repairs can proceed on a 24-hour-a-day basis, you have a very good probability of not only succeeding, but finishing early.

In every case you will raise your chances of success by using a combination of year 2000 repair strategies including date field expansions, bridging, windowing, encapsulation, and data duplexing. You will also raise your chances by using state-of-the-art automation, including year 2000 search engines, year 2000 repair engines, change management tools, complexity analyzers, and other forms of automation that can minimize "brute force" manual methods.

It is far too late to view the year 2000 problem as a normal software activity that uses only a fraction of available resources during one normal business shift. If you had started your year 2000 repair work in 1995 you might have been able to deal with the situation in a semi-leisurely way, but that time is long since past. From this point on, only maximal vigor and full deployment of resources can give you any prospect of success. The need for additional year 2000 personnel brings with it yet another kind of problem—a shortage of programming personnel coupled with the fact that some software professionals refuse to work on the year 2000 problem on the grounds that it is an "old" technology.

Shortage of Programmers and Reluctance to Work on Year 2000 Repairs

After the economic decline of the late 1980s and early 1990s, the software industry has rebounded to a surprising degree. In part, the year 2000 problem is causing a burst of hiring, but also software is expanding in every direction and in every industry that uses computers. Some of the manifestations of the national shortage of programming personnel can be illustrated by these unusual events, which started to occur in 1997:

- Programmers may receive signing bonuses, just as professional athletes do.
- Retired programmers are being asked to return to work, with very attractive incentives.
- College recruitment for programming personnel is accelerating.
- International outsourcing to countries such as India and the Ukraine is increasing.
- International "insourcing" or importing software engineers from abroad is increasing.
- Programmers willing to work on the year 2000 problem may receive substantial bonuses in return for agreeing to work past the year 2000 deadline.

A troubling aspect of the year 2000 problem is the fact that many programmers regard the problem as trivial and don't want to work on it even for attractive compensation packages. This is an unfortunate view, since the year 2000 problem is going to be one of the major software events in all history. Programmers who do work on the year 2000 problem will learn more about testing, maintenance strategies, and other important corporate software issues than may be possible from working on new applications.

Lauris Nance,[14] the year 2000 project manager at Equifax Insurance, makes a strong case that year 2000 programming and project management can be of substantial career value. Over and above the already strong arguments that Nance puts forth in favor of year 2000 programming, the importance of this problem is so great that by 1999 comparatively few kinds of nonyear 2000 programming jobs may be available.

As enterprise after enterprise finally begin to awaken to the seriousness of the year 2000 situation, many other kinds of software projects will be suspended or terminated, which may lead to the short-term situation of more than 50% of the programming jobs in the United States being directly involved with year 2000 repairs during the last half of 1999 and on into the first half of 2000.

Small Companies and the Year 2000 Personnel Shortage

Because the main economic impact of the year 2000 problem is on large companies in the Fortune 500 category, the topic of year 2000 problems within small companies that have less than 10 software personnel, or perhaps none at all, is underreported in the literature. Small companies depend heavily on commercial software packages, and have comparatively little in the way of custom-built software. However, they will experience year 2000 problems with their personal computers, networks, and perhaps serious problems with some of the commercial packages that are not year 2000 compliant or require total replacements to new versions.

Unfortunately, the year 2000 crisis has absorbed so many software personnel for work in large companies that the smaller enterprises are finding it difficult to get assistance. Most of the larger outsourcers are turning away requests for small contracts, and the supply of independent year 2000 specialists is both limited and likely to be heavily booked. Indeed, one of the unexpected byproducts of the year 2000 problem, and the current acute shortage of software personnel, is that some small software companies may be acquired not so much for their current line of business, but because they may provide a pool of available software personnel.

A very interesting business venture would be for one or more year 2000 outsource contractors to help small clients with similar needs form a consortium of 20 to 50 regional companies that can pool their year 2000 expertise, tools, personnel, and information. The best sources of assistance for small companies are the smaller year 2000 tool and outsource groups. Also it is very helpful to join the regional year 2000 associations that have sprung up in almost every major city and to use the World Wide Web and follow the various threads of year 2000 discussion.

Post-2000 Software Personnel Surplus

An aspect of the post-2000 situation that has not been addressed in the year 2000 literature concerns the future of year 2000 service providers and the fact that once the year 2000 repairs are accomplished, many companies may have a surplus of software personnel. As the situation is developing, so many year 2000 repairs will not be accomplished until after the millennium that the repair resources during calendar year 2000 may be at the same or even higher levels than in 1999. Also, because so many of the year 2000 repairs are in the form of encapsulation, windowing, bridging, or other temporary measures, there will be a long-range need for more permanent kinds of repairs for perhaps five years into the next century. Of course, now that many companies have learned how hazardous the year 2000 situation is, noncompliant applications will probably be eliminated at the earliest opportunity. However, by about 2005 the current acute shortage of experienced software personnel should begin to ease up and companies will begin to explore downsizing again, as they did in the late 1980s.

Some of the year 2000 service providers have been in business as outsourcers for many years and will continue to perform their normal business functions. For outsource companies such as Andersen, CSC, EDS, IBM, Keane, Perot Systems, and the like, the year 2000 problem is a significant opportunity, but by no means critical to their long-range business goals. For smaller and more specialized year 2000 companies, and for some of the year 2000 tool vendors, it will be necessary to make the transition to other kinds of work after the year 2000 crisis is resolved. Although it is premature to judge the overall results, it can be hypothesized that the explosive growth of software personnel and start-up year 2000 companies may perhaps be followed by a fairly sharp period of downsizings, layoffs, and possible business failures. Many year 2000 vendors that cannot make the transition to other kinds of work may face an abrupt end to their growth and profitability.

The Emergence of Year 2000 Insurance

Starting circa 1996, a number of insurance companies began to offer insurance policies to guard against some of the financial risks and damages associated with the year 2000 problem. It is premature to judge the final benefits of coverage, since many insurance companies are still creating the policies and they are not yet fully available.

Two general forms of year 2000 insurance are starting to become available, and both are concerned with the risks of business losses caused by the year 2000 problem. In one form, if an enterprise expects that potential year 2000 damages might amount to $100,000,000, then they set aside a significant portion of that amount, such as perhaps $50,000,000, and the insurance company will assume the rest. However, if the risks do not come to pass, the company can regain most of what was set aside except for service payments. The second form is a more traditional assumed-risk form of policy. If anticipated risks are $100,000,000, the premiums might amount to $10,000,000 each year. As with personal insurance, if the risks do not occur the premiums are not refundable.

The topic of year 2000 insurance needs to be evaluated by enterprise executives and risk managers on an individual basis. It is somewhat troubling that not every insurance company is a stellar performer in their own software efforts, and there is a significant chance that some insurance companies will not achieve year 2000 compliance. There is not a direct correlation between insurance coverage and the year 2000 capabilities of insurance companies, but I think that it would be prudent to make inquiries of the insurers as to how they themselves are dealing with the year 2000 problem.

As a corollary to year 2000 insurance, several companies have begun to offer auditing and compliance analysis services to more or less "certify" that a company is year 2000 compliant and hence a low risk for insurance purposes. Here, too, since the year 2000 problem has not yet occurred, it is premature to judge the effectiveness of these compliance audits. However, if insurance companies take these audits at face value and offer reduced costs or lower premiums, then the expenses of the audit may well be worthwhile. But be aware that there is a longstanding historical problem with both certification programs and various kinds of audits and assessments in a software context. There is little empirical evidence that these things actually improve performance.

Although the topic has nothing directly to do with the year 2000 problem, it is an interesting observation on the failure of software certification programs that John Seddon, the keynote speaker at the Software Quality Week conference in San Francisco in May 1997, devoted his talk to the reasons why companies that had been certified to the ISO 9000–9004 quality standards appeared to have worse quality than similar companies that were not certified at all. Hopefully we will not discover too late that companies that have been "certified" as year 2000 compliant may not have fixed all of their year 2000 problems.

The Emergence of Certification for Year 2000 Vendors

The nonprofit Information Technology Association of America (ITAA) has started a voluntary certification program to evaluate at least the basic competence of year 2000 service providers. However, as this book was being written, there was not yet any solid empirical data that indicates that certified organizations can outperform uncertified ones. Companies that take the time and energy to achieve certification are perhaps more serious players in the year 2000 game than uncertified companies.

Unfortunately for software as an industry, many of the certification programs do not actually seem to yield any tangible improvements in the way the work is performed. For example, in unrelated fields, there is no evidence the ISO 9000–9004 certification improves software quality at all. Neither is there any evidence that certification of software quality personnel by the American Society of Quality Control or the Quality Assurance Institute leads to visible quality improvements.[6]

One of the few certification programs in the software industry that actually have any empirical evidence that performance improves is the IFPUG certification program for function point counting. For a technical skill such as counting function points, controlled studies between certified counters and uncertified ones favor the certified counters for both accuracy and counting speed. But counting function points is a fairly discrete technical task involving the application of a number of specific rules. By contrast, the year 2000 problem is amorphous, highly variable from company to company, and the "rules" for successfully containing the year 2000 problem are still evolving.

The Emergence of the de Jager Year 2000 Stock Index

Because so many companies have entered the year 2000 market during calendar years 1996 and 1997, a new stock index has been created based on companies selected by the well-known Canadian year 2000 consultant Peter de Jager. The 18 companies currently selected for this index are a sign that the year 2000 "industry" is reaching significant proportions. It will be interesting to see which companies in this group succeed and which ones fall out or fail, since the year 2000 business is likely to be quite volatile.

Personal Computer Year 2000 Problems

Although Bill Gates, the Chairman of Microsoft, has been widely quoted for his May 1997 statement at his CEO conference that ". . . personal computers don't have the year 2000 problem," it should be noted that his statement is from the point of view of the richest man in America, who obviously can afford to buy the latest models of computers and install the latest versions of every application. If you are not particularly wealthy and are using an older computer (and older software), especially a pre-Pentium computer such as one that uses an Intel 386 or 486 chip or one of the older equivalents, you will experience year 2000 problems in a number of fairly unpleasant ways. Indeed, even if you have the very latest equipment bought in December 1999, you may still have problems in January 2000.

One year 2000 problem that you might notice is that many commercial software applications, including both business applications and games, use commercial installation tools. Unfortunately, the past and current versions (through June 1997) of widely used tools are not year 2000 compliant. This means that if you decide to get a new computer in late 1999 to avoid any potential major year 2000 problems, you may or may not be able to install any of the older software applications that used the popular installation tools. Some games, business tools, word processing packages, and so forth, produced before the end of 1997 or beginning of 1998 may not be capable of being installed after the end of the century, although hopefully the vendors will ensure that they can be installed before the end of the century arrives.

You can test your own computer and software applications to see how your current equipment will respond to the year 2000 problem, but a word of caution: Some of these tests may create unexpected problems that will be difficult from which to recover. My strong suggestion is that you have the tests performed by an expert who can reinstall and reinitialize your applications, including perhaps your DOS or Windows operating systems.

The basic mode of testing personal computers and associated software is to change the clock settings to near midnight at the end of December 31, 1999, or to early in the morning of January 1, 2000, and see if the computer's clock and calendar functions behave properly. You should also try out some other dates, such as February 29, 2000, since the year 2000 is an unusual leap year, which not every software package can handle. If you happen to have a UNIX workstation rather than a Windows PC or an Apple, you might also want to check the dates in the July 2038 time period when the UNIX clock and the C library clock functions expire.

Scorecard of Year 2000 Preparations by Industry

The year 2000 problem is now starting to attract coverage by national magazines, radio stations, and television shows. Unfortunately, almost 50% of US senior executives tend to be lagging behind the optimal time line for dealing with the year 2000 problem within their organizations. Since October 1997 is about the last point in time when it will be possible to complete year 2000 repairs before the end of the century, it is interesting to see the percentages of companies that are more or less on schedule in dealing with the year 2000 issue. The following information has a high margin of error, and is derived from meetings with CIOs and CEOs at year 2000 conferences during 1996 and 1997. Only a dozen selected industries with substantial year 2000 exposure are illustrated in Table 5.15.

Regrettably, almost half or the organizations in the United States are behind a safe time line for completing their year 2000 repairs prior to the end of the century. This is a very hazardous situation for the United States, and for other industrialized nations as well. Unfortunately, government agencies from the national level down through local and community levels seem to be among the organizations that are currently the least prepared for dealing with year 2000 issues.

Table 5.15: Approximate Level of Year 2000 Readiness in 12 US Industries

Industry	Ahead of Schedule	On Schedule	Behind Schedule
Software	10%	65%	25%
Insurance	10%	60%	30%
Banking	5%	65%	30%
Telecommunications	5%	55%	40%
Computer manufacturing	5%	55%	35%
Defense contractors	3%	50%	47%
Public utilities	3%	47%	50%
Health care	3%	46%	51%
Military services	3%	45%	52%
State governments	3%	45%	52%
Federal government	2%	40%	58%
Urban governments	2%	30%	68%
Average	4.5%	50.1%	45.4%

The February 25, 1997, edition of the *Washington Times* contained a story by Doug Abrahams on the year 2000 preparedness of the federal government.[15] The preparedness was derived from a study by the House Subcommittee on Government Management, and used conventional school grades for evaluating major agencies of the US government. The results are summarized in Table 5.16.

To this set of federal agencies might be appended an evaluation of how the executive branch, the Senate, and the House are performing in accelerating governmental year 2000 repair work (Table 5.17).

Recall that the US government is usually not even able to reach agreement on its annual budget in time to keep from shutting down some government agencies. The performance of the US government is not likely to be sufficiently proactive and effective to reach year 2000 compliance, and perhaps not even to provide relief for damaged enterprises and infrastructures after the turn of the century.

As a class, the software organizations in government agencies tend to lag behind the commercial sector in many software-related topics. Compensation levels are often lower, use of contract personnel is somewhat awkward, and the bidding process aims at lowest costs rather than top performance.

At the level of states and provinces, the levels of preparedness vary widely. Some states such as California and Florida have well-designed year 2000 response plans and seem to be doing very well in preparedness. In fact the State of Florida's *Statewide Year 2000 Date Change*

Table 5.16: Scorecard of Federal Government Year 2000 Preparedness

Federal Agency	Grade	Meaning
International Aid	A	Well ahead of schedule
Office of Personnel Management	A	Well ahead of schedule
Small Business Administration	A	Well ahead of schedule
Social Security	A	Well ahead of schedule
Education	B	Ahead of schedule
Nuclear Regulatory Agency	B	Ahead of schedule
Department of State	B	Ahead of schedule
Department of Defense	C	More or less on schedule
Treasury Department	C	More or less on schedule
Science Foundation	C	More or less on schedule
Department of Agriculture	D	Behind schedule
Department of Commerce	D	Behind schedule
Environmental Protection	D	Behind schedule
Health and Human Services	D	Behind schedule
Housing and Urban Development (HUD)	D	Behind schedule
General Services	D	Behind schedule
Veterans Affairs	D	Behind schedule
Department of Justice	D	Behind schedule
Department of Interior	D	Behind schedule
National Aeronautics and Space Administration (NASA)	D	Behind schedule
Federal Emergency Management Agency (FEMA)	F	Dangerously unprepared
Department of Labor	F	Dangerously unprepared
Department of Energy	F	Dangerously unprepared
Department of Transportation	F	Dangerously unprepared

Table 5.17: Addendum to Scorecard

Federal Agency	Grade	Meaning
Executive branch	D	Behind schedule
US Senate	D	Behind schedule
House of Representatives	D	Behind schedule
US courts	D	Behind schedule

Assessment Report of January 1, 1997,[9] is a very useful document that could serve as a model for many other state, provincial, and local governments.

Cautions about Database Repairs Using Date Field Expansion

The work of Kendall has been cited several times in this book. In a new article for *American Programmer* entitled "How to Make the Year 2000 Problem Smaller; How to Make it Bigger" Kendall[16] gives some strong cautions about database year 2000 repairs. He points out that converting database date fields from two digits to four digits will push the year 2000 software repair envelope from less than 25% of applications to almost 100% of applications. At least this might occur for applications that access databases, which is very common for management information systems and client-server applications. Kendall also notes that expanding database fields from two to four digits will cause massive amounts of work and will probably eliminate important data-related topics such as data mining, OLAP, and repositories. He suggests that at the very least, database repairs will entail maintaining two separate versions of databases: the original two-digit date field version and the new four-digit date field, for an indefinite period with extreme difficulties and expenses accruing. (This repair method is actually becoming quite common and is termed *data duplexing*.)

One possible ray of hope for the database repair situation is that the technology of *masking* may turn out to be effective. In the masking technology, an external tool would act as an intermediary between the database and the software that accessed the database, and would handle date logic in a fashion that would not trigger recompilation of the applications or direct repairs within the databases themselves. Examples of masking that might work in the database arena include data duplexing, windowing, encapsulation, and bridging. However, whether or not masking will be totally effective for database year 2000 repairs is unknown as this book is being written.

Masking serves the purpose of allowing databases to continue to be used without actually expanding the date fields, but many of the masking approaches exact a performance penalty that may not be tolerable for high-transaction rate applications such as credit card processing, automated teller machines, telephone directories, and the like. Even if masking *is* effective, it must not be forgotten that masking provides only a *temporary solution* to the year 2000 problem. At some point in the future, it may still be necessary to expand database date fields.

One of the unexpected byproducts of masking technologies is that instead of having the bulk of all year 2000 repair costs accrue before the end of the century, there may be significant waves of year 2000 costs well out into the 2010 to 2020 period. In fact, the last wave of year 2000 repairs may well overlap the UNIX and C library date problem, which will occur in January 2038. Unfortunately the attempts to compress information during the era when computer storage was quite expensive are going to lead to a long stream of unplanned, unanticipated costs that might span a 50-year period from about 1995 through 2045.

Cautions about Dead Code Repair Costs

A communication from Paul Strassmann quoted Tom McCabe's observations based on running his program structure evaluation tools such as ACT (Analysis of Complexity Tool) and Battlemap. (Tom McCabe is the chairman of McCabe Associates, and one of the pioneers in software complexity analysis.) These tools often find significant quantities of dead code in legacy applications. The term *dead code* refers to components or subroutines of software applications with these attributes:

- Unreachable code with no entry points
- Former "go to" statements that have been corrected but not removed
- Copybook code that is no longer used
- Old routines replaced by newer versions but not eliminated

Paul Strassmann cited one system with which he was familiar that totaled 700,000 physical LOC, but perhaps 30% or about 200,000 LOC were dead code that was not active as part of the most recent version of the application. The dead code was kept in the application in the event that some of the newer modifications did not work.

The impact of the dead code phenomenon is that year 2000 vendors whose billing rates are based on gross LOC may end up getting paid for quite a bit of code that, even if it contains the year 2000 problem, need not be fixed because it is never executed. Expressed another way, the count of physical LOC in an application is decoupled from the current features of the application as measured in terms of function points, or from logical statements related to active function points. In other words, the size of a legacy application measured in terms of physical lines is often quite different from a count of logical statements based on the most current version of the application that is actually being executed. This phenomenon could result in the following scenario that would artificially inflate year 2000 repair costs by almost 10:1 in extreme cases, although a more normal inflation might be only about 35% to 50%.

Assume there is a COBOL application with active features that total 1,000 function points. Using logical statements of the software that supports the active features, the application might contain 106,000 active COBOL statements in procedure and data divisions. Note that blank lines, comments, and dead code are excluded from this count. However, since COBOL supports conditional statements that might span a number of physical lines, even though they comprise only one logical statement, a count of the physical LOC for this application might total 200,000. Of these 200,000 physical lines about 100,000 reflect the current working version of the application. However, about 50,000 physical lines might be code that is no longer executed and the other 50,000 might be things such as comments, blank lines, and multiline conditionals that should not be counted as part of the application for year 2000 purposes because they are irrelevant.

If the organization owning this hypothetical application did the repairs themselves with their own personnel, then the actual year 2000 repairs for this application might total about $40,000, which is equivalent to $40 per function point, or $0.37 per logical statement. If the organization had an effective year 2000 search engine augmented by a COBOL year 2000 repair engine, they might even be able to do the repairs for about $25,000, which is equivalent to $25 per function point, or $0.24 per logical statement. However, if the organization uses an external outsource service for these repairs, they will probably be billed in the vicinity of $1.10 per physical LOC, and the billable costs will include the dead code, blank lines, and multiline conditional statements. In other words the costs will be based on 200,000 physical lines and will be about $220,000, or $180,000 more than if the work were done internally and the costs were quantified based on function points or active logical statements rather than gross physical lines.

For COBOL and for many other languages, the usage of cost per physical line of code without regard for dead code, blank lines, logical statements that span multiple physical lines, comments, and other features that have no relevance to the year 2000 problem will tend to generate artificially high costs for the clients, and artificially high profits for the vendors. Although this example is an extreme case, the difference in probable costs based on the use of gross physical lines and the probable costs based on the use of function points for the active application is about 10:1. If the year 2000 problem does nothing else, it will probably demonstrate in a very convincing manner that the usage of physical LOC for contracts and economic purposes is very hazardous indeed in many situations.

Considering only COBOL, the most common language used for business applications, there is a general 2:1 ratio between a count of logical statements in the active portions of the application and a count of gross physical lines, which include dead code, blanks, comments, and other irrelevant features that do not have an impact on the year 2000 problem.

For in-house year 2000 repairs the differences in size and cost based on function points versus physical LOC may not matter very much. But if external contractors are used for year 2000 repairs, the differences can matter a great deal. The ultimate difference in billable costs based on physical LOC and costs based on a more detailed examination of function points or logical statements in the active application can be large enough so that if the differences are examined by auditors, CFOs, boards of directors, or stockholders, there may be some justification for suing the vendor or even the CIO or senior software executive for using a metric with such hazardous characteristics as physical LOC.

On a positive note, the combination of the dead code in active applications, coupled with dormant applications that are not run at all, indicates that perhaps as much as 65% of the software owned by corporations may not need immediate year 2000 repairs. However, ascertaining the actual presence of dead code or the presence of dormant applications is not a trivial undertaking.

Cautions about Missing or Uncompilable Source Code

One of the more difficult issues that the year 2000 problem has brought to light is the fact that for a significant number of aging legacy applications, the source code is missing or was produced using a language and compiler that no longer operate. For applications without any source code it is obvious that repair charges based on cost per source line or on cost per function point will not be possible. In fact, repairs themselves may not be possible and these applications might need to be replaced.

Table 5.18: Probability that Source Code Is Unavailable by Five-Year Period

Year Period Application Entered Production References	Applications Needing Year 2000 Repairs by Age	Probability that Source Code Is Missing or Uncompilable
1995–1999	20%	1%
1990–1994	40%	15%
1985–1989	25%	45%
1980–1984	10%	65%
1975–1979	3%	75%
1970–1974	2%	85%

Table 5.18 illustrates some approximate values for missing source code based on general observations among our clients. The data in Table 5.18 is not particularly accurate, since it stems from informal observations rather than a formal study. However, almost every company will find, if they have not already done so, that a significant percentage of their aging legacy applications lack compilable source code or even lack the source code itself.

The data on missing source code is unreliable, but year 2000 managers and vendors alike should be cognizant of the problem of dealing with possibly important applications where source code is no longer available or cannot be compiled.

Prognosis of Object Code Year 2000 Repairs

On June 20, 1997, the *Wall Street Journal* contained an intriguing column by Thomas Petzinger, Jr.[17] entitled "Bob Bemer Aims 'Silver-Plated Bullet' at Year 2000 Problem." Mr. Bemer is a retired mathematician and IBM software engineer, and has been publishing year 2000 warnings since as early as 1979. He developed a mathematical approach for evaluating whether numerical expressions in object code are or are not calendar dates. For example, dates are never multiplied or divided, so any numerical value with those operations is excluded from consideration as a date candidate. He then uses a variation of compression (for example, using a coded representation so that a two-digit date field can hold the equivalent of a four-digit calendar year) to squeeze four digits of information into a two-digit date field. Mr. Bemer's method is unproved as this book is being written, but is attracting attention and fairly serious interest on the part of both year 2000 experts and also companies that are in urgent need of a quick way of dealing with the problem since they lagged behind in using conventional approaches.

References

1. Jones, Capers. *Software Productivity and Quality Today—The Worldwide Perspective.* Carlsbad, CA: Information Systems Management Group, 1993.
2. Robbins, Brian, and Howard Rubin. *The Year 2000 Planning Guide.* Pound Ridge, NY: Rubin Systems, Inc., 1997.
3. Programart Corporation. "Report on Performance Impact of the Year 2000 Problem." *Enterprise Systems Journal* (December 1966): 31.
4. Levy, Steven, and Katie Haffner. "The Day the World Crashes." *Newsweek* (June 2, 1997): 52–59.
5. Kappelman, Leon A., et al. *How Much Will Year 2000 Compliance Cost?* Version 2.12. Denton, TX: College of Business Administration, University of North Texas, May 30,1997.
6. Jones, Capers. *Software Quality—Analysis and Guidelines for Success.* Boston: ITCP, 1997.
7. Kendall, Robert C. "Management Perspectives on Programs, Programming, and Productivity." In *Programming Productivity—Issues for the Eighties,* edited by Capers Jones, 201–211. Los Angeles: IEEE Computer Society, 1981.
8. Love, Tom. *Object Lessons.* New York: SIGS Books, 1993.
9. Douglas, John. *Statewide Year 2000 Date Change Assessment Report.* Tallahassee, FL: State of Florida, Information Resource Commission, 1997.
10. Jones, Capers. *Assessment and Control of Software Risks.* Englewood Cliffs, NJ: Prentice Hall, 1994.
11. Jones, Capers. *Patterns of Software Systems Failure and Success.* Boston: ITCP, 1996.
12. Jones, Capers. *Applied Software Measurement.* 2nd ed. New York: McGraw-Hill, 1996.
13. Strassmann, Paul. *The Squandered Computer.* New Canaan, CT: The Information Economics Press, 1997.
14. Nance, Lauris. "The Impact of the Year 2000 on Career Opportunities." *American Programmer* 10(June 1997): 20–24.
15. Abrahams, Doug. "Federal Government Year 2000 Preparedness Scores." *Washington Times.* February 25, 1997.
16. Kendall, Robert. "How to Make the Year 2000 Problem Smaller; How to Make it Bigger." *American Programmer* 10(June 1997): 25–28.
17. Petzinger, Jr., Thomas. "Bob Bemer Aims 'Silver-Plated Bullet' at Year 2000 Problem." *Wall Street Journal,* B1. June 20, 1997.

6 | Testing, Test Case Errors, and Repairing Software Regression Test Libraries

*T*ESTING YEAR 2000 repairs will be one of the critical activities for successful year 2000 work, and also one of the most expensive. Between testing individual applications to be sure the year 2000 repairs work, and regression testing the application to be sure that the updates have not damaged existing functions, from 30% to more than 70% of the year 2000 costs can go to testing and more than half of the elapsed time requirements.

Because the year 2000 problem originated as an explicit software requirement and then entered design specifications, the normal testing process for software applications has not been effective in finding two-digit date fields. Even worse, many test cases not only failed to find the problem but they actually *enforced* the erroneous two-digit format! As a result, not only source code but also many test cases in regression test libraries must be updated and repaired. Unfortunately, this aspect of the year 2000 problem has been underreported in the year 2000 literature.

In round numbers it takes about five test cases to test one function point. A simple rule of thumb for predicting overall test case volumes of new applications is to raise the size of the application in function points to the 1.25 power. However, the year 2000 problem is not the same as building new applications. The numbers of test cases required will vary based on the specific form or variant of year 2000 repair selected. Table 6.1 illustrates six hypotheses for the number of test cases in response to six year 2000 repair alternatives, ranked in descending order by the overall number of test cases that may be needed.

The most questionable assumption is the low number of regression test cases. Year 2000 repairs for some kinds of applications that link with many other external applications may require 10 times as many regression test cases as the number shown here. Indeed, the year 2000 problem will create a need for a special kind of regression testing with

Table 6.1: Probable Numbers of Test Cases for Alternate Year 2000 Strategies[a]

Year 2000 Repair Alternative	New Test Cases	Regression Test Repairs	Total Test Cases
Compression	708	30	738
Date expansion	501	30	531
Bridging	501	30	531
Windowing	178	30	208
Encapsulation	89	30	119
Duplexing	89	30	119
Average	344	30	374

[a]A COBOL application of 1,000 function points or 100,000 code statements is assumed.

little or no empirical data available. Applications that communicate across company boundaries, such as those involved with EDI, need to be tested at both ends of the connection. This means that some year 2000 regression testing will involve multiple companies. It may even occur that these companies are direct competitors, such as telephone companies or retail establishments that accept other companies' credit cards.

In the context of Table 6.1, the "compression" alternative assumes that rather than expanding date fields from two digits to four digits, the two-digit format is preserved but some form of encoding is used to indicate the century, such as storing the date in binary form rather than in decimal form. This method is very tricky and will require substantial testing, including stress and performance testing since this method will degrade performance. The assumption here is that raising the function point total of the application to the 0.95 power will yield a rough approximation of the number of test cases needed.

The date expansion alternative is the normal repair strategy for the year 2000 problem of expanding date fields from a two-digit size to a four-digit size. The testing for these repairs must also be thorough, and the assumption used here is that raising the function point total to the 0.9 power will yield a rough approximation for the number of test cases needed.

The bridging alternative is a combination of date field expansions in software coupled with a windowing approach, used concurrently. Although bridging may sometimes be more complex than normal date field expansion, I have used the same assumption for the number of test cases, which is raising the function point total of the application to the 0.9 power. Unfortunately, not enough empirical data is yet available to be certain of the implications of bridge testing, so readers are urged to explore their own results if they use this alternative.

The windowing alternative keeps the current two-digit date fields intact, but creates an external port to the application that converts dates going in and coming out into values that can be safely processed. My assumption is that raising the function point total of the application to the 0.65 power will yield an approximate number of test cases for ascertaining whether or not the windowing alternative is working correctly. The window concept is mathematically simple. It consists of establishing a range of a fixed number of years. Many companies use a 100-year interval as the window, such as the years 1950 through 2049, although other periods may also be used. A base year within this window is specified, such as 1970. Because each two-digit year will occur only once in the 100-year window, any incoming or outgoing date can be assigned to the correct century mathematically.

For example, suppose the incoming year is 1998, recorded as 98. Since 98 is *greater than* the base year value of 70, it would be assigned to the twentieth century as 1998. Now suppose the incoming year is 2001, recorded as 01. Since 01 is *smaller than* the base year of 1970, then this date would be assigned to the twenty-first century as 2001.

The encapsulation alternative is more or less similar to windowing, and simply modifies incoming and outgoing dates by subtracting 28 years from the true value. Thus the year 2003 would have 28 subtracted from it and would temporarily become 1975. The value of 28 is used because that brings the days of the week (Monday, Tuesday, Wednesday, and so on) and calendar dates (October 6, 7, 8, and so on) into correct synchronization. Since encapsulation is fairly straightforward, my assumption is that raising the function point total of the application to the 0.65 power should generate an approximate number of test cases.

The duplexing alternative is suitable for batch database applications, but probably not for on-line applications. With duplexing, a database is replicated and the replica has four-digit dates instead of the original two-digit date fields. Using this alternative, applications that are year 2000 compliant and expect four-digit dates can run against the replica, while older applications that are not yet year 2000 compliant can run against the original version.

Here, too, since duplexing is fairly straightforward, I have assumed that raising the function point total of the application to the 0.65 power should be sufficient to predict, roughly, the number of test cases needed. Although the data duplexing approach sounds simple, keeping both versions synchronized is not a trivial undertaking. Unfortunately, true date field expansion for databases is such a complex issue that temporary compromises are becoming the norm, and some of these temporary measures are tricky in their own right.

Note that all of the powers shown in this chapter are based on very preliminary observations and can have a large but unknown margin of error. Using function point metrics for test case prediction is still an emerging technology with considerable uncertainty even for standard software development work. Using a partly experimental method to predict a novel situation like year 2000 testing is pushing the methodology past the bounds of known results.

Over and above creating new test cases for the year 2000 problem, many existing test cases will probably have to be corrected because if they look for dates at all, they look for two-digit date fields. My preliminary hypothesis, with a high margin of error, is that the costs of repairing and upgrading software regression test libraries will amount to about 15% of the costs of making year 2000 repairs to source code itself. This is merely a rough estimate based on examining the test case situation among a number of our clients. There is not enough available data on the test library implications of the year 2000 problem to be certain.

Not every company maintains a formal library of regression test cases, but almost every software organization has regression test cases in either formal or informal libraries. The informal libraries are maintained by individual programmers, who may not even realize that they need updating until the next time the test cases are run. Ironically, the next time the test cases are run may be to validate the change from two-digit to four-digit date format, and many of the test cases will indicate errors because they do not expect the correct four-digit format! (Incidentally, the whole topic of errors in test cases is underreported in the software quality literature. Preliminary studies indicate that the error density of bugs or defects in test cases is actually somewhat higher than the numbers of bugs in the software the test cases are written to test!)

General Forms of Software Testing and the Year 2000 Problem

The testing section of my book published just before starting this year 2000 book—*Software Quality—Analysis and Guidelines for Success*[1]—

discusses 18 forms of testing. It is interesting to consider the impact of these various testing methods on the year 2000 problem, since most of them will probably be used.

These "general" forms of software testing are used for all kinds of software: systems software, commercial software, military software, information systems, and so forth. While the general forms of software testing are common and well understood, not all companies use the same vocabulary to describe them. The following brief definitions explain the general forms of testing in a year 2000 context.

Subroutine testing is the first line of defense in year 2000 testing. Each time a year 2000 date field is expanded, it should be immediately tested before moving on to the next. Subroutine testing is the lowest level of testing noted among our clients. Recall that a subroutine is a small collection of code that may constitute less than 10 statements or perhaps one tenth of a function point. By interesting coincidence, this is also about the size of typical year 2000 date field repairs.

Subroutine testing is performed almost spontaneously by developers and is very informal. Essentially this form of testing consists of executing a just-completed subroutine to see if it compiles properly and performs as expected. Subroutine testing is a key line of defense against errors in algorithms in spite of its being informal and underreported in the testing literature. Subroutine testing is a "white-box" form of testing.

Unit testing is the lowest level of testing discussed in the testing literature. Unit testing is the execution of a complete module or small program that usually ranges from perhaps 100 to 1,000 source code statements, or roughly from 1 to perhaps 10 function points. Here, too, unit testing is a key defensive strategy for the year 2000 problem. Unfortunately for some companies, this may be the last form of testing due to excessive schedule pressures to complete year 2000 work.

Although unit testing may often be performed informally, it is also the stage at which actual test planning and test case construction begins. Unit testing is usually performed by the programmers who write the module, and hence seldom has available data on defect levels or removal efficiency, and this is especially true in a year 2000 context.

Unit testing is often plagued by bad test cases, which themselves contain errors. Indeed, there are often more errors in the test cases than in the products for which the test cases are created. The topic of bad test cases is underreported in the quality and testing literature, and as far as can be determined, has not yet been discussed in the year 2000 literature at all. The bad news is that errors can be expected to occur often, so additional year 2000 costs will be expended on test case repairs.

New function testing is often teamed with regression testing, and both forms are commonly found when existing applications are being updated or modified. As the name implies, new function testing is aimed at validating new features that are being added to a software package. Ideally, new functions would not be added to software at the same time that year 2000 repairs are occurring. However, in the United States the costs for year 2000 repairs must be expensed in the current year *unless* new functions and features are added too! This questionable policy by the Financial Accounting Standards Board (FASB) may force US companies to attempt enhancements on top of the already tight schedules for the year 2000 repairs themselves, with probably unfortunate results. For entirely new projects, as opposed to enhancements, this form of testing is also known as *component testing*, since it tests the combined work of multiple programmers whose programs in aggregate may comprise a component of a larger system.

New function testing is normally supported by formal test plans, planned test cases, and occurs on software that is under full configuration control. While this rigor would be desirable for the year 2000 tests, the time crunch of many year 2000 test efforts often causes rigor and planning to be truncated, if not eliminated. Here, too, the eventual consequences may be serious.

Regression testing is the opposite of new function testing. The word *regression* means to slip back, and in the context of testing regression means accidentally damaging an existing feature as an unintended byproduct of adding a new feature. Regression testing also checks to ensure that prior known bugs have not inadvertently stayed in the software after they should have been removed. Regression testing is a key line of defense in year 2000 repairs, since bad fixes or fresh bugs are common problems in repairing other kinds of defects, and should have a significant impact on year 2000 repairs as well.

After a few years of software evolution, regression testing becomes one of the most extensive forms of testing because the library of available test cases from prior releases tends to grow continuously. Also, regression testing involves the entire base code of the application, which for major systems can exceed 10,000,000 LOC or 100,000 function points.

A special problem for regression testing in a year 2000 context is the fact that a significant percentage of regression test cases may need to be repaired themselves. Any regression test case that deals with dates probably uses two-digit date logic. Imagine the trouble that will occur when after expanding date fields from two digits to four digits, every date-related regression test case fails when run against the new version!

Regression testing can be performed by developers, professional test personnel, or software quality assurance personnel. Regardless of who performs regression tests, the application is usually under full configuration control.

Regression test libraries, though often extensive, are sometimes troublesome and have both redundant test cases and test cases that themselves contain errors. These problems will obviously be troublesome for year 2000 regression testing. In addition, the year 2000 problem is going to be particularly troublesome for applications that span multiple companies, such as EDI, telephone switching systems, fund transfers between banks, and even electronic payment of bills via home computers. This means that regression testing involving multiple companies will be part of the year 2000 testing scenario, and some of these companies may even be direct competitors. Not only will this form of testing be complex, but you may now understand why I strongly recommend assembling and publishing industrywide directories of year 2000 contact points and project managers.

Integration testing, as the name implies, is testing a number of modules or programs that have come together to comprise an integrated software package. Since integration testing may cover the work of dozens or even hundreds of programmers, it also deals with rather large numbers of test cases. The role of integration testing in a year 2000 context is somewhat ambiguous. If only year 2000 repairs are made, with no added features, then this form of testing may be used only seldom or even bypassed. But if new features are added while the year 2000 problems are being fixed, then integration testing might well occur. Integration testing often occurs in "waves," as new builds of an evolving application are created. Microsoft, for example, performs daily integration of developing software projects and hence also performs daily integration testing. Other companies may have longer intervals between builds, such as weekly or even monthly builds.

Applications undergoing integration testing are usually under formal configuration control. Integration testing normally makes use of formal test plans, planned suites of test cases, and formal defect reporting procedures. Integration testing can be performed by developers themselves, by professional test personnel, or by software quality assurance pesonnel.

System testing of a full application is usually the last form of internal testing before customers get involved with field testing (beta testing). For large systems, a formal system test may take many months and may involve large teams of test personnel. For year 2000 repairs, system testing will probably be somewhat abbreviated.

System testing demands formal configuration control and also deserves formal defect tracking support. It can be performed by developers, professional test personnel, or by quality assurance personnel.

For software that controls physical devices (such as telephone switching systems) the phrase *system test* may include concurrent testing of hardware components. In this case, other engineering and quality assurance specialists may also be involved, such as electrical or aeronautical engineers dealing with the hardware. Microcode may also be part of system test. For complex hybrid products, system test is a key event. Testing hybrid products in which both software and microcode are involved with year 2000 dates is not yet well discussed in the literature, but will certainly be troublesome and complex.

System testing may sometimes overlap a specialized form of testing termed *lab testing,* which is when special laboratories are used to house complex, new hardware and software products that will be tested by prospective clients under controlled conditions. Lab testing will be a key line of defense for year 2000 problems in telephone switching systems, military applications, and other kinds of specialized software that operates large and complex physical devices, such as medical instruments.

Specialized Forms of Software Testing and the Year 2000 Problem

Specialized forms of software testing occur with less frequency than the general forms. The specialized forms of testing are most common for systems software, military software, commercial software, contract software, and software with unusually tight criteria for things like high performance or ease of use.

Stress or *capacity testing* is a specialized form of testing aimed at judging the ability of an application to function when nearing the boundaries of its capabilities in terms of the volume of information used. This form of testing may not be very significant in a year 2000 context. Capacity testing is usually performed by testing specialists rather than by developers, and may be a separate test stage or performed as a subset of integration or system testing. Usually it cannot be performed earlier, since the full application is necessary.

Performance testing is a specialized form of testing aimed at judging whether or not an application can meet the performance goals set out for it. For many applications performance is only a minor issue, but for some kinds of applications it is critical. For example, weapons systems, aircraft flight control systems, fuel injection systems, access methods, and telephone switching systems must meet stringent performance goals or the devices that the software is controlling may not work. As it happens, several of the methods used for year 2000 repairs will degrade software performance significantly. For example, windowing, bridging, compression, and encapsulation can all affect performance to a greater or lesser degree. Therefore performance testing will be a major issue in a year 2000 context, and especially so for companies with high transaction rates, such as credit card processing.

Performance testing is often performed by professional testers and sometimes supported by performance or tuning specialists. Some aspects of performance testing can be done at the unit test level, but the bulk of performance testing is associated with integration and system testing since interfaces among the full product affect performance. Performance of software applications is often monitored by special hardware or software tools that can identify areas that may be causing performance degradation.

Viral protection testing is rapidly moving from a specialized form of testing to a general one, although it still has been noted on less than half of our clients' projects. The introduction of software viruses by malicious hackers has been a very interesting sociological phenomena in the software world. Viruses number in the thousands and more are being created daily. Virus protection has now become a minor but growing subindustry of the software domain. Virus testing is a whitebox form of testing. Although commercial virus protection software can be run by anybody, major commercial developers of software also use special proprietary tools to ensure that master copies of software packages do not contain viruses.

The implications of viruses in a year 2000 context have not yet been considered by most of the year 2000 authors, but they are alarming. Since a lot of changes will be happening under very tight schedules, it would be very easy for viruses to enter software applications as an unintended byproduct of year 2000 repairs! Indeed, one potentially devastating form of virus would be one that caused dates to change. In the midst of frantic year 2000 repairs and testing, such a virus could do incalculable harm.

Security testing is most commonly used to test sophisticated military software and software that deals with very confidential information such as bank records, medical records, tax records, and the like. The organizations most likely to use security testing include the military services, National Security Agency (NSA), Central Intelligence Agency (CIA), Federal Bureau of Investigation, and other organizations that use computers and software for highly sensitive purposes.

Security testing is a special form of testing usually performed by highly trained, specialized personnel. Indeed, some military projects use *penetration teams,* who attempt to break the security of applications by various covert means including hacking, theft, bribery, and even picking locks or breaking into buildings. The implications of security testing in a year 2000 context are not well understood, but for most of the software industry our security criteria are fairly mild compared to the CIA or to the Mossad.

Platform testing is a specialized form of testing found among companies with software that operates on different hardware platforms under different operating systems. Many commercial software vendors market the same applications for Windows 95, Windows NT, OS/2, UNIX, and sometimes for other platforms as well. Microsoft, for example, is known to have international versions of applications such as Windows 95, that are not quite identical to US versions, so testing on other countries' versions is desirable. While the features and functions of the application may be identical on every platform, the mechanics of getting the software to work on various platforms requires separate versions and separate test stages for each platform. Platform testing in a year 2000 context will occur for every company with software applications that span multiple platforms.

Another aspect of platform testing is to ensure that the software package correctly interfaces with any other software packages that might be related to it. For example, when testing software cost-estimating tools, this stage of testing would verify that data can be passed both ways between the estimating tool and various project management tools. For example, suppose a cost-estimating tool such as Checkpoint is intended to share data with Microsoft Project under Windows 95. This is the stage where the interfaces between the two would be verified. This aspect of platform testing is obviously important in a year 2000 test situation. Even if your software is century compliant, you may be interfacing with other applications that are noncompliant; hence, platform testing should occur.

Platform testing is also termed *compatibility testing* by some companies. Regardless of the nomenclature used, the essential purpose remains the same—to ensure that software that operates on multiple hardware platforms, under multiple operating systems, and interfaces with multiple applications can handle all varieties of interconnection.

Year 2000 testing is the most recent form of specialized testing noted among our clients. The first companies among our clients to begin serious attempts to find and fix the year 2000 problem only started in 1994, although perhaps other companies may have started earlier. Year 2000 testing may look for date expansions, but newer forms of year 2000 testing have been started for alternate repair strategies such as windowing, encapsulation, data duplexing, compression, or bridging. Each of these requires its own special form of testing.

Independent testing is very common for military software, since it is required by Department of Defense standards. It can also occur for commercial software, and indeed there are several commercial testing companies who do testing on a fee basis. However independent testing is very rare for management information systems (MIS), civilian systems software projects, and outsource or contract software. Independent testing, as the name implies, is performed by a separate company or at least a separate organization from the one that built the application. It is not likely that independent testing will occur for the year 2000 problem, because schedules are so short. However, military standards in some countries may still require it and if so, then independent testing may take place for year 2000 repairs, like it or not.

Another form of independent testing is found among some commercial software vendors who market software developed by subcontractors or other commercial vendors. The primary marketing company usually tests the subcontracted software to ensure that it meets their quality criteria. This form of testing will occur in a year 2000 context, and indeed is starting already. For example, the very widely used software installation utilities are not currently year 2000 compliant. This means, perhaps, that many software packages that were acquired in 1996 through mid 1997 may not install properly if they need to be reinstalled after the turn of the century.

Forms of Testing Involving Users or Clients

For many software projects, the clients or users are active participants at various stages along the way, performing activities such as requirements gathering, prototyping, inspections, and several forms of testing. The testing stages in which users participate are described in the following paragraphs.

Usability testing is a specialized form of testing that is sometimes performed in usability laboratories. It involves actual clients who use the software under controlled and sometimes instrument-monitored conditions so that their actions can be observed. Usability testing is common for commercial software produced by large companies such as IBM and Microsoft. However, this form of testing will probably not be used in a year 2000 context.

Field (beta) testing is a common testing technique for commercial software. Its use in testing stems from a testing sequence used by hardware engineers that included alpha, beta, and gamma testing. For software, alpha testing more or less dropped out of the lexicon circa 1980 and gamma testing was almost never part of the software test cycle. Beta testing is an external software test involving customers. Although beta testing may occur with year 2000 repairs, it is not likely to be a very common form of year 2000 testing since it occurs too late to be effective.

Lab testing is a special form of testing found primarily with hybrid products that consist of complex physical devices that are controlled by software, such as telephone switching systems, weapons systems, and medical instruments. It is obvious that conventional field or beta testing of something like a PBX switch, a cruise missile, or a computed tomographic scanning machine is infeasible due to the need for possible structural modifications to buildings, special electrical wiring, heating and cooling requirements, to say nothing of zoning permits and authorization by various boards and control bodies. Lab testing for year 2000 repairs is already occurring among the world's major telecommunication manufacturers, and also among other manufacturers of specialized equipment such as computers, aircraft, medical instruments, weapons systems, and the like.

Customer acceptance testing is commonly done for contract software and often for MIS, systems software, and military software. The only form of software for which acceptance testing is rare or does not occur is that of high-volume, commercial "shrink-wrapped" software. Even here, some vendors and retail stores provide a money-back guarantee, which permits a form of acceptance testing. How the customers go about acceptance testing varies considerably, and is an interesting but unknown factor for the year 2000 problem.

Clean room statistical testing is found only in the context of clean room development methods. The clean room approach is unusual in that the developers do not perform unit testing, and the test cases themselves are based on statistical assertions of usage patterns. Clean room testing is inextricably joined with formal specification methods and proofs of correctness. The implications of clean room testing for the year 2000 problem are not discussed in the literature and are unknown. It should be pointed out that, theoretically, the clean room method should have found and eliminated the year 2000 problem long ago, but obviously this did not happen.

Numbers of Testing Stages for Year 2000 Software Projects

Looking at the data from another vantage point, if each specific kind of testing is deemed a testing stage, it is interesting to see how many discrete testing stages are likely to occur for software projects. The overall range of testing stages among our clients and their software projects runs from a low of 1 to a high of 16 of the 18 testing stages discussed here (Table 6.2).

As you can see from the distribution of results in Table 6.2, the majority of normal development software projects in the United States

Table 6.2: Approximate Distribution of Year 2000 Testing Stages for US Software Projects

No. of Testing Stages	Percent of Development Projects and Test Stages	Percent of Year 2000 Projects and Test Stages
1	2%	15%
2	8%	20%
3	12%	35%
4	14%	15%
5	16%	6%
6	18%	4%
7	5%	3%
8	5%	2%
9	7%	0%
10	5%	0%
11	3%	0%
12	1%	0%
13	1%	0%
14	1%	0%
15	1%	0%
16	1%	0%
17	0%	0%
18	0%	0%
Total	100%	100%

(70%) use six or fewer discrete testing stages, and the most common pattern of testing observed includes the following:

- Subroutine testing
- Unit testing
- New function testing
- Regression testing
- Integration testing
- System testing

However, for year 2000 testing the number of testing stages is skewed toward the low end of the spectrum. The normal set of year 2000 test stages consists of:

- Subroutine testing
- Unit testing
- Regression testing
- System testing

It is an important but currently unknown situation as to whether the truncated testing patterns being used on the year 2000 problem will be sufficient. Since even the larger test patterns for normal development projects leave bugs in the code, it is reasonable to assume that the shorter suite of tests used for the year 2000 problem will also leave two-digit year 2000 date fields still latent in the code.

Testing Stages Noted in Lawsuits Alleging Poor Quality

My colleagues at SPR and myself have worked as expert witnesses in a number of lawsuits between outsourcers and clients in which poor quality was one of the key issues. All of these suits were remarkably similar in their claims, and the essence of the litigious quality topics were summarized in *Conflict and Litigation Between Software Developers and Clients*.[2] This discussion is an excerpt from that report.

It is an interesting observation that for outsource, military, and systems software that ends up in court for litigation involving assertions of unacceptable or inadequate quality, the number of testing stages is much smaller, while formal design and code inspections are not used at all. Table 6.3 shows the typical patterns of defect removal activities for software projects larger than 1,000 function points in size when the client sued the developing organization for producing software with inadequate quality levels. Table 6.3 simply compares the pattern of defect removal operations observed for reliable software packages with high

---

Table 6.3: Defect Removal and Testing Stages Noted during Litigation for Poor Quality

Defect Removal and Testing Stage	Reliable Software	Software Involved in Litigation for Poor Quality
Formal design inspections	Used	Not used
Formal code inspections	Used	Not used
Subroutine testing	Used	Used
Unit testing	Used	Used
New function testing	Used	Rushed or omitted
Regression testing	Used	Rushed or omitted
Integration testing	Used	Used
System testing	Used	Rushed or omitted
Performance testing	Used	Rushed or omitted
Capacity testing	Used	Rushed or omitted

---

quality levels to the pattern noted during lawsuits when poor quality and low reliability were part of the litigation.

The phrase *rushed or omitted* indicates that the vendor departed from best standard practices by eliminating a stage of defect removal or by rushing it to meet an arbitrary finish date or commitment to the client. There is a strong lesson here for the year 2000 community. Truncating and abbreviating year 2000 testing may lead to litigation, and will certainly not benefit the overall work of year 2000 repairs!

It is interesting that during the depositions and testimony of the litigation, the vendor often countercharges that the shortcuts were made at the direct request of the client. In fact, from observing the deposition materials and testimonies from a number of software lawsuits, it usually happens that both sides have made mistakes. Seldom does a breach-of-contract lawsuit do anything but reveal errors of judgment on the part of both the plaintiff and the defendant. Sometimes the vendors assert that the client ordered the shortcuts even in the face of warnings that the results might be hazardous. When year 2000 litigation begins, this same set of statements will probably be observed.

Using Function Points to Estimate Test Case Volume

Function point and the related feature point metrics are starting to provide some preliminary but interesting insight into test case volume. This is not unexpected, since the fundamental parameters of both function points and feature points all represent topics that need test coverage:

- Inputs
- Outputs
- Inquiries
- Logical files
- Interfaces
- Algorithms (feature points only)

Table 6.4 shows preliminary data on the number of test cases that have been noted among our clients, using test cases per function point as the normalizing metric. The Development Average column shows probable test cases per function point for normal development projects. The Year 2000 Average column shows the probable number for testing year 2000 problems, assuming that any data exists. This table has a high margin of error, but as with any other set of preliminary data points, it is better to publish the results in the hope of future refinements and corrections than to wait until the data is truly complete.

The size referred to in the table is the size of the overall project, expressed in function points. Thus for a 1,000-function point application, about 40 unit test cases might be constructed. If year 2000 test

Table 6.4: Ranges of Test Cases per Function Point for Software Projects

Testing Stage	Development Average	Year 2000 Average
Clean room testing	1.00	—
Regression testing	0.60	0.45
Unit testing	0.45	0.40
New function testing	0.40	0.30
Integration testing	0.40	0.20
Subroutine testing	0.30	0.25
Independent testing	0.30	—
System testing	0.25	—
Viral testing	0.20	—
Performance testing	0.20	0.20
Acceptance testing	0.20	—
Lab testing	0.20	—
Field (beta) testing	0.20	—
Usability testing	0.20	—
Platform testing	0.15	—
Stress testing	0.15	—
Security testing	0.15	—
Year 2000 testing	0.15	0.5
Total	5.50	2.30

data is not shown by a particular form of test, which occurs for more than half of the numbers of test stages, it is because no data is available to the author.

The usage of function point metrics provides some rough rules of thumb for predicting the overall volumes of test cases that are likely to be created for software projects.

- Raising the function point total of the application to the 1.2 power will give an approximation of the minimal number of test cases during normal development.
- Raising the function point total to the 1.3 power gives an approximation of the average number of test cases.
- Raising the function point total to the 1.4 power gives an approximation of the maximal number of test cases.
- Raising the function point total of the application to the 0.75 power will give an approximation of the minimal number of year 2000 test cases.
- Raising the function point total of the application to the 0.85 power will give an approximation of the average number of year 2000 test cases.
- Raising the function point total of the application to the 0.95 power will give an approximation of the maximal number of year 2000 test cases.

These rules of thumb are based on observations of software projects with sizes that range between about 100 function points and 100,000 function points. Rules of thumb are not accurate enough for serious business purposes such as contracts, but are useful in estimating "sanity checks."

The year 2000 rules are obviously very preliminary and need much more research and validation. Because of combinatorial complexity, it is usually impossible to write and run enough test cases to exercise fully a poorly structured software project larger than about 100 function points in size. The number of permutations of inputs, outputs, and control flow paths quickly becomes astronomical. For really large systems that approach 100,000 function points in size, the total number of test cases needed to test every condition fully can be regarded, for practical purposes, as an infinite number. Also, the amount of computing time needed to run such a test suite would also be an infinite number, or at least a number so large that there are not enough computers in any single company to approach the capacity needed. Therefore the volumes of test cases shown here are based on empirical observations, and the numbers assume standard reduction techniques such as testing boundary conditions rather than testing all intermediate values, and compressing related topics into equivalency classes.

References

1. Jones, Capers. *Software Quality—Analysis and Guidelines for Success.* Boston: ITCP, 1997.
2. Jones, Capers. *Conflict and Litigation Between Software Clients and Developers.* Version 4. Burlington, MA: SPR, May 1997. Available on SPR Web site http://www.spr.com.

7 Repairing Databases, Repositories, and Data Warehouses

*T*HE YEAR 2000 impact on databases, repositories, and data warehouses is currently the least understood aspect of the entire year 2000 problem, but appears to be among the most severe and costly domains of year 2000 repairs. As stated, software costs and economic studies of software can be expressed by means of function point metrics. Unfortunately there is no equivalent metric for dealing with the volume of information stored in databases, repositories, and data warehouses. In other words, the industry lacks a data point metric. As a result, there are no published statistics on the volumes of data and information owned by corporations and government agencies. Also, there is no easy way to perform an economic analysis of the data impact on the year 2000 problem. Thus, as this book is being written, the impact of the year 2000 problem on databases, repositories, and data warehouses is still uncertain. However, preliminary indications of relative costs lead to the following hypothesis: For every dollar spent on changing software applications, it will probably be necessary to spend almost another dollar on changing databases. However, for data-intensive industries such as insurance and finance, and for data-intensive government agencies such as Social Security, the data-repair costs will perhaps be twice those of fixing the software itself!

Unfortunately, changing date references in databases from two-digit to four-digit form would have an enormous impact on the software that used the data and would far more than double the overall repair costs. As a result, the most common form of database repairs will probably be some form of masking, such as windowing or creating an external tool that converts incoming and outgoing dates from their true values into dates that are less than 1999. Another set of masking approaches are bridging, which expands date fields in software but not in databases, and data duplexing, which calls for creating both two-digit and four-digit replicas of databases, which are otherwise identical except for the size of the date fields.

Due to the lack of data metrics, the volume of on-line information can only be approximated. Table 7.1 and some of the other work in this chapter are based on the data quality concepts from one of my previous books, *Software Quality—Analysis and Guidelines for Success.*[1] Table 7.1 shows the approximate amount of data maintained by large corporations such as IBM and AT&T with perhaps 250,000 total employees.

Table 7.1: Relative Volumes of Stored Information in Major Corporations

Kind of Information	No. of Pages Stored	Percent Stored On-Line	Year 2000 Impact?
Customer information	90,000,000	50%	Yes
Product information	50,000,000	50%	Yes
Software applications	40,000,000	75%	Yes
Email messages	30,000,000	95%	No
Reference information	15,000,000	20%	No
Personnel information	12,500,000	50%	Yes
Graphics/images	10,000,000	50%	No
Correspondence	5,000,000	10%	No
Defect information	2,500,000	50%	Yes
Supplier information	1,500,000	25%	Yes
Tutorial/training material	1,000,000	50%	No
Litigious/legal information	1,000,000	25%	Yes
Total volume	258,500,000	—	—

Since the example shown here is a corporation stated to have 250,000 employees, it is interesting to note that the total volume of corporate information stored by the case study corporation amounts to more than 1,000 pages per employee. How much of this information will require year 2000 changes is an important but currently unanswered question.

Table 7.2 shows the hypothetical costs of data repairs with a very large but unknown margin of error. Unfortunately, because database repair productivity rates are essentially a topic with no citations in the literature, the information presented here for the costs of data repairs is largely speculative.

Table 7.2: Hypothetical Database Repair Costs for the Year 2000 Problem

Industry	Software Cost	Database Cost	Total Cost
Military	$13,363,636,364	$12,027,272,727	$25,390,909,091
Finance	$4,950,000,000	$5,445,000,000	$10,395,000,000
Manufacturing	$4,444,444,444	$3,111,111,111	$7,555,555,556
Communications	$4,235,294,118	$2,964,705,882	$7,200,000,000
Services	$4,166,666,667	$3,333,333,333	$7,500,000,000
Insurance	$4,050,000,000	$5,062,500,000	$9,112,500,000
Wholesale	$3,882,352,941	$2,911,764,706	$6,794,117,647
Federal	$3,400,000,000	$3,060,000,000	$6,460,000,000
Defense	$2,933,333,333	$2,640,000,000	$5,573,333,333
Retail	$3,093,750,000	$2,010,937,500	$5,104,687,500
Software	$1,740,789,474	$1,392,631,579	$3,133,421,053
Municipal	$1,020,000,000	$765,000,000	$1,785,000,000
Health care	$892,500,000	$624,750,000	$1,517,250,000
States	$770,000,000	$616,000,000	$1,386,000,000
Energy	$700,000,000	$525,000,000	$1,225,000,000
Transportation	$656,250,000	$459,375,000	$1,115,625,000
Other	$14,400,000,000	$10,800,000,000	$25,200,000,000
Total	$68,699,017,341	$57,749,381,839	$126,448,399,179

As pointed out in his critique of year 2000 repair strategies, Kendall[2] suggests that actual date field expansion in databases will be prohibitively expensive. Actually expanding the date fields in databases and data warehouses can elevate the costs of the year 2000 problem from "very large" to "astronomical" due to the fact that so many applications would be affected. Therefore most of the immediate repairs to databases will probably not consist of date field expansions, but rather one of the masking alternatives such as windowing, encapsulation, or duplexing. These alternative strategies are temporary measures that can delay the onset of permanent database repairs for a number of years, but will probably not prevent the real repairs from being necessary in the future since most of the masking alternatives will degrade performance, perhaps to unsatisfactory levels. The cost impact of these temporary database alternatives is to reduce the near-term database repair costs over the next few years until 2000, but eventually the real date expansions must take place.

Few of the commercial database and data warehouse vendors have issued reports or bulletins on the year 2000 problem. This is surprising because the year 2000 problem, in theory, could put an abrupt end to a number of key activities, including data mining, data warehousing, and OLAP.

The problems of database architectures have been mentioned several times earlier in this book, but because the message is important it does not hurt to repeat it. The fundamental database technologies have long been blinded by the need to conserve space, so that after the year 2000 crisis has subsided, there is a need for a major rethinking of data base architectures. Two key research agendas are urgently needed in the database and data warehouse domains.

1. Develop database architectures that do not implicitly assume destructive updating of records so that past values are lost when new values are added.
2. Develop a database size metric similar to function points for expressing data volumes, quality, costs, productivity, and so on. The lack of a data point metric means that any attempt to explore the economics of data is likely to be unsuccessful, since there is no known way of expressing database sizes or defect levels.

Possibly the enormous costs of the year 2000 problem for databases will lead to substantial improvements in what is actually a rather primitive and flawed technology.

References

1. Jones, Capers. *Software Quality—Analysis and Guidelines for Success.* Boston: ITCP, 1997.
2. Kendall, Robert. "How to Make the Year 2000 Problem Better; How to Make it Worse." *American Programmer* (June 1997).

8 | Litigation and Liability Potential for the Year 2000 Problem

*T*HE COSTS OF repairing the year 2000 problem can be quantified with acceptable precision for software, and guessed at for database repairs. The last and most alarming component of the year 2000 problem is the potential expense for litigation and possible damages for *not* fixing the year 2000 problem. As stated earlier, six kinds of litigation can be envisioned in the context of the year 2000 problem.

1. Litigation filed by clients whose products, finances, or investments have been damaged
2. Litigation filed by shareholders of companies whose software does not safely make the year 2000 transition
3. Litigation associated with any deaths or injuries derived from the year 2000 problem
4. Class-action litigation filed by various affected customers of computers or software packages
5. Litigation filed by companies that used outsource vendors, contractors, consultants, or commercial year 2000 tools, but year 2000 problems still slipped through and caused damage
6. Litigation against hardware manufacturers such as computer companies and defense contractors if the year 2000 problem resides in hardware or embedded microcode as well as software

Potential litigation is not easy to predict. Further, when litigation does occur the *outcome* is not easy to predict. Unfortunately, the United States is a very litigious country and damage awards are often set at astronomical values. It is possible that litigation expenses (and any damages if suits are lost) for the year 2000 problem can exceed the direct costs of repairs by as much as 20:1 in cases when negligence and violation of fiduciary duty are proved or at least confirmed by jury decisions.

However, so many companies will be countersuing, or suing other companies, that the net gain or loss is very difficult to predict. Suppose your company is sued for $50,000,000 for noncompliance with a year 2000 factor that causes huge damages to one of your major clients. Also, suppose that your company sues 10 subcontractors or vendors, who provided some of the software in question, for $5,000,000 apiece. Under this scenario, if your company lost the suit against you but won the suits against your subcontractors, the actual transfer of money would be marginal, except that legal fees are not yet considered.

Table 8.1 shows the litigious potential for the industries discussed thus far for four of the six kinds of litigation. Suits against vendors are subsumed under the Client Suits column rather than being shown separately. Suits against hardware vendors would be distributed across the other categories.

Senior executives of corporations have what is called a *fiduciary responsibility* to act in the best interests of the shareholders of the companies they serve. Failure to take action to repair the year 2000 problem has at least the potential to damage or even end the careers of about half of the senior executives in the United States. Incidentally, executives may not be able to escape the consequences of not taking appropriate year 2000 actions by retiring before the end of the century or by changing jobs. Any top executive at the CEO, CFO, or CIO level

Table 8.1: Litigation Potential for Failure to Repair the Year 2000 Problem

Industry	Client Suits	Shareholder Suits	Injury Suits	Class-Action Suits
Military	Low	Low	Very high	Low
Finance	High	High	Low	High
Manufacturing	High	High	High	High
Communications	High	High	Low	High
Services	High	High	Low	High
Insurance	High	High	Low	High
Wholesale	High	High	Low	Low
Federal	High	None	High	High
Defense	High	High	High	High
Retail	High	High	Low	High
Software	High	High	Low	High
Municipal	High	None	Low	High
Health Care	High	High	High	High
States	High	None	High	High
Energy	High	High	Low	High
Transportation	High	High	Very high	High

who is in a position of fiduciary responsibility will probably be held accountable if employed during the years 1996 and 1997, which is the last time during which year 2000 repairs should have started. Any executive of a public company who ignored the year 2000 problem during 1996 and the remainder of 1997, and who retires in 1997 or 1998, will probably find that shareholders will still bring suit. The year 2000 problem brings to mind the aphorism: You can run, but you can't hide. If you are a top executive in a software-intensive organization, your only viable option is to take quick and effective action regarding the year 2000 problem.

Of course, not everyone believes that the year 2000 problem will be serious. It has been rumored that some well-known software personalities, such as Bill Gates, the Chairman of Microsoft, have been quoted as saying the year 2000 problem is of limited importance and consultants are exaggerating it to make more money.[1] However, consider the game theory implications of the year 2000 software problem.

>   If the year 2000 problem is *not* serious, then those of us who caution executives that it is serious will be embarrassed, but no real harm will occur other than the fact that authors of books like this one will look a bit foolish.

>   If the year 2000 problem is *very* serious, and executives fail to take the warnings seriously and plan corrective actions, then they will be called into court on charges of violation of fiduciary duty. Indeed, if year 2000 problems should cause accidental deaths or injuries, possible criminal charges might occur.

From a game theory point of view, it is prudent to regard the year 2000 problem as a serious issue, because the consequences are much less drastic that way.

Attorney fees and damage awards for the year 2000 problem are difficult to estimate using any kind of historical data, since a problem of this magnitude has not occurred before. For the United States as a whole, I suspect that legal fees associated with year 2000 lawsuits will come to close to $2,000,000,000 between about 1997 and 2005, which is the window of major year 2000 litigation. Damages and punitive damages are even harder to assess, but possibly $100,000,000,000 is a likely number for the United States as a whole. Expressed another way, a major bank, insurance company, or Fortune 500 company in general might expect to pay about $750,000 a year in year 2000 legal fees between 1997 and 2005.

Since major companies are very likely to end up suing each other, the potential of damage paid out might be offset by damage payments that come in. However, it would be surprising if less than $100,000,000 per company ends up being paid out for year 2000 damages among the Fortune 500 class of enterprises. What is likely to occur is a "ring" of lawsuits that might resemble the illustration in Figure 8.1. Assuming that each company sues for the same amount, say $50,000,000, and each one wins its case, the net result can be marginal in financial terms, except for the rather large costs associated with legal fees plus the disruption of the work time caused by participating in litigation preparation, depositions, and the litigation hearings themselves.

On the whole, the results of litigation are unpredictable and therefore the overall impact of the year 2000 problem on litigation is really outside the scope of standard economic analysis. However, the number and seriousness of possible year 2000 lawsuits should cause every corporate executive and government official with software responsibilities to behave in a prudent fashion.

Note that other estimates of litigation potential are even higher than the ones shown here. For example, in the US congressional testimony during the hearings in March of 1997, the Giga Group (founded by Gideon Gartner, who also founded the Gartner Group) estimated the year 2000 litigation costs as perhaps topping one trillion dollars.[2]

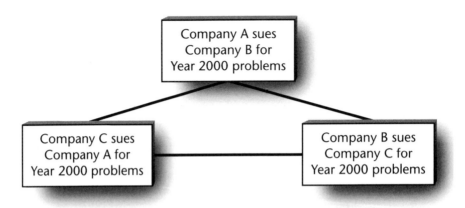

Figure 8.1 Potential loop of interlocking year 2000 lawsuits.

This estimate was cited at a year 2000 conference hosted by the well-known insurance company Lloyds of London, and then rapidly traveled around the world, only being attributed to the well-known Lloyds organization rather than to the comparatively obscure Giga Group. It is interesting that the confusion between Lloyds and Giga surfaced on the Internet, and much of the discussion surrounding this situation occurred via email or Web messages. The year 2000 problem is the first major business issue to occur during the explosive growth of the Internet and the close to universal availability of email messages.

From discussions with attorneys, no one can really predict the number of lawsuits that will be filed, their outcome, or the total amount of money that might be paid in damages or punitive damages. Even basic litigation expenses such as legal fees and court costs are not very easy to predict. The only thing that can be said about year 2000 lawsuits with any real certainty is:

- Year 2000 lawsuits will occur.
- Year 2000 lawsuits will be expensive.
- Year 2000 lawsuits will involve both corporations and executives.
- Year 2000 lawsuits will involve government agencies and executives.

I recommend that all corporate executives seek advice from their own and their corporations' attorneys. However, some very useful surveys of year 2000 legal and liability issues can be found in the recent reports of attorneys who are at least temporarily specializing in year 2000 legal issues, such as those by Jeff Jinnett[3] and Vito Peraino.[4] Although not an attorney, the consultant Warren Reid[5,6] specializes in the effects of litigation on software, and is one of the more visible speakers and authors dealing with year 2000 legal issues.

Financial Disclosure and Executive Year 2000 Liabilities

Many software personnel have been aware of the year 2000 problem for more than 10 years, and it was first discussed as a possible problem more than 25 years ago. However, the year 2000 problem was not a major business issue for many companies until about 1996. Also in 1996, a congressional hearing on the year 2000 problem started in the United States, as did parliamentary hearings in the United Kingdom.

It was only in 1997, with the publication of a special feature in *Newsweek*, June 2, 1997,[7] that the seriousness of the year 2000 problem achieved widespread public awareness. Now that a major national magazine such as *Newsweek* has broken the ice, it can be expected that most other national journals will do the same.

On the whole, the editorial staffs of general business journals have done a disservice to their readers by not offering feature articles for top executives before it was almost too late to take effective action. The editors of major national journals such as the *Economist*, the *Harvard Business Review*, *Business Week*, *Forbes*, and *Fortune* are remiss for not featuring this problem in 1995 and 1996, which is when repairs should have started. While these business magazines did make some reference to the year 2000 problem from time to time, there was no sense of editorial urgency, and certainly no warnings that if companies wait until 1997 or 1998 they may have waited too long to complete the work. (Indeed, one of the problems with "news" journals is that what constitutes news is often limited to what is happening right now, in the current month. Important topics that may have a longer range impact are seldom discussed.)

Year 2000 Disclosure Requirements for US Public Companies

As the end of the century approaches, new information about the year 2000 problem is becoming increasingly plentiful. Many organizations are already well advanced on their year 2000 repairs, so empirical data is starting to replace speculation as the basis of year 2000 cost and effort projections. This section discusses some of the "hot" topics that are now significant in the year 2000 problem domain.

The Securities and Exchange Commission (SEC) requires that public companies file financial reports, including a management report on factors that can affect earnings, profits, and the financial health of corporations.[8] Obviously the year 2000 problem will require disclosure and reporting, since it will have a major impact. Of course, all of the Fortune 500 companies are in the same boat. The specific filing of this kind of information also occurs at the level of state requirements as well as federal requirements. This means that between now and the end of the century, a variety of public documents such as forms 10-K, 10-Q, 8-K, and others will have to disclose year 2000 cost data. Further, when financial results are audited, the auditors' report will also deal with the year 2000 effect on financial performance, and the audit statement will doubtless reflect the auditors' opinion of the prudence and thoroughness of the year 2000 responses.

The Generally Accepted Auditing Standards (GAAS) no. 53 requires that auditors detect and report on errors and irregularities.[9] Failure to disclose year 2000 costs would certainly comprise an irregularity or an error. (In addition to SEC release no. 6835, FASB has made a ruling that year 2000 repairs must be charged to current-year expenses. See the Emerging Issue Task Force [EITF] report 98–14.[10])

Because of the high costs of the year 2000 repairs coupled with the fact that they must be treated as current-year expenses, many public companies will have reduced or negative profitability during years 1997 through 2000, and probably during 2001 and 2002. (Private companies may be in the same situation, of course, but the reporting criteria are not the same.) The impact of reduced profitability or even losses by a large number of companies at the same time will certainly affect the stock market, at least temporarily. The exact effects on investments and stock values are problematic, but investors should exercise due diligence from this point on. Further, reduced profitability or even reported losses will depress local, county, state, and federal tax revenues. Several financial analysts within municipal, county, and state governments have contacted the author and expressed concern that income projections for 1998 through 2001 may be overestimated and fail to take into account the impact of the year 2000 problem.

Directors and officers of certain industries are going to be very seriously affected by the year 2000 problem. For example, officers and directors of US banks are held to much higher levels of accountability than directors of nonfinancial corporations. Indeed, bank directors are required to take an oath to be diligent and honest. Obviously bank officers and directors should be well ahead of any other industry in year 2000 repairs and strategies.

Another aspect of the year 2000 problem concerns the Employee Retirement Income Security Act (ERISA) of 1974. Under this act, directors have a fiduciary duty to be very careful with pension plans, benefits, welfare plans, and other topics affecting the well-being of employees. The ERISA situation is rather complex in the year 2000 context, because quite a few employee-related dates are very difficult to find in software applications. One of the more troubling forms of the date problem with the year 2000 issue are dates associated with personnel transactions. Some of these dates are not explicitly recorded but may be calculated dynamically and used only in working storage during program execution. However, if they are calculated incorrectly, the results can be very harmful. These dates include:

- Salary review dates
- Hire dates
- Performance review dates
- Benefit enrollment dates
- Benefit eligibility dates
- Dates of stock options
- Physical examination dates
- Dates of last salary change
- Payroll deduction start/end dates
- Retirement dates

The rather stringent ERISA requirements make it imperative that year 2000 plans deal with personnel and benefits applications in a very thorough fashion. Every corporation with pensions and retirement plans needs to be sure that the problem has no adverse effects on salaried employees, contractors, and craft employees.

However, the problems of directors and officers between now and 1999 are comparatively small compared to the problems they may face starting January 1, 2000. From that point on, the year 2000 financial reports will switch from the topic of year 2000 repairs to the much more serious topics of reporting year 2000 damages, litigation, and recovery costs.

Accounting Standards for Year 2000 Costs

In the United States the FASB has made a controversial 1996 ruling on how the expenses for year 2000 repairs should be treated from an accounting standpoint.[10] A very clear discussion, by Pucciarelli[11] of the Gartner Group, of the FASB ruling was published in December 1996. The EITF, which is one of the working committees of FASB, decided that in general year 2000 expenses must be charged to current-year expenses,[10] rather than being capitalized and amortized beyond the current fiscal year. The Gartner Group report[11] suggests that the FASB ruling will motivate organizations to replace software rather than repair it because of the ability to capitalize and amortize replacements, which is now lacking in making the year 2000 repairs themselves. Unfortunately, this view will collide with the fact that it is not technically possible to construct major new applications before the end of the century, and for many kinds of large and specialized software systems, no commercial replacements are available.

As this book is being written, the maximal size of applications that might be constructed prior to the end of the century is roughly 2,000 function points or 200,000 source code statements in a procedural language such as COBOL. Many of the key corporate systems top 10,000 function points or 1,000,000 source code statements, and could not be redeveloped in less than 48 calendar months. Adding to the poor prognosis for replacement, with every month that passes the largest size of application that might reasonably be complete before the end of the century drops by perhaps 50 function points or 5,000 source code statements.

Another year 2000 researcher, Lauris Nance,[12] has hypothesized that an unexpected byproduct of the FASB ruling may be to push year 2000 repairs offshore to countries such as India or the Ukraine, where current-year expenses may be much lower than in the United States. Of course, establishing a long-range international outsourcing agreement is not without its own difficulties. For example, encrypted information cannot be exported, contact with the vendor is often difficult, and should the work turn out to be unacceptable, achieving a remedy can be expensive, time-consuming, and uncertain. Nance also points out that FASB accounting standards are different from the accounting standards in many other countries, so that the United States may find itself at a financial disadvantage concerning the year 2000 problem compared with many other countries.

As stated, under the FASB ruling the year 2000 repairs themselves must be a current-year expense. If, however, a company decides to add new features to software while it is being repaired or to make functional enhancements, then it is possible to capitalize the costs and amortize them. The accounting implications of the FASB ruling are complicated and not completely consistent with prior FASB work. They add another dimension of complexity to the year 2000 problem, and it is a dimension that requires specialized assistance to choose a cost-effective path.

One alarming aspect of the FASB ruling is just starting to be explored by state, county, and municipal governments, and may affect the federal government as well. The FASB ruling may accidentally give a "double hit" of year 2000 problems to various levels in the government and may have unexpected tax revenue consequences:

- At every level, governments will have unexpectedly high costs for achieving their own year 2000 repairs. These costs may be high enough to raise taxes.

- The FASB ruling will cause many businesses to report significant losses rather than profits for several years in a row, possibly for five years in a row, which will reduce tax revenues by a significant amount.

The combined results of higher than budgeted governmental expenses coupled with lower than expected tax revenues could conceivably affect the bond ratings of many municipal governments, and may even cause bankruptcy of urban and country governments.

Possible Year 2000 Tax Credits for US Companies

An intriguing speech was given by J. Peter Harries[13] of Coopers & Lybrand when he addressed the Arizona Millennium Group in September 1996. Coopers & Lybrand notes that perhaps some portion of the year 2000 repair costs may, under certain circumstances, be eligible for federal tax benefits under the Research and Experimentation (R&E) Tax Credit, although this is not a clear-cut situation.

The R&E tax credit is very complex and requires specialized tax assistance. To qualify, the project needs to pass a number of stringent criteria.

- The project must eliminate business uncertainty.
- The project must be technological in nature.
- The project must be somewhat experimental rather than proved.
- The project has to result in a new and improved business function.
- The project must deal with a significant economic risk.

For software tools, the project must be internal, since it is aimed at software tools built for private use and excludes commercial packages, although some package modifications might be acceptable.

At first glance, the year 2000 problem would seem to be able to pass all of these criteria, but with taxes and the government, achieving useful ends is not always as easy as it seems. Further, if 30,000 or so companies including all 500 of the Fortune 500 companies attempt this route at once, the IRS is likely to balk. Some of the things that are eligible under the R&E tax credit include 80% of employee wages, 65% of consultants' wages, supplies, and computer time. After the allowable costs are accumulated, the tax credit is 20% of the research expenditures. Because this is a novel and complicated tax issue, it may or may not pay off. You should check with your tax accountants and legal staff to find out if the R&E credit situation is still in effect, and if it might be relevant to your organization.

Possible US Tax Consequences of Reusable Year 2000 Repairs

The June 1997 "article of the month" on the de Jager Year 2000 Web site (http://year2000.com) is entitled "International Tax Consequences of Year 2000 Fix Costs" and was written by Joan Paul[14] of the law firm of Thelen, Marrin, Johnson & Bridges LLP. The article raises a number of important topics that large, multinational corporations would be well advised to consider. Indeed, the article raises concerns that transcend the year 2000 problem, and may pose substantial and unwitting tax exposures for any form of large-scale software reusability including:

- Object-oriented class libraries in large corporations
- Component-based development in large corporations
- Formal corporate reuse programs

The central point of concern for both reusable year 2000 repairs and other forms of possible large-scale corporate reuse is section 482 of the IRC. The essence of IRC 482 is that when one division or affiliate in a controlled group of related corporations (such as a conglomerate or multinational company) performs technical services that benefit other divisions or affiliates, the technical services may be treated by the IRS as though they were taxable income for the receiving divisions that benefited from them. In other words, if Division A of Mega Company in San Jose develops a year 2000 windowing tool that is used by Division B in Cambridge and Division C in New York, then the IRS may treat the reuse of this tool as taxable income by Divisions B and C, even though neither one actually paid anything for the tool. Under the same reasoning, a class library or collection of reusable components developed by any of the three divisions but used by the other divisions might also constitute taxable incomes for the divisions that benefit from the reuse.

It is obvious the IRC 482 might potentially drive a stake through the heart of software reusability, by requiring that companies charge fair-market value for reusable objects shared among divisions and locations of the same company. Such an interpretation of IRC 482 would degrade the economic value of reusable components and class libraries in a significant way, and would perhaps impede several technologies that have notable value for moving software away from a labor-intensive craft and toward a manufacturing model based on reusable components.

This situation is even more complex for multinational enterprises when the reusable material is developed overseas, but extensively deployed and reused in the United States. The reverse situation is also complex—when reused materials are exported from the United States to overseas subsidiaries.

For small quantities of reusable materials shared informally, IRC 482 may not be a problem or its existence even known to the software community. But the year 2000 problem is a special case, since the costs are extraordinarily large and companies are actively seeking cost-effective strategies for lowering these costs and speeding up the year 2000 repair schedules. If the IRC 482 regulation adds a notable increase to corporate tax loads in a year 2000 context, or even triggers penalties for failing to comply with the rather complex IRC 482 criteria, then an already bad situation could grow decidedly worse.

Incidentally, the article cited here (the June 1997 "article of the month" from the de Jager Year 2000 Web site) does not differentiate among the various kinds of software artifacts that are potentially reusable. Presumably IRC 482 would cover all major kinds of reusable software artifacts, such as:

- Reusable requirements
- Reusable designs and specifications
- Reusable source code
- Reusable user documentation
- Reusable test cases

Evaluating the IRC criteria is a job for a tax specialist or a tax attorney. However, even specialists may be troubled by the fact that the IRC 482 interpretation for year 2000 reuse may be in the process of being changed.

Adding to the complexity and need for professional counsel by tax attorneys and accountants, the year 2000 problem is a multinational situation that will affect software in every industrialized country in the world at more or less the same time. This means that not only US tax regulations have to be explored and evaluated, but also the tax laws of every other country where a US corporation does business.

The worst-case scenario under IRC 482 is that some of the enormous expenses already going to year 2000 repairs may have to be treated as taxable income, which will add to the costs and depress earnings even more. This is a complex and troublesome issue, and one that may require congressional legislation to minimize additional harmful year 2000 consequences. Of course, the best-case scenario would be for the IRS to state that IRC 482 will not apply to year 2000 tools and repair materials, and perhaps not to other forms of software reuse either, such as class libraries.

References

1. Gates, Bill. Unpublished response to a question on the seriousness of year 2000 at his CEO forum, May 1997, circulating via email and the internet.
2. Testimony of Ann Coffou, Managing Director of Giga Information Group, before the US House of Representatives Science Committee. March 20, 1997.
3. Jinnett, Jeff. "Legal Issues Concerning the Year 2000 'Millennium Bug.'" *The Computer Lawyer.* (December 1996): 3.
4. Peraino, Vito. "Corporate Director Liabilities and the Year 2000 Problem." *Delaware Corporate Litigation Reporter.* (February 27, 1997).
5. Reid, Warren. *You Can Lose Your House and Yacht.* Encino, CA: WSR Consulting Group, 1997.
6. Reid, Warren. "The Year 2000 Crisis." *American Programmer* 10 (June 1997): 31–41.
7. Levy, Steven, and Katie Haffner. "The Day the World Crashes." *Newsweek* (June 2, 1997): 52–59.
8. SEC. release no. 6835. Washington D.C.: Government Printing Office (1996).
9. GAAS no. 53. Washington D.C.: Government Accounting Standards Board (1997).
10. *Financial Accounting Standards Board (FASB) Emerging Issue Task Force (EITF)* Report 98–14. 1996.
11. Pucciarelli, J. "Inside Gartner Group." (December 1996).
12. Nance, Lauris. Unpublished correspondence on FASB accounting standards. April–June 1997.
13. Harries, Peter J. of Coopers & Lybrand, LLP, speaking at the Arizona Millennium Group meeting, September 18, 1996, Tempe, AZ. In: Janet Butler, ed. *Managing System Development.* Scottsdale, AZ: Applied Computer Research, (October 1996): 7.
14. Paul, Joan. *International Tax Consequences of Year 2000 Fix Costs.* June 1997 article of the month. de Jager year 2000 Web site, http://www.year2000.com/archive/taxes.html.

9 | Risk of Business Failure Due to the Year 2000 Problem

ONE OF THE most serious potential problems associated with the year 2000 crisis is that some companies may go bankrupt or fail either as a direct result of the year 2000 problem or as a possible defensive measure to stave off massive damages due to year 2000 litigation. There is insufficient data to predict the probable number of business failures that might be attributed to the year 2000 problem with any degree of accuracy, but from observing the recent history of business failures for other causes it is possible to form some preliminary hypotheses.

There are four ways of examining the business failure potential associated with the year 2000 crisis:

1. Failure potential based on the size of the company
2. Failure potential based on the industry in which the company competes
3. Failure potential based on the financial health of the company
4. Failure potential based on probable year 2000 litigation against the company

The following paragraphs are some preliminary observations on failure potential based on these four criteria.

Business Failure Potential Based on Company Size

In evaluating the potential for business failure based on company size, the preliminary conclusion is that mid-size corporations with 1,000 to 10,000 total employees are probably at greater risk than either larger or smaller enterprises. Very large companies in the Fortune 500 class will be greatly affected by year 2000 repairs, but many are already engaged in making those repairs and most have adequate financial resources to complete the task either on their own or with the assistance of specialized year 2000 tool and service vendors. My estimate is that the chance of a business failure among the Fortune 500 class is only about 1%, unless some of them declare bankruptcy as an emergency measure to avoid damages due to litigation.

Very small companies with fewer than 100 total employees will be affected by the year 2000 problem, and sometimes severely, but these companies usually do not own very much software so they can probably deal with the situation. My estimate is that the chance of failure for small companies as a direct impact of the year 2000 problem is about 3%, unless they are a direct target of year 2000 litigation for some reason. (Of course small companies fail all the time for a variety of reasons, so my 3% estimate is a delta on top of the already notable failure rate of small enterprises that exceeds 50% in the first two years after incorporation.)

Mid-size corporations with 1,000 to 10,000 total employees historically show a distressing tendency to use quite a lot of software, but to be only marginally competent in how they build and maintain this software. In the year 2000 context, mid-size corporations will probably be late in getting started on their year 2000 repairs, will underestimate and underbudget for their year 2000 work, will not bring in the appropriate tools and specialists, and will probably not have any contingency plans in place on what to do with applications that don't make the changes in time. I place the failure probability of mid-size US corporations at about 5% to 7%.

There are about 30,000 companies in the mid-size range in the United States, and a 5% to 7% business failure rate would mean that 1,500 to perhaps 2,100 companies might close or file for bankruptcy as a result of the year 2000 problem. This is a significant number and it is an open question as to whether the impact of the year 2000 problem is severe enough to trigger a recession.

Business Failure Potential Based on Industry

In considering the probability of year 2000 problems causing failures by industry, the industries that are most likely to be affected are those that use software for key business operations: banks, brokers, credit unions, health care, insurance, manufacturing, retail, and wholesale.

All of these probably have at least a 2% chance of going out of business or declaring bankruptcy to stave off damages and litigation.

Somewhat more ominous is the possibility that industries not always recognized as software intensive will fail due to the year 2000 problem. City governments, county and provincial governments, and public utilities and telephone companies may also fail. Perhaps the most hazardous of any of these is not an industry at all. The effect of the year 2000 problem on state, provincial, county, and city government operations may well cause a rash of bankrupt government organizations or at least drastic reductions in the services they provide.

In the United States many local government agencies use computers and software for a variety of revenue and disbursement purposes. Unfortunately governments as a class are often not very sophisticated about building or maintaining their software. They are typically underfunded and many can't even afford to bring in year 2000 consultants. The probable result will be a rash of lawsuits against a wide variety of government organizations. In any case, the impact of the year 2000 problem will no doubt reduce many government services because the money to fix the year 2000 problem has got to come from somewhere.

Public utilities and all telephone companies use software for both technical and administrative purposes. Some of these organizations are large and sophisticated in how they build software, but others have been somewhat careless. The year 2000 problem may cause some of these utility companies to fail, and in any case will probably raise the costs of their services to consumers.

Business Failure Potential Based on Financial Health

The year 2000 problem is going to be very expensive no matter how the repairs are accomplished. This obvious fact means that companies with cash flow and finances that are already marginal will have a significant probability of failing under the added expenses of the year 2000 problem. Since perhaps 10% of small- to mid-size companies in the United States are already in some kind of financial distress, the added burden of the year 2000 problem may put many of them out of business.

What is not so obvious is that the venture capital community will be seriously affected by the year 2000 problem. Right now venture capital is pouring into new year 2000 start-ups, and into many other kinds of software start-ups as well. The venture capital community should have included year 2000 compliance as part of the due diligence process starting in about 1994, but hardly any venture group even thought about the problem. When the costs of year 2000 repairs to venture-backed companies is factored into business plans, the anticipated 10:1 yield that venture capitalists expect will shrink to nothing. This means that second, third, or additional rounds of financing may evaporate.

Business Failure Potential Based on Litigation

Readers of John Grisham's book *The Rainmaker*[1] are aware of how a lawsuit against an insurance company triggered a deliberate bankruptcy filing to stave off having to pay damages. The year 2000 problem will obviously cause a lot of litigation, and hence many organizations will consider filing for bankruptcy rather than face having to pay year 2000 damage claims. Indeed, some insurance companies themselves may seek this kind of protection, although hopefully they will be prepared for the year 2000 problem.

Although the insurance industry was a pioneer in the use of both software and databases, and has a very large population of software personnel, the insurance industry has not been a stellar performer in software quality and maintenance productivity, with a few exceptions such as Hartford Insurance. In the greater Hartford area, where many insurance companies are located, a "typical" life or property and casualty company routinely spends more than 50% of their annual software budgets on maintaining huge inventories of aging legacy applications, none of which are getting any younger and all of which will need year 2000 repairs.

About 12 years ago Hartford Insurance embarked on a very successful "geriatric" program that lowered their annual maintenance costs down to about 19%. Some of these same methods would seem relevant to the year 2000 problem, so in summary these are the approaches used (I formerly worked for the ITT corporation, which is the parent company of Hartford Insurance).

- All active applications (dormant ones were excluded) were given a thorough complexity analysis using one or more of the commercial software complexity analyzers.
- Active applications for which the cyclomatic and essential complexity were at dangerous levels were restructured using one or more of the COBOL restructuring engines, such as Recorder, SuperStructure, or Structured Retrofit.

- As a byproduct of the complexity analysis and restructuring, some latent errors were found, dead code was removed, and error-prone modules were eliminated.
- For critical, strategic applications (but not for minor or peripheral applications) programmers examined the code and made sure the naming conventions were appropriate and the data dictionaries had correct information.

The net result of these geriatric undertakings was roughly a 300% increase in maintenance productivity over about a four-year time period, which was remarkably good progress. Curiously, although Hartford Insurance gave public speeches on what they did, few other insurance companies (if any) in the Hartford area tried to replicate their success story. More recently, the discovery in Massachusetts that Blue Cross/Blue Shield did not control their software applications well enough to even realize they were losing money does not bode well for making complex updates such as those required by the year 2000 problem.

Overall, because of the enormous volumes of software and huge databases, the insurance industry will be more heavily affected by the year 2000 problem than many other industries. It remains to be seen if the insurance industry's response to the year 2000 problem will be fully adequate. At least all of the major insurance companies are moving to contain the year 2000 problem.

The year 2000 crisis is likely to focus legal attention on three topics that have not been significant to software professionals and software companies in the past, but may well become major topics as the year 2000 problem manifests itself:

- Professional malpractice
- Violation of fiduciary duty
- Consequential damages

The topic of professional malpractice has long been a major source of litigation for medical practitioners, and a significant source of litigation against attorneys and some forms of engineers such as civil engineers. The claim of professional malpractice has not been levied against software personnel very often, but the year 2000 problem may cause this to change. In particular, year 2000 vendors who contract to make repairs but fail to do so may find this charge brought against them. It is somewhat ironic that the very insurance companies that offer malpractice insurance for physicians may find the same charges brought against them if they fail to repair the year 2000 problem in time.

The concept of professional malpractice is that a knowledge worker failed to perform duties in a way that matched the standard level of acceptable behavior for the topic in question. One likely target of professional malpractice claims may be some of the year 2000 tool and service providers. It often happens when problems of a significant nature occur that a great many marginal organizations and even outright frauds move into the arena to make a quick profit. Companies seeking year 2000 assistance are cautioned to be alert to this fact and to use due diligence when seeking year 2000 service providers.

Executives and boards of directors of corporations have what is called a *fiduciary duty* to act in the best interests of their corporations. Since the onrushing year 2000 problem is a very obvious one, the boards and top executives of companies that do not take effective and rapid action to solve the problem may find themselves sued by shareholders.

Note that public companies are required by the SEC[2] to publish management warnings in their financial reports about any business factors that might affect earnings. Obviously the year 2000 problem is such a factor. Furthermore, auditors are required by the GAAS[3] to point out situations that might affect the financial stability and earnings of the companies they audit. Here, too, the year 2000 problem is such a situation. These two requirements mean that the executives of public companies must face the year 2000 issue squarely and deal with it, hopefully, in a competent manner or face very severe prospects of major litigation by shareholders.

Of course, every one of the Fortune 500 companies and most smaller companies are going to face the year 2000 problem at exactly the same time, so all executives in the industrialized world are in the same boat, which hopefully will not become the Titanic of the end of the century and sink beneath them with great losses.

The software industry has not yet encountered the risk of consequential damages for the bugs and errors that are common in software. The idea of consequential damages is that in addition to paying for repairs or replacement of a defective product, the vendor may have to pay for any lost business or secondary damages that result. For example, suppose you use a $200 spreadsheet to calculate a bid for a $1,000,000 contract. If there is an error in the spreadsheet that causes you to not get the contract, then under the concept of consequential damages the vendor might be ordered to pay you not only for your out-of-pocket $200 for the defective spreadsheet, but an additional $1,000,000 for the business you lost due to using the spreadsheet. Since the year 2000 problem permeates almost every piece of financial and long-range planning software ever written, the year 2000 problem is likely to elevate the topic of consequential damages to a very significant place in software litigation.

Codicil: Business Failures Based on Loss of Essential Services

Most business failures in the United States are based on problems arising from cash flow or financial problems. The year 2000 problem may conceivably lead to a kind of business failure that is usually associated only with major natural disasters such as earthquakes, hurricanes, tidal waves, floods, and tornadoes, which often destroy the physical facilities of the businesses. The year 2000 problem will not, of course, lead to the physical destruction of office buildings and their equipment, but may very well lead to the loss of essential services for such a long period that some businesses may not survive.

In the industrialized world we are so used to electric power, telephones, computers, and the other attributes of a modern high-technology world that we may have lost the ability to transact business in a meaningful way if these essentials are taken away for an extended period. There is a reasonable possibility that the year 2000 problem will disrupt electric power for a period that may be as long as a week. Telephone services may also be lost for a week or more, while computer systems may be shut down or inoperable for a period that might exceed 10 days. These problems, in turn, will disrupt manufacturing, the ability to place orders, the shipment of products (ground, air, and sea), billing operations, and many of the other business activities that we have learned to take for granted. Should the year 2000 problem lead to the loss of these essential services for more than a five-day period, then business failures could reach a level that would disrupt national economies, and indeed throw the global economy into turmoil and economic depression.

Hopefully these essential services will not be lost at all, not lost at national levels, or lost for more than a period of a few hours. However, if the year 2000 problem does affect essential services for extended periods, then the damages will be much more severe than anything yet discussed in this book. The damages might be so severe that they could introduce a "year 2000 winter" that will have the same chilling effect on the global economy as a nuclear winter would have on the natural ecology.

References

1. Grisham, John. *The Rainmaker.* New York: Bantam Doubleday Dell Publishing Group, 1995.
2. SEC release no. 6835.
3. GAAS no. 53. Government Accounting Standards Board.

10 | The Emergence of the Year 2000 Repair Industry

SINCE THIS BOOK was first begun, a new subindustry of year 2000 repair companies has come into being. Indeed, new companies are entering the year 2000 market faster than almost any industry in human history. Approximately 25 companies a month have begun to announce year 2000 repair tools and services starting roughly in January 1995. This new subindustry is beginning to coalesce into three broad categories:

1. Companies that sell year 2000 analysis and repair tools for various languages
2. Companies that sell year 2000 consulting and programming assistance (outsourcing)
3. Companies that sell both year 2000 tools and programming assistance

It is an interesting but still partly unknown question as to how many of these companies will be effective, how many will be marginal, and how many will fail in their stated business of finding and repairing year 2000 damages. (As of the second half of 1997 about 65% of our clients who use outsourcers or contractors for year 2000 work have been reasonably satisfied, but 35% have felt that the work was not effective, was overpriced, or both.)

Prior to the year 2000 issue SPR has often been asked to compare the overall results of software contractors and outsource vendors to the results achieved by their clients. In fact, we've been doing assessment and benchmark studies of contract and outsource projects for more than 12 years.[1] Maintenance of software projects is not a new phenomenon, and the year 2000 problem overlaps a number of other problems that have been addressed more or less successfully for many years.[2] A whole suite of "geriatric" tools have been in existence for almost 10 years, including:

- Complexity analysis tools
- Code-restructuring tools
- Change control tools
- Reverse-engineering tools
- Reengineering tools
- Defect-tracking tools

Outsourcing and the Year 2000 Problem

Some outsourcing and contracting organizations have specialized in maintenance and the use of geriatric technologies, so they are already equipped to deal with the year 2000 problem, even if the schedule is more stringent and the risks are higher than normal maintenance problems.

The general conclusions of our benchmark assessment studies are that outsource vendors usually had higher productivity and shorter schedules than their clients, as well as somewhat better quality control.[3] In addition, large outsourced projects in the 10,000-function point range (and higher) had a somewhat better probability of being finished on time, and a lower probability of being canceled, than similar projects done internally by information systems development groups.[4] These results are based on assessments involving the larger US outsource organizations such as Andersen, CSC, EDS, IBM's ISSC division, and Keane.

A recent major problem with outsource agreements drafted prior to about 1995 is that most of them are totally silent on the topic of year 2000 repairs. (The fact that my colleagues and I have served as expert witnesses in litigation between clients and outsourcers is a sign that not all agreements satisfy both parties.) The absence of specific year 2000 language in outsource agreements may lead to yet another form of litigation. The clients contend that year 2000 repairs are included in blanket maintenance outsource agreements, while the vendors are claiming that the year 2000 repairs are a special case outside the agreement. The absence of specific year 2000 language and the broad assertions of maintenance responsibilities in many outsource agreements are going to cause severe strains between clients and outsource vendors as the twentieth century winds down. Already in 1997, litigation on this topic is starting to occur, and more can be anticipated.

On the down side of outsourcing, my colleagues and I have worked several times each year as expert witnesses in US lawsuits between clients and outsourcers or contractors where breach of contract, poor quality, or some other form of contractual violation is one of the charges levied by the client.[5] We have not yet been asked to serve as expert witnesses in international outsource litigation, although we have worked with several companies where such litigation may occur due to dissatisfaction with the delivered projects.

Although litigation potentials vary from client to client and contractor to contractor, it is reasonable to assume that the results of hiring outsource vendors to perform year 2000 repairs will approximate the overall results of other kinds of outsourcing within the United States. Some common motives for seeking outsource partners include (1) dissatisfaction with the performance of the in-house software organization, (2) a desire to reduce software expenses, (3) a belief that software is not a core competency for the organization's main business, and (4) a belief that professional software groups can build applications faster than ordinary information systems groups.

Paul Strassmann's[6] analysis of more than 50 outsource agreements concluded that factor 2—a desire to reduce expenses—was actually the primary motivating factor. His study also indicated that companies that opted for outsource arrangements were often in some kind of financial difficulty and that the outsource arrangement did not usually reverse the financial problems.

Very preliminary results from a sample of roughly 50 of our clients indicate that year 2000 outsourcing is slightly less satisfactory overall than conventional outsourcing. However, the sample is small and the results need to be reexamined as time passes. The distribution of outsource results presented in Table 10.1 is based on 18 to 24 months of contractual operations, which is likely to be the same time period needed to accomplish year 2000 repairs for a large enterprise that owns in excess of 250,000 function points of software in its operational portfolio.

As mentioned previously, from process assessments performed within several large outsource companies and analysis of projects produced by outsource vendors, our data indicates slightly better than average quality control approaches when compared with the companies and industries who engaged the outsource vendors. This statement is true for management information systems. Outsourcers in the systems and military domain are approximately equal to their clients, but the systems and military domains have higher quality than the MIS domain already. However, our data is still preliminary and needs refinement for year 2000 repairs, which is still so new a task that we have not yet been commissioned to explore the success or failure of year 2000

Table 10.1: Approximate Distribution of US Outsource Results after 24 Months

Results	Nonyear 2000 Outsource Arrangements	Year 2000 Outsource Arrangements
Both parties generally satisfied	70%	65%
Some dissatisfaction by client or vendor	15%	17%
Dissolution of agreement planned	10%	12%
Litigation between client and contractor probable	4%	6%
Litigation between client and contractor in progress	1%	0%

vendors in a significant way, although we have come across many year 2000 outsource projects in the course of our standard assessment and benchmark studies on other topics.

Hazardous Year 2000 Charging Practices

In the context of the year 2000 problem, a great many clients are disturbed at what appears to be a very questionable charging structure for year 2000 repairs. Many year 2000 service vendors are charging rates of between $1 and more than $2 per physical source line of code for all software submitted to them, regardless of the fact that usually only 1% to perhaps 5% of the code consists of date references that need repair.

The situation is made worse by two additional phenomena. First, a significant quantity of code in aging legacy applications is dead code left over from previous repairs and no longer executed. Possibly more than 20% of the entire volume of code may be in the dead code category, which obviously does not need year 2000 repairs. Second, a significant quantity of applications in software portfolios are dormant and may not be executed again. A study by Robert Kendall of IBM data centers found about half of all applications were in this dormant status.

If dormant applications and dead code are included in year 2000 repair efforts at a rate of between $1 and $2 per source line, the results can be overcharges of such a huge magnitude that auditors are very likely to include a negative discussion of this situation in audited financial reports.

The issue of using physical LOC for year 2000 repairs is causing such a bad business situation that the more sophisticated companies are using their own personnel for year 2000 repairs, and going to outsource vendors for other kinds of work for which the pricing structures are not so one sided in favoring the vendor rather than the client. Indeed, many companies that rushed into the year 2000 outsource market in the expectation of making a quick profit are finding that clients are choosing to do their own year 2000 repairs. A major reason for keeping year 2000 repairs in-house is because the pricing structures based on the simplistic costs of between $1 and $2.50 per line of source code would penalize the clients and provide windfall profits for the vendor. So long as year 2000 vendor charges are based on a simplistic gross physical LOC basis it makes better business sense to keep the year 2000 repairs in-house and, if outsourcing is necessary, to use the outsource vendors for more conventional work.

A better form of year 2000 pricing by outsourcers and vendors is to use activity-based costing. It should include the following activities:

- Year 2000 searches for active software (no dormant applications)
- Year 2000 repairs for the code actually affected (dead code excluded)
- Year 2000 testing for the code actually repaired (dead code excluded)
- Year 2000 masking (windowing tools, bridge tools, and so on) built on time and materials or a fixed-price basis

Using this pricing model, the clients and the vendors would have to keep fairly good records, and the clients would need to do some preparatory work in (1) separating the active from the dormant applications and (2) identifying dead code.

There are a host of smaller outsource vendors and contractors where we have encountered only a few projects, or sometimes none at all, since our clients have not used their services. Further, we have not yet been commissioned to explore the specific performance of outsource vendors in the year 2000 repairs, so these observations are incidental byproducts of other kinds of studies.

Outsourcing is possible for development projects, maintenance projects (defect repairs), enhancement projects (adding new features to existing software), conversion projects (moving software to a new platform), or all of these. A special kind of outsource project—fixing year

2000 problems—is now exploding through the contract and outsource domains, and in particular is moving offshore toward India for US enterprises, and toward Eastern Europe for enterprises in the European Union. Of course, not all kinds of software can or should be outsourced. If the software offers very significant competitive advantages, contains trade secret algorithms, deals with military issues, or is encrypted or uses encrypted data it may not be safe to deal with outsourcers of any kind. Indeed, in the presence of encryption, it is not even legal to export some forms of encrypted information and encryption tools outside the United States.

Because the US and Western European outsource companies tend to charge on the high side, and especially so if they are using costs per LOC for an entire portfolio, the year 2000 problem is giving a major surge of business to offshore companies in countries where labor and burden costs are well below US and European norms.

In terms of pure year 2000 outsourcing, the results to date are mixed. Some clients are fairly pleased with the outsourcing results on year 2000 repairs, but some problems are starting to emerge. Not every year 2000 outsource vendor can provide capable personnel who are skilled in the languages used. Further, as the available programmers are being sucked up for year 2000 work by Fortune 500 companies with fairly good pay scales and benefits, some of the outsource vendors are finding that not only is it difficult to hire programmers, but they are in danger of losing some of their current programmers because the year 2000 work may pay better within a Fortune 500 company than within the outsource vendor community. Indeed, some programmers with valuable skills for the year 2000 problem are receiving signing bonuses, just like athletes.

Year 2000 Staffing Problems

The demand for programmers is also triggering some questionable business practices, such as companies raiding other companies for software personnel. This situation may add yet another kind of litigation to the already litigious year 2000 situation—suits for unfair business practices by one company when raiding another company for personnel. If the raided company is in the same business as the raider, then lawsuits for theft of trade secrets or misappropriation of confidential information might become yet another form of year 2000-related litigation. This is not to say that the raiding companies are necessarily seeking trade secrets, but when a company is acquiring programmers, it is likely that they possess some trade secrets, so due diligence is indicated.

Although the results vary from situation to situation, the overall results from the outsource data we have collected indicate the following in terms of how the outsource world compares with similar projects carried out by client companies that produce MIS. Table 10.2 is based on a sample of about 300 projects analyzed between 1987 and 1997, and is compared with similar projects done by in-house software personnel.

Although this data is very preliminary and needs additional validation, the early indications are that at least the larger of the specialized year 2000 outsource vendors are capable of finding and fixing year 2000 problems somewhat faster and more thoroughly than their clients who attempt the work themselves. Not every year 2000 outsource project is a success, however, and some clients are dissatisfied enough to cancel agreements and take the work back themselves. It does help to perform "due diligence" of outsource vendors and check with other clients before committing to a long-range contract. If the results are not successful, it may be too late or too costly to terminate the agreement and still achieve year 2000 compliance.

One troublesome aspect of the data is the fact that the outsource project personnel in the year 2000 domain had considerably more experience in year 2000 repairs than the in-house groups, who usually were just getting started. Recent data within large corporations in the Fortune 500 class indicates that their in-house year 2000 repairs speed up with practice. By the time half a dozen applications have been repaired, the in-house year 2000 repair teams are achieving results that

Table 10.2: Comparison of Outsource Results with Projects Produced by Clients

Project Type	Outsource Results versus Clients		
	Schedule Reductions	Productivity Levels	Defect Levels
New software projects	−10%	+ 15%	−12%
Maintenance projects	−50%	+ 50%	−45%
Enhancement projects	−10%	+ 20%	−35%
Conversion projects	−20%	+ 30%	−30%
Year 2000 repair projects	−30%	+ 45%	−45%
Average	−24%	+ 32%	−33%

can equal the results of the software year 2000 contract and outsource community.

The most visible advantage in the domain of year 2000 projects is the specialized staff and tools available within the outsource community that are more plentiful than in-house tools and personnel. However, for large corporations with adequate year 2000 tool and repair budgets, results can often favor the in-house repair teams.

The year 1996 was the last year in which a mid-size corporation could have hoped to tackle the year 2000 problem in a 500,000-function point portfolio with a reasonable chance of finishing before the end of the century using their own staff and manual search methods on a "business as usual" basis. Now the choices have narrowed to immediate outsourcing or adopting unusual strategies to finish in time. Moving from less than 15% deployment of personnel on year 2000 work to more than 50% deployment and use of automated search engines can move the deadline to sometime in 1998 for common languages such as COBOL. However, if your portfolio has languages with limited year 2000 search engines such as MUMPS, CHILL, Algol, or APL, there is little or no time remaining to commence year 2000 repairs. From 1998 onward, it will be necessary to employ unusual methods to raise the probability of completing year 2000 repairs prior to the end of the century. Some of these unusual methods have already been discussed, but include:

- Suspending work on all other software projects except emergency repairs and statutory changes, so that the available year 2000 personnel can rise from the current average of about 15% to a maximum of about 85% of all software personnel
- Moving from one-shift, eight-hour year 2000 repairs to 24-hour around-the-clock year 2000 repairs by establishing global repair facilities located eight hours apart
- Joining or forming collaborative, industrywide year 2000 consortia, and pooling year 2000 resources and expertise (This latter approach assumes that antitrust regulations will not be applied to solving the year 2000 problem in a cooperative manner.)

Note that the performance edge that year 2000 outsource contractors have over their clients in terms of work effort does not translate into a direct dollars and cents advantage, because the outsource fees and charges include burden rates and enough to make a normal profit.

When evaluating the tools and services of a proposed year 2000 vendor, the following checklist of key capabilities may be of use.

Year 2000 Outsource Vendor Checklist

1. Does the vendor exclude dead code and dormant applications from charges?
2. Does the vendor exclude blank lines and comments from charges?
3. Does the vendor have satisfied clients with whom you can discuss performance?
4. Does the vendor have any ongoing litigation from dissatisfied clients?
5. Does the vendor have tools that support your primary programming languages?
6. Does the vendor have tools that support mixed-language projects?
7. Does the vendor have tools for searching databases for year 2000 references?
8. Will the vendor's search tools find more than 99% of year 2000 instances?
9. Will the vendor's repair tools safely repair more than 95% of year 2000 instances?
10. How many undetected year 2000 instances are likely to be left in your software?
11. Does the vendor guarantee to repair bad fixes or new defects introduced by their work?
12. Will the vendor's year 2000 repairs damage throughput or performance?
13. Does the vendor have adequate personnel for repairing your entire portfolio?
14. Will the vendor offer a warranty or guarantee of year 2000 compliance?
15. Will the vendor provide references from prior year 2000 clients?

The year 2000 consulting, repair, and tool business is so new that a full evaluation of its effectiveness is still largely unknown. Hopefully the major vendors in this domain are fully qualified and capable for the work at hand. However, a word of caution is indicated. Problems of the seriousness of the year 2000 problem will attract many vendors with marginal capabilities. Exercise due diligence in selecting an outsource vendor for performing year 2000 repairs. If the vendor fails to repair the year 2000 problem in your portfolio safely, it will be too late to resolve the problem via arbitration or litigation and still get your software repaired. Even if the vendor is technically qualified, you should check very carefully with the way year 2000 repair costs are going to be calculated. Using a simplistic rate based on gross charges per line of code when total physical lines are used can lead to overcharges of a very significant nature. If these charges are noted by your auditors and shareholders, you may have to deal with possible litigation.

Since the year 2000 problem is a major business issue, there are now a number of available sources for selecting and performing due diligence on year 2000 tool vendors and outsource partners. Many organizations have published directories of year 2000 vendors and outsourcers that describe their capabilities. The Applied Computer Research (ACR) catalog for year 2000 vendors,[7] the ITAA catalog,[8] and the Management Support Technology (MST) catalog[9] are three examples of the kind of year 2000 vendor resource guides now available. Since year 2000 vendors are entering the market at a very rapid rate, it is also desirable to explore the vendor listings available on the Internet, such as the vendor section of Peter de Jager's well-known year 2000 Web site.[10]

Almost every large city and many regions have formed nonprofit year 2000 associations where companies can pool their information and experiences. It is highly advantageous to join such groups, since you can discuss vendor performance with companies similar to yours that have actually used their services.

References

1. Jones, Capers. *Evaluating the Pros and Cons of Software Outsourcing. SPR Knowledge Base.* Vol. 3, no. 2. Burlington, MA: SPR, September 1994.

2. Jones, Capers. *Geriatric Care for Legacy Systems.* Burlington, MA: SPR, March 1994.

3. Jones, Capers. *Applied Software Measurement.* 2nd ed. New York: McGraw Hill, 1996.

4. Jones, Capers. *Patterns of Software Systems Failure and Success.* Boston: ITCP, 1996.

5. Jones, Capers. *Conflict and Litigation Between Software Clients and Developers.* Version 4. Burlington, MA: SPR, May 1997. Also available on SPR Web site http://www.spr.com.

6. Strassmann, Paul. *The Squandered Computer.* New Canaan, CT: Information Economics Press, 1997.

7. ACR. *Guide to Year 2000 Tools and Vendors.* Phoenix: ACR, 1997.

8. ITAA. *Year 2000 Solution Providers.* Arlington, VA: ITAA, 1996.

9. Management Support Technology (MST). *The Year 2000 Resource Book.* Framingham, MA: MST, 1996.

10. de Jager, Peter. Vendor section of year 2000 Web site http://www.year2000.com.

11 | The Emergence of Masking as a Year 2000 Repair Alternative

IN ADDITION TO going into software applications and repairing the actual year 2000 problem, an alternative repair method is being discussed that may be appropriate for some kinds of software applications, and for some database year 2000 problems as well. This alternative method consists of masking the problem rather than actually repairing it. To effect this repair a special software shield is constructed, more or less similar to a virus intercept package. Each time a date is encountered entering or leaving an application, the masking software intercepts the date and converts it into one that the application can handle.

I selected the generic term *masking* to describe this approach because there was no other single term that encompassed all of the various discrete forms of year 2000 circumvention. These forms include windowing, compression, encapsulation, bridging, and object code date interception.

Windowing, an external technology for dealing with dates in databases and software, does not require date field expansion. It establishes a 100-year (or some other fixed interval) time period, such as 1915 to 2014, and uses program logic to deal with all dates within that period. Windows can either be fixed or sliding. However, windowing exacts a performance penalty and assumes that everyone using the data knows about the existence of the windowing routines.

Compression is a form of encoding within the allotted two-digit date space that represents any conceivable date. By using a binary or hexadecimal representation rather than a decimal representation, the available two-digit date field can handle dates over almost any period. However, this method requires knowledge of the specific compression technique used by all applications accessing the data. There are also performance reductions associated with this alternative, but they are not as severe as windowing.

Encapsulation, interestingly, is the one that Bill Gates, the Chairman of Microsoft, recommended in response to a query from the floor at his CEO summit meeting in Spring 1997. This method simply shifts all dates downward by 28 years so that the year 2000 would be represented as 1972. The rationale for using 28 years is that a 28-year shift will bring the days of the week (Monday, Tuesday, Wednesday, and so on) and the calendar dates (October 6, 7, 8, and so on) into synchronization. Encapsulation has the advantages of being fairly easy to do and does not need much in the way of testing. However, here too there is a performance penalty.

Bridging is a hybrid method used for database applications in which the software itself is converted from two-digit to four-digit form but the underlying database is not, due to the excessive difficulties associated with database date field expansion. A fixed or sliding window, or encapsulation, are used with the database. Here, too, a performance penalty is exacted.

As this book is being written, experimental methods for intercepting dates in executable object code are being researched.[1] These methods do not yet have commercial tools, and may not even work, but the current research looks promising. In particular, object code year 2000 interception may provide a way of dealing with a very knotty and difficult problem: How to make year 2000 repairs in aging legacy applications when the source code is missing or uncompilable, but the software is still being executed.

Masking in every form has the advantage of not requiring any potentially hazardous changes to the aging legacy applications or to databases. The down sides of the masking approach are (1) it is not certain if deep, indirect, or subtle year 2000 problems will be intercepted and (2) the performance impact of the masking methods and tools will degrade throughput by a finite and possibly significant amount. The technology of masking is still in rapid evolution, and holds some potential advantages. Masking may perhaps be effective for at least some applications written in proprietary or obscure programming languages for which there are no effective year 2000 search engines nor any trained programmers available.

All of the masking approaches should be viewed as temporary methods, since they do not cure the underlying problem of using only two digits for dates. However, if applications are gradually phased out over the next 10- to 15-year period and replaced by compliant applications, then masking may be an acceptable solution for software that does not have stringent performance needs.

For databases, data warehouses, repositories, and other forms of data storage masking is a temporary expedient that eventually must be replaced by true date field expansion. However, masking may provide an ability to defer true date field expansions until after the end of the century, when they can be pursued at leisure rather than being rushed and hurried. The database repair issue is turning out to be much more troublesome than the source code repair issue in the year 2000 problem domain.[2]

However, *all* forms of year 2000 repairs, and the masking forms in particular, have two negative implications that need to be evaluated very carefully: (1) most forms of year 2000 repair will degrade the performance or execution speed of applications and (2) for every change made to a software application, there is a small but finite probability that the change will introduce a fresh error, termed a *bad fix*. Table 11.1 illustrates these two troublesome phenomena by showing some rough approximation based on early client experiences with various forms of year 2000 repairs and masking approaches. The data in Table 11.1 is sorted in order of decreasing values for performance loss or degradation. Leading the way with the greatest negative or harmful impact on software performance are the two methods of expanding date fields, coupled with the assumption that testing will be rushed and inadequate. At the other end of the spectrum, with no apparent performance losses of any kind, would be date field expansions accompanied by careful performance tuning and of course thorough testing. The data in Table 11.1 is preliminary and is included only to emphasize the fact that performance issues and bad-fix injection rates are both important aspects of the overall year 2000 repair equation.

For additional data on the performance impact of various year 2000 repair strategies, refer to the independent studies performed by Robbins and Rubin[3] and by the Programart Corporation.[4]

Although there are hundreds of tools and vendors aimed at the huge COBOL, C, and FORTRAN markets, there are many other languages without a single commercial year 2000 search engine, nor are any year 2000 service providers available. For example, software written in CHILL, CORAL66, or in proprietary languages such as ESPL/I have essentially zero tools and zero year 2000 service providers as this book is being written, other than the in-house tools and staff by the companies that use these languages. However, the technology of masking may open up at least a possibility of generalized year 2000 protection for obscure languages. This niche in the year 2000 domain is a potential business opportunity for vendors. Since the tools and services for

Table 11.1: Performance Reduction and Bad-Fix Injection Potentials for Selected Year 2000 Repair and Masking Strategies

Year 2000 Containment Strategy	Performance Reduction	Bad-Fix Potential
Year 2000 date field expansion, inadequate testing	−20.00%	12.00%
Database date field expansion, inadequate testing	−20.00%	20.00%
Year 2000 date field expansion, novice programmers	−17.00%	15.00%
Database date field expansion, no performance tuning	−15.00%	5.00%
Year 2000 date field expansion, no performance tuning	−10.00%	7.00%
Bridging for database applications	−10.00%	7.00%
Compression (two-digit encoding)	−10.00%	20.00%
Encapsulation (date shifting)	−7.00%	2.00%
Windowing (fixed)	−5.00%	2.00%
Windowing (sliding)	−5.00%	2.00%
Data duplexing (batch applications)	−3.00%	1.00%
Year 2000 date field expansion, expert programmers	−2.00%	4.00%
Year 2000 date field expansion, performance tuning	0.00%	2.00%
Database date field expansion, performance tuning	0.00%	2.00%
Average	−8.86%	7.21%

primary languages such as COBOL are now reaching the saturation point, far-sighted vendors could conceivably capitalize on the hundreds of languages that thus far have been left out of the year 2000 commercial tool domain.

Applications written in common languages such as FORTRAN, COBOL, C, and PL/I comprise about 65% of the software applications that will need year 2000 repairs. The other 35% of applications that need year 2000 repairs are divided among almost 450 other languages and dialects, for which few if any search engines are available. This situation means that each of the obscure languages has too small and too fragmented a client base to be, individually, an attractive market for a customized year 2000 search engine. However, a generalized set of year 2000 masking tools that supported all languages would find a substantial and unexploited market.

Masking may turn out to be a viable technology for the problem of year 2000 repairs in databases, repositories, and data warehouses. Indeed, masking may turn out to be the only viable technology for this critical year 2000 topic and could enable at least rudimentary repairs to be accomplished before the end of the century. For a broad and rather useful overview of all possible masking technologies see Dr. Dick Lefkon's[5] latest book, which is revised annually.

References

1. Petzinger Jr., Thomas. "Bob Bemer Aims 'Silver-Plated Bullet' at Year 2000 Problem." *Wall Street Journal,* page B1. June 20, 1997.
2. Kendall, Robert C. "Year 2000: How to Make the Problem Smaller; How to Make it Bigger." *American Programmer* 10 (June 1997): 25–28.
3. Robbins, Brian and Howard Rubin. *The Year 2000 Planning Guide.* Pound Ridge, NY: Rubin Systems, Inc., 1997.
4. Shea, Brian. "Report on the Performance Impact of the Year 2000 Problem." *IBM Enterprise Systems Journal* (December 1996): 31.
5. Lefkon, Dick, ed. *Year 2000 Best Practices for Y2K Millennium Computing:* New York: AITP—SIG Mainframe, 1997.

12 | International Year 2000 Repair Effort for 30 Countries

*T*HE YEAR 2000 problem is an interesting one because it affects industrialized nations more severely than those that are less dependent on computers and software for business and government operations. The United States, Japan, Germany, France, the United Kingdom, and Brazil will probably be the most heavily impacted. Conversely, countries such as India and the Ukraine may find themselves in an advantageous position as a result of the year 2000 problem, since they will probably have a surplus of skilled programming personnel available during a period that the heavy software countries are mired down in year 2000 repair work.

Year 2000 Repairs by Country

The first topic of interest is the year 2000 repair costs in the countries that have the most software personnel employed and the largest volumes of software in production. Table 12.1 gives a rough approximation of the year 2000 software repair effort in some 30 countries with software populations derived from a 15-year survey of global software demographics, which is still ongoing and is updated on a semiannual basis.[1]

There is a high margin of error in the data in Table 12.1, and it should be noted that some of the data is derived from previous US data and extrapolated for other countries. The demographic data for software personnel is limited to professionals and ignores end-user programming. Although the cost data in Table 12.1 is probably incorrect (on the low side), the relative rankings of effort by country should reflect the overall software populations and hence should be of some utility in projecting year 2000 costs on a demographic basis. The portfolio sizes are based on ratios of US portfolios, and the volume of year

2000 software changes is artificially held constant at 9.5%, which means that just under 10% of the code in global applications is assumed to require year 2000 updates. This is a questionable assumption, but a reasonable starting place. The effort to make the year 2000 changes is also held constant at 16 function points per staff-month. Here, too, the assumption is questionable, but it is at least a starting place for more detailed analysis. Note that this rate of 16 function points per staff-month is derived from the work of date field expansions in common programming languages such as COBOL and C. Expressed in terms of LOC per staff-month, the equivalent value using logical statements would be roughly 1,600 source code statements per staff-month. Other year 2000 repair strategies such as encapsulation, bridging, windowing, and so forth, can proceed at rates of at least twice the nominal values associated with standard date field expansion. However, these other methods are temporary in nature, and may introduce performance degradation of a significant amount.

Table 12.1: Estimated Year 2000 Software Repair Effort for 30 Countries

Country	Software Staff (professional)	Portfolio (function points)	Year 2000 Hits (function points)	Year 2000 Repairs (mo)	US Effort
United States	1,920,000	1,570,560,000	149,203,200	9,325,200	100.00%
Japan	900,000	738,000,000	70,110,000	4,381,875	46.99%
Russia	770,000	539,000,000	51,205,000	3,200,313	34.32%
Germany	550,000	440,000,000	41,800,000	2,612,500	28.02%
United Kingdom	390,000	312,000,000	29,640,000	1,852,500	19.87%
Brazil	475,000	308,750,000	29,331,250	1,833,203	19.66%
France	385,000	308,000,000	29,260,000	1,828,750	19.61%
China	990,000	297,000,000	28,215,000	1,763,438	18.91%
Italy	375,000	290,625,000	27,609,375	1,725,586	18.50%
India	750,000	225,000,000	21,375,000	1,335,938	14.33%
South Korea	300,000	210,000,000	19,950,000	1,246,875	13.37%
Ukraine	260,000	195,000,000	18,525,000	1,157,813	12.42%
Mexico	275,000	178,750,000	16,981,250	1,061,328	11.38%
Spain	235,000	170,375,000	16,185,625	1,011,602	10.85%
Canada	185,000	144,300,000	13,708,500	856,781	9.19%
Turkey	210,000	141,750,000	13,466,250	841,641	9.03%
Thailand	175,000	105,000,000	9,975,000	623,438	6.69%
Poland	190,000	104,500,000	9,927,500	620,469	6.65%
Taiwan	125,000	93,750,000	8,906,250	556,641	5.97%
Australia	110,000	85,250,000	8,098,750	506,172	5.43%

Continued on next page

Table 12.1: Estimated Year 2000 Software Repair Effort for 30 Countries, *continued*

Country	Software Staff (professional)	Portfolio (function points)	Year 2000 Hits (function points)	Year 2000 Repairs (mo)	US Effort
The Netherlands	100,000	77,500,000	7,362,500	460,156	4.93%
Argentina	110,000	77,000,000	7,315,000	457,188	4.90%
Indonesia	175,000	74,375,000	7,065,625	441,602	4.74%
Egypt	145,000	68,875,000	6,543,125	408,945	4.39%
The Philippines	145,000	66,700,000	6,336,500	396,031	4.25%
Pakistan	135,000	57,375,000	5,450,625	340,664	3.65%
South Africa	75,000	56,250,000	5,343,750	333,984	3.58%
Belgium	65,000	50,375,000	4,785,625	299,102	3.21%
Portugal	65,000	45,500,000	4,322,500	270,156	2.90%
Sweden	60,000	45,000,000	4,275,000	267,188	2.87%
Total	10,645,000	7,076,560,000	672,273,200	42,017,075	—

It should be noted once again that Table 12.1 is built on a series of assumptions and hypotheses that may be incorrect. There are possible errors in every column, and the data is only suitable for discussion and for preliminary economic analysis. However, the importance of the year 2000 problem is such that publishing preliminary data with a high margin of error may be better than waiting for corrected data, since the end of the twentieth century is approaching very rapidly.

Table 12.2 shows approximate costs for repairing software in 30 countries. This table uses a number of simplifying assumptions, such as basing all salary and burden rates on percentages of US norms. This means that the costs are rough and only approximate, but should be within the ballpark for the countries in question.

Table 12.2: Estimated Expenses for Year 2000 Software Repairs in 30 Countries

Country	Monthly Salary and Burden	Effort (staff-months)	Year 2000 Repair Costs
United States	$8,000	9,325,200	$74,601,600,000
Japan	$9,600	4,381,875	$42,066,000,000
Russia	$4,000	3,200,313	$12,801,250,000
Germany	$9,200	2,612,500	$24,035,000,000
United Kingdom	$9,200	1,852,500	$17,043,000,000

Continued on next page

Table 12.2: Estimated Expenses for Year 2000 Software Repairs in
           30 Countries, continued

Country	Monthly Salary and Burden	Effort (staff-months)	Year 2000 Repair Costs
Brazil	$7,760	1,833,203	$14,225,656,250
France	$9,200	1,828,750	$16,824,500,000
China	$1,000	1,763,438	$1,763,437,500
Italy	$7,760	1,725,586	$13,390,546,875
India	$1,200	1,335,938	$1,603,125,000
South Korea	$7,200	1,246,875	$8,977,500,000
Ukraine	$3,600	1,157,813	$4,168,125,000
Mexico	$7,200	1,061,328	$7,641,562,500
Spain	$6,800	1,011,602	$6,878,890,625
Canada	$8,400	856,781	$7,196,962,500
Turkey	$7,400	841,641	$6,228,140,625
Thailand	$5,200	623,438	$3,241,875,000
Poland	$6,000	620,469	$3,722,812,500
Taiwan	$7,520	556,641	$4,185,937,500
Australia	$7,760	506,172	$3,927,893,750
The Netherlands	$8,800	460,156	$4,049,375,000
Argentina	$7,200	457,188	$3,291,750,000
Indonesia	$3,600	441,602	$1,589,765,625
Egypt	$6,000	408,945	$2,453,671,875
The Philippines	$3,200	396,031	$1,267,300,000
Pakistan	$1,000	340,664	$340,664,063
South Africa	$7,600	333,984	$2,538,281,250
Belgium	$9,600	299,102	$2,871,375,000
Portugal	$7,200	270,156	$1,945,125,000
Sweden	$9,200	267,188	$2,458,125,000
Total(T)/Average(A)	$6,580(A)	42,017,075(T)	$297,329,248,438(T)

Because Table 12.2 uses generic data and rounded values, the overall
results are slightly different from the more detailed data shown earlier by
language and industry. Given the overall uncertainty of year 2000 costs,
this difference (while noticeable) is not significant. The costs should be
alarmingly high no matter how precisely they are stated. Because global
information on software costs is difficult to gather and in short supply, it
may be of interest to examine some of the global cost data produced by
Dr. Howard Rubin[2] in his annual software economic reports.

Note that Table 12.2 shows only software repair costs. Other
expense elements over and above software repairs will be found that
may more than double the costs shown in the table. Some of these additional cost elements include:

- Database repairs
- Test library repairs
- Year 2000 insurance
- Masking of software rather than actual repairs
- Hardware upgrades
- Retuning of applications
- Litigation costs
- Damages awarded from litigation

The data in the international tables reveals a potential problem for the US software industry. Since the United States is the country with the largest software portfolio, it will be the most greatly affected by year 2000 repairs. This fact may give other countries a chance to make significant headway in global software markets in several fashions:

- By offshore outsourcing of year 2000 repairs
- By offshore outsourcing of other development and maintenance projects while US software personnel are entangled in the year 2000 morass

A possible business outcome of the year 2000 problem is that the United States will lose its dominant market position in the software industry, while countries such as India, China, Russia, and the Ukraine will gain market shares since they are not as greatly affected by year 2000 work and will have a substantial surplus of software technical personnel while the United States enters a period of shortage.

Another important factor not addressed in this study, nor in the similar Gartner Group study, is the long-range impact of inflation on year 2000 repair costs. Note that the financial data shown in this book assumes current 1997 dollars. By the year 2000, inflation will no doubt raise the dollar and other currency amounts significantly and perhaps alarmingly. The year 2000 problem is already driving software compensation packages upward at double-digit rates, so the potential costs of year 2000 repairs may rise faster than shown here or discussed in similar reports by other organizations.

Table 12.3 shows year 2000 repair costs in descending order of magnitude, starting with the United States. Although year 2000 repairs will be troublesome everywhere, it can be hypothesized that countries in the top half of Table 12.3 will have a much greater set of problems than those in the lower half. Indeed, it is possible for the countries with the lowest year 2000 repairs to expand their software markets significantly by outsourcing surplus software engineering capacity to the countries with software personnel who are likely to be preempted by emergency year 2000 upgrades. Note that Table 12.3 deals only with software repair costs and does not include hardware upgrades, database repairs, or litigation expenses. The future is hard to predict, but the economic consequences of the year 2000 problem are likely to be severe for industrialized nations and potentially advantageous for countries that lagged behind in early automation and computerization.

Table 12.3: Ranking of Relative Year 2000 Software Repairs for 30 Countries

Country	Year 2000 Repair Costs	Percent of US Year 2000 Costs
United States	$74,601,600,000	100.00%
Japan	$42,066,000,000	56.39%
Germany	$24,035,000,000	32.22%
United Kingdom	$17,043,000,000	22.85%
France	$16,824,500,000	22.55%
Brazil	$14,225,656,250	19.07%
Italy	$13,390,546,875	17.95%
Russia	$12,801,250,000	17.16%
South Korea	$8,977,500,000	12.03%
Mexico	$7,641,562,500	10.24%
Canada	$7,196,962,500	9.65%
Spain	$6,878,890,625	9.22%
Turkey	$6,228,140,625	8.35%
Taiwan	$4,185,937,500	5.61%
Ukraine	$4,168,125,000	5.59%
The Netherlands	$4,049,375,000	5.43%
Australia	$3,927,893,750	5.27%
Poland	$3,722,812,500	4.99%
Argentina	$3,291,750,000	4.41%
Thailand	$3,241,875,000	4.35%
Belgium	$2,871,375,000	3.85%
South Africa	$2,538,281,250	3.40%
Sweden	$2,458,125,000	3.30%
Egypt	$2,453,671,875	3.29%
Portugal	$1,945,125,000	2.61%
China	$1,763,437,500	2.36%
India	$1,603,125,000	2.15%
Indonesia	$1,589,765,625	2.13%
The Philippines	$1,267,300,000	1.70%
Pakistan	$340,664,063	0.46%
Total	$297,329,248,438	—

Table 12.4 gives a rough approximation of the total number of staff-months per capita for year 2000 repairs in the 30 countries selected for inclusion. There is of course a high margin of error, but if the year 2000 problem is as serious and pervasive as believed, then the software development capacities of the industrial nations may be seriously degraded by the huge amount of effort absorbed by year 2000 repairs. If up to 6 months of effort per capita on the part of most industrialized software personnel is really needed for year 2000 repairs, then many other kinds of software development and maintenance projects will be slipped or canceled.

Table 12.4: Staff-Months of Effort per Capita for Year 2000 Software Repairs in 30 Countries

Country	Staff-Months	Percent of US Effort
Japan	4.87	100.24%
United States	4.86	100.00%
Germany	4.75	97.80%
United Kingdom	4.75	97.80%
France	4.75	97.80%
Canada	4.63	95.35%
Italy	4.60	94.74%
Australia	4.60	94.74%
The Netherlands	4.60	94.74%
Belgium	4.60	94.74%
Ukraine	4.45	91.69%
Taiwan	4.45	91.69%
South Africa	4.45	91.69%
Sweden	4.45	91.69%
Spain	4.30	88.63%
Russia	4.16	85.57%
South Korea	4.16	85.57%
Argentina	4.16	85.57%
Portugal	4.16	85.57%
Turkey	4.01	82.52%
Brazil	3.86	79.46%
Mexico	3.86	79.46%
Thailand	3.56	73.35%
Poland	3.27	67.24%
Egypt	2.82	58.07%
The Philippines	2.73	56.23%

Continued on next page

Table 12.4: Staff-Months of Effort per Capita for Year 2000 Software Repairs in 30 Countries, continued

Country	Staff-Months	Percent of US Effort
Indonesia	2.52	51.96%
Pakistan	2.52	51.96%
China	1.78	36.67%
India	1.78	36.67%
Average	3.95	81.31%

As can be seen, the range of effort to make year 2000 repairs varies substantially. It is likely that the companies where the effort exceeds about 4.5 staff-months per software professional will probably seek outsource assistance from the countries farther down the list. By coincidence, independent research by Dr. Leon Kappelman[3] and the SIM reached conclusions similar to those in Table 12.4. Their study found that year 2000 software repairs were roughly equal to 30% of annual software budgets, which would be approximately 4 months of staff effort.

The Year 2000 Problem and 35 Urban Areas

Software development is normally an urban occupation that takes place within a 30-mile radius of a major metropolitan area. Table 12.5 shows the approximate number of software workers and the year 2000 repair effort for a total of 35 international cities. Some American cities are also included to give an overall picture of the impact of the year 2000 problem on a number of urban economies where software is a major occupation. An interesting implication of Table 12.5 is that software business failures are very likely to be concentrated in the cities where there are the largest numbers of software companies.

The possible impact of the year 2000 problem on software employment is somewhat alarming for those of us in the software industry: What comes to mind is the rapid deployment of air bags in automobile accidents—an explosive expansion followed almost at once by deflation. The data on software employment in response to the year 2000 problem indicates these two trends:

1. A sharp, almost explosive increase in software hiring through 1999 as enterprises staff up for year 2000 repairs

2. A significant surplus of software workers and major unemployment among software occupations early in the twenty-first century due to either completing year 2000 repairs or business failures and bankruptcies.

The cities shown in Table 12.5 are the global areas most likely to experience the "air bag" cycle of explosive growth of software employment followed by abrupt deflation after the year 2000 crisis passes. Incidentally, among the most severely affected during the deflation cycle will be the year 2000 service providers, with a corporate life expectancy from 1997 that is probably five years or less, unless they have other kinds of services to take up the slack.

Table 12.5: Year 2000 Software Repairs by City for 35 International Cities

International City	Software Personnel in Urban Area	Year 2000 Effort (mo/staff member)	Burdened Monthly Salary	Year 2000 Costs per City
Tokyo	165,000	4.87	$9,600	$7,714,080,000
London	136,000	4.75	$9,200	$5,943,200,000
Los Angeles	127,000	4.86	$9,000	$5,554,980,000
New York	116,000	4.86	$9,000	$5,073,840,000
Paris	85,000	4.75	$9,200	$3,714,500,000
Yokohama	75,000	4.87	$9,600	$3,506,400,000
Seoul	112,000	4.16	$7,200	$3,354,624,000
Sao Paulo	110,000	3.86	$7,760	$3,294,896,000
Osaka	67,000	4.87	$9,600	$3,132,384,000
Toronto	80,000	4.63	$8,400	$3,111,360,000
Mexico City	110,000	3.86	$7,200	$3,057,120,000
Chicago	75,000	4.86	$8,300	$3,025,350,000
Berlin	65,000	4.75	$9,200	$2,840,500,000
Montreal	68,000	4.63	$8,400	$2,644,656,000
Sydney	66,000	4.65	$8,400	$2,577,960,000
Washington, DC	50,000	4.86	$8,200	$1,992,600,000
Rio de Janeiro	64,000	3.86	$7,760	$1,917,030,400
Moscow	112,000	4.16	$4,000	$1,863,680,000
San Jose	36,000	4.86	$9,000	$1,574,640,000
Stockholm	35,000	4.75	$9,200	$1,529,500,000
San Francisco	33,000	4.86	$9,000	$1,443,420,000
Rome	40,000	4.60	$7,760	$1,427,840,000
Hong Kong	38,000	4.60	$7,700	$1,345,960,000
Madrid	46,000	4.30	$6,800	$1,345,040,000

Continued on next page

Table 12.5: Year 2000 Software Repairs by City for 35 International Cities, continued

International City	Software Personnel in Urban Area	Year 2000 Effort (mo/staff member)	Burdened Monthly Salary	Year 2000 Costs per City
Bangkok	70,000	3.56	$5,200	$1,295,840,000
Cairo	75,000	2.82	$6,000	$1,269,000,000
Buenos Aires	40,000	4.16	$7,200	$1,198,080,000
Lima	40,000	4.16	$6,000	$998,400,000
Leningrad	56,000	4.16	$4,000	$931,840,000
Jakarta	62,000	2.52	$3,600	$562,464,000
Beijing	90,000	1.78	$1,000	$160,200,000
Bombay	60,000	1.78	$1,200	$128,160,000
Shanghai	70,000	1.78	$1,000	$124,600,000
Delhi	58,000	1.78	$1,200	$123,888,000
Karachi	41,000	2.52	$1,000	$103,320,000
Total(T)/Average(A)	2,573,000(T)	4.03(A)	$6,768(A)	$79,881,352,400(T)

Showing year 2000 expenses by urban area is in some ways more shocking than considering national levels. Most of us live in or near a city and know the numbers and kinds of companies in the area that employ software personnel. Dividing the urban costs by the number of local software employers leads to a very alarming economic picture.

The Overlap of the Year 2000, European Currency, and Leap Year Conversions

In what must be regarded as one of the most unwise and hazardous public policy decisions in all of human history, the European Community has scheduled the completion of conversion to a unified currency for the beginning of calendar year 1999, without any apparent regard or concern for the fact that the year 2000 problem and the European currency conversion will be in direct competition for scarce software resources. Of course it would be an exciting thing to start the new century with a new currency, so you can see why the European Union wanted to make the currency change before the twenty-first century. Unfortunately, the glamour of the standard currency blinded the political leaders to the painful fact that Europe does not have enough software personnel to do both the currency conversion and year 2000 repairs at the same time. (The somewhat smaller technical problem of ensuring that all software applications recognize the year 2000 as a leap year will also have an impact.)

The net result of the unwise conversion schedule set by the European Union is that the Western European countries have been devoting most of their available surplus software resources to the currency conversion problem and are not yet expending even minimal resources on the year 2000 problem. A much wiser policy would have been to defer the European currency conversion until after the year 2000 problem, and not plan for full conversion until about 2003 at the earliest or perhaps even 2005, which should be after the bulk of the year 2000 problem is behind us.

The European currency conversion impact on software applications is as large as the impact of the year 2000 problem in many industries, and in two industries—banking and retailing—will probably be even more expensive. However, the European currency situation only affects software dealing with finance and is not a major factor in weapons systems, telephone switching, aircraft flight control, and some of the other areas in which the year 2000 problem may cause safety hazards. Further, the impact of failing to achieve the European currency conversion target date will only result in financial and political problems, even if they are severe ones. Failing to achieve year 2000 conversion, on the other hand, can result in much more serious problems involving possible disruption of air traffic, shutdown of power and telecommunication facilities, and potential injury or death due to failure of medical instruments, airline navigation equipment, or railroad control devices.

The most probable result of the unwise policy of having the schedule for the European currency conversion overlap the schedule for the year 2000 problem will be the following: Through 1997 the Western European countries will continue to devote most of their software efforts to the European currency problem and pay little or no attention to the year 2000 problem. In about late 1997 or early 1998 the Western European countries will realize the far more serious hazards associated with the year 2000 problem and begin emergency repairs. Since software resources are as limited in Europe as they are in the United States, some of the resources for year 2000 repairs will probably be diverted from the currency conversion projects. Since there are not enough software resources available in Western Europe to complete both the year 2000 repairs and the currency conversion work on parallel schedules, the dilution of effort between these two enormous problems will probably result in these three disturbing phenomena:

1. Western Europe will not achieve year 2000 compliance for even 65% of the applications that need year 2000 repairs.

2. The simultaneous attempts to perform year 2000 repairs and currency conversion work on nearly identical schedules will cause both efforts to slip well beyond their deadlines. Western Europe will probably not be able to complete the currency conversion work until about 2005, and will probably not be fully recovered from the year 2000 crisis until at least 2003.

3. Since the most convenient pools of surplus software personnel reside in Eastern Europe, the Eastern European countries of Russia, the Ukraine, the Czech Republic, and others will probably end up with very significant outsource contracts, and will grow to become major software powers while Western Europe may face losses and reductions in software staffing after the two crises have passed.

Although these three software problems are all important, the potential severity of the year 2000 problem is much greater than either the European currency issue or the leap year problem (Table 12.6).

While the European currency conversion problem is a major topic in Western Europe in 1997, many US companies are not yet even dealing with it, although US companies will be affected when the new currency becomes operable. It would not be surprising to find that the

Table 12.6: Impact of Year 2000, Leap Year, and European Currency Changes

Industry	Year 2000	Leap Year	European Currency Conversion	Average
Airlines	5.00	3.00	4.00	4.00
Defense	5.00	2.00	3.00	3.33
Health care	5.00	2.00	3.00	3.33
Railroads	5.00	2.00	3.00	3.33
Manufacturing	4.00	2.00	3.00	3.00
National government	4.00	3.00	4.00	3.67
Finance	4.00	4.00	4.00	4.00
Insurance	4.00	2.00	3.00	3.00
Local government	4.00	2.00	3.00	3.00
Public utilities	4.00	3.00	3.00	3.33
Telecommunications	4.00	3.00	3.00	3.33
Wholesale/retail	4.00	3.00	4.00	3.67
Average	4.33	2.58	3.33	3.42

1.0 = none; 2.0 = minor; 3.0 = significant; 4.0 = severe (financial hazards);
5.0 = major (life threatening)

unwise scheduling of the European currency conversion in 1999—only one year before the year 2000 and leap year problems hit—will end up by damaging the Western European economies severely, while perhaps strengthening the software balance of trade for Eastern Europe and the Pacific Rim, and perhaps South America as well. Table 12.7 shows a preliminary assessment of how various geographic regions may end up in terms of achieving repairs on all three software issues.

Although the future is hard to envision, one possible result of the year 2000, the leap year, and the currency conversion problems is that the software industries in South America, the Pacific Rim, and Eastern Europe will receive a major jolt of new business in the form of outsource contracts to handle either the three software problems themselves or to perform software work that Western Europe and the United States is unable to perform because we have devoted all available resources to the three software problems.

Once the developing geographic regions achieve a major presence in world software markets, it is unwise to assume that they will lose their market shares when the crises are past. The most likely conclusion from the combination of the year 2000, leap year, and the European currency conversions is that the current software powers—the United States and Western Europe—will lose software market shares while Eastern Europe, South America, and the Pacific Rim will gain software market shares.

The European currency conversion problem is not the focus of this book; however, since the costs and effort for the year 2000 problem and for the European currency conversion will occur almost simultaneously and interfere with each other, it is advantageous to consider both problems as part of one enormous problem for the European Union.

Table 12.7: Readiness for Year 2000, Leap Year, and European Currency Conversions

Region	Year 2000	Leap Year	European Currency	Average
South America	75%	95%	75%	82%
Pacific Rim	80%	95%	70%	82%
Eastern Europe	80%	95%	60%	78%
Western Europe	60%	90%	85%	78%
North America	85%	95%	55%	78%
Average	76%	94%	69%	80%

Table 12.8 shows a rough comparison of the two software undertakings for the 15 countries in the European Union. The European currency effort is merely set at 90% of the year 2000 effort, on the grounds that fewer applications will be affected. This assumption is both arbitrary and questionable, and is only a preliminary judgment.

If the data in Table 12.8 is close to reality, then roughly eight months of programming effort on the part of every software professional in the European Union may be devoted to year 2000 or European currency work over the next two and one-half years. The inescapable conclusion must be that the European Union will fall far behind other geographic regions in terms of the ability to build new applications and become a major software vendor in the world market.

Although Table 12.8 does not show the information, the costs for damages, litigation, and recovery of unrepaired software packages in the European Union should be much larger than almost any other geographic region, since Western Europe has lagged in year 2000 repairs.

- Expect about $4 in year 2000 damages for every $1 on year 2000 repairs, on the grounds that the European Union will probably not be much more than 50% compliant at the end of the century.
- Expect around $1 in damages for every $1 spent on the European currency conversion issue, on the grounds that the year 2000 work and the European currency work will compete head on and will delay both activities.

The most likely beneficiary of the European Union software problems will probably be Eastern Europe, since a surplus of trained software personnel are available who will not be preempted by either the year 2000 or the European conversion problems. It is quite unfortunate that the European Union is moving into a very hazardous first decade of the next century. The timing of the European currency conversion could hardly have been worse, and illustrates the basic human problem of *tunnel vision*, failing to understand how one topic connects to other topics.

Aggregate of Global Year 2000 Repair Expenses

The previous international tables show only the 30 largest countries in terms of their software populations, and hence anticipated software expenses. Since there are roughly 200 countries in the United Nations, an interesting question is that of the magnitude of effort and costs for the 170 or so countries that are not shown separately. My overall global

Table 12.8: Comparison of European Currency Conversion and Year 2000 Effort

Country	Software Staff	Portfolio Size (function points)	Year 2000 Effort (mo)	Currency Effort (mo)	Total Effort, European Union
Germany	550,000	440,000,000	2,612,500	2,351,250	4,963,750
United Kingdom	390,000	312,000,000	1,852,500	1,667,250	3,519,750
France	385,000	308,000,000	1,828,750	1,645,875	3,474,625
Italy	375,000	290,625,000	1,725,586	1,553,027	3,278,613
Spain	235,000	170,375,000	1,011,602	910,442	1,922,044
The Netherlands	100,000	77,500,000	460,158	414,142	874,300
Belgium	65,000	50,375,000	299,102	269,192	568,294
Portugal	65,000	45,500,000	270,156	243,140	513,296
Greece	60,000	45,000,000	249,600	224,640	474,240
Sweden	60,000	45,000,000	267,188	240,469	507,657
Austria	51,000	39,525,000	237,150	213,435	450,585
Denmark	34,000	27,200,000	159,800	143,820	303,620
Finland	32,000	24,800,000	147,200	132,480	279,680
Ireland	24,000	19,200,000	111,600	100,440	212,040
Luxembourg	3,000	2,325,000	13,710	12,339	26,049
Total	2,429,000	1,897,425,000	11,246,602	10,121,942	21,368,544
Costs	—	—	$94,471,456,800	$85,024,311,120	$179,495,767,920

demographic data indicates that the world population of software professionals circa 1996 totals about 12,500,000 (with a high margin of error). The 30 countries enumerated here had a total professional population of just over 7,000,000. Assuming both sets of assumptions are true, the absent 170 countries would have a combined software population of about 5,500,000.

It is interesting that the average software population for the 30 countries that are enumerated here is about 233,000 per country. The average software population for the 170 countries that are not shown separately averages about 32,000 per country. Assuming that the ratio of year 2000 expenses is similar to the ratio of software personnel (a questionable assumption but at least a starting point), then the year 2000 expenses for the missing 170 countries would total about $233,000,000,000. This amounts to about $1,371,000,000 per country. By contrast, the average cost for the 30 countries that are shown separately is about $9,900,000,000 per country. Of course "averages" are not very meaningful when whole countries are considered, but the results do give a sanity check to the approximate costs on a global basis.

Adding the invisible costs for the missing countries to the visible costs for the 30 countries shown here yields an approximate global cost of $530,000,000,000 for year 2000 software repairs. For year 2000 software repairs, the US total of roughly $70,000,000,000 amounts to about 13.2% of the global total of $530,000,000,000. This raises an interesting question as to the entire total of all year 2000 repairs on a global basis when software, hardware, databases, and litigation are all considered. Table 12.9 is an attempt to assemble a global picture of all major year 2000 cost elements simply to judge the rough magnitude of costs. For every cost element except litigation, the US ratio of 13.2% of global totals was used. Note that unlike the earlier tables that only showed 30 countries, Table 12.9 is based on the assumption that all of the approximately 200 countries constituting the United Nations will have year 2000 expenses. For litigation, the United States is assumed to have a much higher total of global costs than for the other year 2000 expense elements. I estimate that US litigation will amount to about 33% of world totals. The rationale for this assumption is because the United States is a much more litigious country than the other major industrial powers such as Japan, Germany, France, the United Kingdom, and many others. My assumption on litigation percentages may well be wrong, but I'm not aware of any other data on this topic.

Table 12.9: Overall Total of Global Year 2000 Expense Elements

Year 2000 Topic	Global Year 2000 Costs
Initial software repairs	$530,000,000,000
Secondary bad-fix software repairs	$50,000,000,000
Test library repairs	$75,000,000,000
Database repairs	$454,000,000,000
Hardware chip replacements	$76,000,000,000
Hardware performance upgrades	$150,000,000,000
Litigation and damages	$300,000,000,000
World total	$1,635,000,000,000

No matter how things turn out, it is certain that the software industry in every country will be undergoing a major transformation between the years 1996 and 2005 in reaction to the year 2000 problem. One of the problems faced by the software industry is sociological. Some think that we have not been regarded by the older professions such as electrical and mechanical engineers as being true engineers or even true professionals. The fact that the software industry, collectively, has brought about one of the most expensive and hazardous problems in human history when it could easily have been avoided is going to lower our status even more.

Not only is the year 2000 problem one of the most expensive problems in human history, it is also one of the most embarrassing. This problem has been theoretically discussed for more than 25 years, and its significance has been hypothesized with increasing alarm for more than 10 years. It is not a credit to the human race nor to the software industry that such an obvious problem with such a straightforward technical solution should have reached the magnitude that is likely to occur. On the other hand, the year 2000 problem is symptomatic of a general human tendency to avoid trying to solve problems until the evidence is overwhelming. The historical difficulties that medical researchers such as Lister and Semmelweis had in introducing sterile surgical procedures, and the early resistance to Jenner's concept of vaccination, illustrate that software is not the only learned profession that does not move swiftly to minimize potential risks.

References

1. Jones, Capers. *Software Productivity and Quality Today—The WorldWide Perspective*. Carlsbad, CA: Information Systems Management Group, 1993.
2. Rubin, Howard. *Worldwide Software Benchmark Report for 1996*. Pound Ridge, NY: Rubin Systems, Inc., 1996.
3. Kappelman, Leon A., et al. *How Much Will Year 2000 Compliance Cost?* Version 2.12 Denton, TX: College of Business Administration, University of North Texas, May 30, 1997.

13 | Why Do Year 2000 Costs Vary?

*T*HIS BOOK, as well as similar reports by other organizations, such as the Gartner Group, tries to express many aspects of the year 2000 problem in terms of costs. Software cost estimates are a complicated issue, and the year 2000 problem is much more complicated than usual. It is important to explain some aspects of why software costs vary and why the year 2000 costs will vary by several hundred percent based on specific situations.

Although year 2000 software productivity measurements based on human effort in terms of work hours or work months can now be measured with acceptable precision, the same cannot be said for software costs. There are several major problems in the cost domain that have existed for more than 50 years, but have escaped notice as long as software uses inaccurate metrics like LOC, which tends to mask a host of other important problems. These same problems occur for other industries besides software, incidentally. They tend to be more troublesome for software than for most other industries because software is so labor intensive, and hence they need to be discussed in a year 2000 context, which is perhaps the most labor-intensive problem in human history.

The topic of software costs has a very large range of variability within any given country, and an even larger range for international software studies. There are six interconnected sets of cost factors that need to be evaluated to determine software costs, and every one is an independent variable:

1. Variations due to industry compensation averages
2. Variations due to company size
3. Variations due to geographic regions or locations
4. Variations due to merit appraisals or longevity
5. Variations due to burden rate or overhead differences
6. Variations due to work patterns and unpaid overtime

A fundamental problem with software cost measures is the fact that salaries and compensation vary widely from job to job, worker to worker, company to company, region to region, industry to industry, and country to country. For example, among SPR's clients in the United States the basic salary of the occupation of "software project manager" ranges from a low of about $42,000 per year to a high of almost $100,000 per year. When international clients are included, the range for the same position runs from less than $10,000 per year to more than $120,000 a year. Table 13.1 shows 1996 averages and ranges for project management compensation for 20 US industries taken from among SPR's client organizations. The table shows average results in the left column, and then shows the ranges observed based on company size and on geographic region. In general, large corporations pay more

Table 13.1: 1996 Annual Compensation Levels for Software Project Managers in 20 Industries in the United States

Industry	Average Annual Salary	Range by Company Size (+ /−)	Range by Geographic Region (+/−)	Maximal Annual Salary	Minimal Annual Salary
Banking	$72,706	$18,000	$6,000	$96,706	$48,706
Electronics	$71,750	$15,000	$6,000	$92,750	$50,750
Telecommunications	$71,500	$15,000	$6,000	$92,500	$50,500
Software	$71,250	$15,000	$6,000	$92,250	$50,250
Consumer products	$69,929	$14,000	$5,500	$89,429	$50,429
Chemicals	$68,929	$13,000	$5,500	$87,429	$50,429
Defense	$65,828	$13,000	$5,500	$84,328	$47,328
Food/beverages	$63,667	$12,000	$5,000	$80,667	$46,667
Media	$62,125	$12,000	$5,000	$79,125	$45,125
Industrial equipment	$62,009	$12,000	$5,000	$79,009	$45,009
Distribution	$60,900	$11,000	$5,000	$76,900	$44,900
Insurance	$59,117	$10,000	$5,000	$74,117	$44,117
Public utilities	$57,214	$7,500	$4,500	$69,214	$45,214
Retail	$57,105	$7,000	$4,500	$68,605	$45,605
Health care	$55,459	$7,500	$4,500	$67,459	$43,459
Nonprofit agencies	$53,883	$7,500	$4,500	$65,883	$41,883
Transportation	$53,448	$7,000	$4,500	$64,948	$41,948
Textiles	$52,583	$7,000	$4,500	$64,083	$41,083
Government	$51,990	$6,000	$4,000	$61,990	$41,990
Education	$50,176	$6,000	$4,000	$60,176	$40,176
Average	$61,578	$11,026	$5,079	$78,284	$46,073

than small companies. For example, large urban areas such as the San Francisco Bay area or the urban areas in New York and New Jersey have much higher pay scales than do more rural areas or smaller communities. Also, some industries such as banking and financial services, and telecommunications and manufacturing tend to have compensation levels that are far above US averages, while other industries such as government service and education tend to have compensation levels that are significantly lower than US averages. These basic economic facts mean that it is unsafe and inaccurate to use "US averages" for cost comparisons of software. At the very least, cost comparisons should be within the context of the same or related industries, and comparisons should be made against organizations of similar size and located in similar geographic areas.

Other software-related positions besides project management have similar ranges, and there are now more than 50 software-related occupations in the United States, most of which are involved in year 2000 work. This means that to do year 2000 software cost studies it is necessary to address major differences in costs based on industry, company size, geographic location, the kinds of specialists that are present on any given project, and years of tenure or merit appraisal results.

Table 13.2 illustrates the 1996 ranges of basic compensation (exclusive of bonuses or merit appraisal adjustments) for 15 software occupations in the United States. As you can see, the range of possible compensation levels runs from less than $30,000 to more than $100,000. Over and above the basic compensation levels shown in Table 13.2, a number of specialized occupations are now offering even higher compensation levels than those illustrated. For example, programmers who are familiar with the SAP R/3 integrated system and the ABAP programming language can expect compensation levels about 10% higher than average, and may even receive a signing bonus similar to those offered to professional athletes.

Although year 2000 specialists were not included in the original 1996 data, information on year 2000 compensation packages is now starting to become available, so the approximate ranges were included in Table 13.2 in italics simply to show what might be expected for this fast-growing specialty. Year 2000 specialists are already above average in terms of compensation, and this trend can be expected to continue and indeed to become more skewed as the year 2000 approaches.

Even if only basic compensation is considered, you can see easily that year 2000 software projects by large companies in large cities such as New York and San Francisco will have higher cost structures than

Table 13.2: 1996 Variations in Compensation for Selected Software Occupational Groups in the United States

Occupation	Average Annual Salary	Range by Company Size (+ /–)	Range by Geographic Region (+/–)	Range by Industry (+ /–)	Maximal Annual Salary	Minimal Annual Salary
Software architect	$77,000	$13,000	$4,500	$7,500	$102,000	$52,000
Senior systems programmer	$75,000	$12,000	$4,500	$6,000	$97,500	$52,500
Senior systems analyst	$67,000	$11,000	$4,000	$6,000	$88,000	$46,000
Systems programmer	$60,000	$11,000	$4,000	$5,500	$80,500	$39,500
Systems analyst	$55,000	$10,500	$3,750	$5,000	$74,250	$35,750
Process analyst	$53,000	$10,500	$3,750	$5,000	$72,250	$33,750
Database analyst	$52,000	$12,000	$3,750	$6,000	$73,750	$30,250
Metrics specialist	$50,000	$12,000	$3,750	$5,000	$70,750	$29,250
Programmer/analyst	$50,000	$11,000	$3,500	$5,000	$69,500	$30,500
Applications programmer	$50,000	$10,000	$3,500	$5,000	$68,500	$31,500
Maintenance programmer	$50,000	$10,000	$3,500	$5,000	$68,500	$31,500
Quality assurance specialist	$49,000	$7,500	$3,500	$5,000	$65,000	$33,000
Test specialist	$49,000	$7,500	$3,500	$5,000	$65,000	$33,000
Technical writer	$40,000	$5,000	$3,500	$3,000	$51,500	$28,500
Customer support	$37,000	$2,000	$3,500	$2,000	$44,500	$29,500
Year 2000 specialists	*$60,000*	*$10,000*	*$4,000*	*$6,000*	*$80,000*	*$40,000*
Average	$54,267	$9,667	$3,767	$5,067	$72,767	$35,767

the same applications developed by small companies in smaller cities. This is true for in-house year 2000 projects. When the work involves contractors or outsource vendors, even larger ranges can occur!

For information on software compensation, many public and private sources are available. For example, Computerworld publishes annual software compensation reports[1] and many organizations pool their compensation data to generate industry averages. Also, compensation variations by industry are published on an annual basis in a number of guides, of which the well-known "Hoover's guides" are fairly representative for international studies,[2] software,[3] and other industries.[4] In addition, several years ago AT&T commissioned my company to explore various kinds of specialization in large software employers such as IBM, Texas Instruments, and the US Air Force. This study included hiring practices, sources of specialists, and of course typical compensation packages. Excerpts from this report were published in one of my earlier books entitled *Patterns of Software Systems Failure and Success.*[5]

Although the topic is not illustrated and the results are often proprietary, there are also major variations in compensation based on merit appraisals and/or longevity within grade. This factor can add about another ±$7,500 to the range of compensation for technical positions, and even more for executive and managerial positions. Also not illustrated are the bonus programs and stock equity programs that many companies offer to software technical employees and to managers. For example, in California some COBOL programmers are getting bonuses that amount to a year's salary in exchange for agreeing to work through the completion of the year 2000 crisis. Other forms of benefits include stock equity. For example the stock equity program at Microsoft has become famous for creating more millionaires than any similar program in US industry. Overall, software compensation packages are better than many other kinds of knowledge work and will be getting even larger as the chronic shortage of software personnel continues over the next few years.

Variations in Burden Rates or Overhead Costs

An even more significant problem associated with software cost studies is the lack of generally accepted accounting practices for determining the burden rate or overhead costs that are added to basic salaries to create a metric called *the fully burdened salary rate,* which corporations use for determining business topics such as the charge-out rates for cost centers. The fully burdened rate is also used for other business purposes such as contracts, outsource agreements, and ROI calculations.

The components of the burden rate are highly variable from company to company. Some of the costs included in burden rates can be social security contributions, unemployment benefit contributions, various kinds of taxes, rent on office space, utilities, security, postage, depreciation, portions of mortgage payments on buildings, various fringe benefits (medical plans, dental plans, disability, moving and living expenses, vacations, and so on), and sometimes the costs of indirect staff (human resources, purchasing, mail room, and so on).

One of the major gaps in the software literature as of 1997, and for that matter in accounting literature as well, is the almost total lack of international comparisons of the typical burden rate methodologies used in various countries. So far as can be determined, there are no published studies that explore burden rate differences between countries such as the United States, Canada, India, the European Union countries, Japan, China, and so forth. Among SPR's clients, the range of burden rates runs from a low of perhaps 15% of basic salary levels to a high of approximately 300%. In terms of dollars, that range means that the fully burdened charge rate for the position of senior systems programmer in the United States can run from a low of about $15,000 per year to a high of $350,000 per year. Unfortunately, both the general software literature and the year 2000 software literature are almost silent on the topic of burden or overhead rates. Indeed, many of the articles on software costs not only fail to detail the factors included in burden rates, but often fail to even state whether the burden rate itself was used in deriving the costs that the articles are discussing!

Table 13.3 is taken from the author's prior book *Applied Software Measurement*[6] and illustrates some of the typical components of software burden rates, and also how these components might vary between a large corporation with a massive infrastructure and a small start-up corporation that has very few overhead cost elements.

When the combined ranges of basic salaries and burden rates are applied to software projects in the United States, they yield almost a 6:1 variance in billable costs for year 2000 projects for which the actual number of work months or work hours are identical! When the salary and burden rate ranges are applied to international year 2000 projects, they yield about a 15:1 variance between countries such as India or the Ukraine at the low end of the spectrum, and Germany, Switzerland, or Japan at the high end of the spectrum. For additional information on overseas software costs, the annual reports of Dr. Howard Rubin[7] are a useful source of comparative data for most industrialized countries. Bear in mind that this 15:1 range of cost variance is for projects for which the actual number of hours worked is identical. When productivity differences are considered too, there is more than a 100:1 variance between the most productive year 2000 projects in companies with the lowest salaries and burden rates, and the least productive year 2000 projects in companies with the highest salaries and burden rates.

Variations in Work Habits and Unpaid Overtime

The software industry is a highly labor-intensive one, and the year 2000 problem is adding extra labor on top of an already huge amount of work. So long as the year 2000 repairs depend primarily on using human effort, all of the factors associated with work patterns and overtime will continue to be significant.

Table 13.3: Generic Components of Typical Burden or Overhead Costs in Large and Small Companies

	Large Company		Small Company	
Average annual salary	$50,000	100.0%	$50,000	100.0%
Personnel burden				
Payroll taxes	$5,000	10.0%	$5,000	10.0%
Bonus	$5,000	10.0%	0	0.0%
Benefits	$5,000	10.0%	$2,500	5.0%
Profit sharing	$5,000	10.0%	0	0.0%
Subtotal	*$20,000*	*40.0%*	*$7,500*	*15.0%*
Office burden				
Office rent	$10,000	20.0%	$5,000	10.0%
Property taxes	$2,500	5.0%	$1,000	2.0%
Office supplies	$2,000	4.0%	$1,000	2.0%
Janitorial service	$1,000	2.0%	$1,000	2.0%
Utilities	$1,000	2.0%	$1,000	2.0%
Subtotal	*$16,500*	*33.0%*	*$9,000*	*18.0%*
Corporate burden				
Information systems	$5,000	10.0%	0	0.0%
Finance	$5,000	10.0%	0	0.0%
Human resources	$4,000	8.0%	0	0.0%
Legal	$3,000	6.0%	0	0.0%
Subtotal	*$17,000*	*34.0%*	*0*	*0.0%*
Total burden	$53,500	107.0%	$16,500	33.0%
Salary + burden	$103,500	207.0%	$66,500	133.0%
Monthly rate	$8,625	—	$5,542	—

Assume that a typical US work month contains four work weeks, each comprised of five eight-hour working days. The combination of 4 weeks × 5 days × 8 hours = 160 available hours in a typical month. However, at least in the United States, the *effective* number of hours worked each month is often less than 160, due to factors such as coffee breaks, meetings, slack time between assignments, classes, and the like. Thus in situations where there is no intense schedule pressure, the effective number of work hours per month may only amount to about 80% of the available hours, or about 128 hours per calendar month.

On the other hand, software projects are often under intense schedule pressures and overtime is quite common. This is about to become the mode of working on the year 2000 problem, as company after company realizes that they are late in getting started. Thus for situations where schedule pressures are intense, not only might the software team work the available 160 hours per month, but the team would also work late in the evenings and on weekends too. Therefore, on "crunch" projects, the work might amount to 110% of the available hours, or about 176 hours per week.

Table 13.4 compares two versions of the same project—in this case a 1,000-function point information systems application written in COBOL that is a replacement for an older application that was not year 2000 compliant. The first version is a "normal" version, when only about 80% of the available hours are worked each month. The second version shows the same project in "crunch" mode when the work hours comprise 110%, with all of the extra hours being in the form of unpaid overtime by the software team. (The majority of professional US software personnel are termed *exempt,* which means that they do not receive overtime pay for work in the evening or on weekends. Indeed,

Table 13.4: Differences Between Normal and Intense Software Work Patterns

Activity	Work Habits Project 1 Normal	Work Habits Project 2 Intense	Difference	Percent
FP size	1,000	1,000	0	0.00%
Size in LOC	100,000	100,000	0	0.00%
LOC per FP	100	100	0	0.00%
A-scope (FP)	200	200	0	0.00%
Nominal P-rate (FP)	10	10	0	0.00%
Availability	*80.00%*	*110.00%*	*30.00%*	*37.50%*
Hours per month	*128.00*	*176.00*	*48.00*	*37.50%*
Salary per month	$5,000.00	$5,000.00	$0.00	0.00%
Staff	5.00	5.00	0.00	0.00%
Effort months	125.00	90.91	−34.09	−27.27%
Schedule months	31.25	16.53	−14.72	−47.11%
Cost	$625,000	$454,545	−$170,455	−27.27%
Cost per FP	$625.00	$454.55	−$170.45	−27.27%
Work hours per FP	16.00	16.00	0.00	0.00%
Virtual P-rate (FP)	8.00	11.00	3.00	37.50%
Cost per LOC	$6.25	$4.55	−$1.70	−27.27%
LOC per month	800	1100	300	37.50%

FP = function point; LOC = lines of code; A-scope = assignment scope; P-rate = production rate.

many software cost-tracking systems do not even record overtime hours. Since exempt software personnel are normally paid on a monthly basis rather than an hourly basis, the differences in apparent results between "normal" and "intense" work patterns are both significant and also tricky when performing software economic analyses.)

As seen in Table 13.4, applying intense work pressure to a software project such as year 2000 repairs in the form of unpaid overtime can produce significant and visible reductions in software costs and software schedules. However, there may be invisible and harmful results in terms of staff fatigue and burnout.

Table 13.4 introduces five terms that are significant in software measurement and also year 2000 cost estimating, but that need definition. *Assignment scope* (abbreviated *A-scope*) is the quantity of function points normally assigned to one staff member. *Production rate* (abbreviated *P-rate*) is the monthly rate in function points at which the work will be performed. *Nominal production rate* (abbreviated *Nominal P-rate*) is the rate of monthly progress measured in function points without any unpaid overtime being applied. *Virtual production rate* (abbreviated *Virtual P-rate*) is the apparent rate of monthly productivity in function points that will result when unpaid overtime is applied to the project or activity. *Work hours per function point* simply accumulates the total number of work hours expended and divides that amount by the function point total of the application.

Because software staff members are paid monthly but work hourly, the most visible impact of unpaid overtime is to decouple productivity measured in work hours per function point from productivity measured in function points per staff-month. Assume that a small 60-function point project would normally require two calendar months or 320 work hours to complete. Now assume that the programmer assigned worked double shifts and finished the project in one calendar month, although 320 hours were still needed. If the project had been a normal one, stretched over two months, the productivity rate would have been 30 function points per staff-month and 5.33 work hours per function point. By applying unpaid overtime to the work and finishing in one month, the virtual productivity rate appears to be 60 function points per staff-month, but the actual number of hours required remains 5.33 work hours per function point.

Variations in work patterns are extremely significant when dealing with international software projects. There are major national differences in terms of work hours per week, quantities of unpaid overtime, number of annual holidays, and annual vacation periods. In fact, it is very dangerous to perform international studies without taking this phenomenon into account. Variations in work practices are a major differentiating factor for international software productivity and schedule results. Table 13.5 makes a number of simplifying assumptions and does not deal with the specifics of sick time, lunch and coffee breaks, meetings, courses, and nonwork activities that might occur during business hours. The data in the table is derived from basic assumptions about national holidays and average annual vacation times, and ignores telecommuting, home offices, flex time, and a number of other factors that are important for detailed analyses. Since there are significant local and industry differences within every country, the data in Table 13.5 should be used just as a starting point for more detailed exploration and analysis.

Software is currently among the most labor-intensive commodities on the global market. Therefore work practices and work effort applied to software exerts a major influence on productivity and schedule results. In every country, the top software personnel tend to work rather long hours, so this table can only be used for very rough comparisons.

Dr. Howard Rubin and I have two of the largest collections of international software data. Although we are competitors from time to time, we also collaborate on joint studies as well. A frequent topic of collaboration is in the international software measurement and metric domain, since we both work overseas and collect global data. For an example of a collaborative study between SPR and Dr. Rubin, refer to

Table 13.5: Approximate Number of Work Hours per Year in 10 Countries

Country	Work Days per Year	Work Hours per Day	Overtime per Day	Work Hours per Year	Percent of US Results
Japan	260	9.00	2.5	2,990	139%
China	260	9.00	1.5	2,730	127%
India	245	8.50	2	2,573	120%
Italy	230	9.00	1	2,300	107%
United States	239	8.00	1	2,151	100%
Brazil	234	8.00	1	2,106	98%
United Kingdom	232	8.00	1	2,088	97%
France	230	8.00	1	2,070	96%
Germany	228	8.00	0	1,824	85%
Russia	230	7.50	0	1,725	80%
Average	238.8	8.30	1.1	2,245	104%

our recent international benchmark report.[8] For an earlier study on global software demographics and international variations in software productivity rates, although published before the year 2000 problem was notable, refer to my 1993 book on global software variations in productivity and quality.[9] Useful information on global software variations can also be found by reviewing the annual issues that many software journals publish, such as *Software Magazine*.[10]

The year 2000 problem will be particularly labor intensive as time passes and companies that are late in starting their year 2000 work begin to realize the pressure of the approaching end of the century. Indeed, it is reasonable to assume that massive doses of overtime (both paid and unpaid) will probably accrue starting in 1997, and by 1999 will be the normal situation for the year 2000 repair teams. Of course, companies that were proactive and started their year 2000 repairs early will be winding up and planning vacations while the laggards are working around the clock.

The differences in national work patterns compounded with differences in burdened cost structures can lead to very significant international differences in software costs and schedules for the same size and kind of application. Table 13.6 illustrates how wide the global cost variances can actually be. This table examines the cost ranges of building exactly the same 1,000-function point year 2000 replacement project in 10 countries throughout the world. Table 13.6 artificially holds the effort constant at

Table 13.6: International Cost Comparison for 1,000 Function Points

Country	Work Hours per FP	Effort (work hours)	Cost per Work Hour	Project Cost	Cost per FP	Percent of US Effort
Germany	20	20,000	$57.56	$1,151,200	$1,151.20	129%
France	20	20,000	$46.92	$938,400	$938.40	105%
United States	20	20,000	$44.74	$894,800	$894.80	100%
United Kingdom	20	20,000	$41.09	$821,800	$821.80	92%
Brazil	20	20,000	$37.60	$752,000	$752.00	84%
Italy	20	20,000	$37.30	$746,000	$746.00	83%
Japan	20	20,000	$36.70	$734,000	$734.00	82%
Russia	20	20,000	$10.08	$201,600	$201.60	23%
India	20	20,000	$4.46	$89,200	$89.20	10%
China	20	20,000	$3.70	$74,000	$74.00	8%
Average	20	20,000	$32.02	$640,300	$640.30	72%

FP = function points

20 work hours per function point, and then applies typical local compensation levels and burden rates for the 10 countries illustrated.

Although there are very large ranges within each country, you can see that there also are very large national differences as well. Expressed in terms of development cost per function point, the observed range for the exact same size and kind of software project around the world spans amounts that run from less than $75 per function point on the low end to more than $1,500 per function point on the high end. It is possible to calculate the arithmetic mean, harmonic mean, median, and mode of software costs, although any such cost value would be dangerous to use for estimating purposes when the ranges are so broad. This is why I have long been reluctant to publish general software cost data, and instead prefer to use costs only in the context of industry, regional, and project norms. In fact, cost data varies so much that work hours or person-months are much more stable for year 2000 software productivity studies. Obviously for international comparisons, the daily fluctuations in currency exchange rates and the longer fluctuations in national rates of inflation also need to be considered.

When clients ask for data on "average year 2000 cost per function point" or on "average costs per line of code" so that they can use this data for estimating purposes, the only safe answer is that costs vary so much due to compensation and burden rate differences that it is better to base the comparison on the client's own industries and geographic locales. General year 2000 cost data is much too variable for casual comparisons at national levels.

However, due to the fact that many software research organizations such as Gartner Group, Meta Group, and Giga Group all publish data on cost per LOC for the year 2000 problem, SPR also gets many requests for data expressed in these terms.

After considering the pros and cons of withholding cost data or publishing it with caveats to explain why it may be hazardous to use, it seems best to publish the data and explain as fully as possible why year 2000 costs can fluctuate very widely and why "average cost per LOC" and "average cost per function point" are unsafe metrics for the year 2000 problem unless they are given in context with specific industries, geographic locations, company sizes, and skill mixes.

References

1. Computerworld. *Salary and Job Satisfaction Survey '95–'96.* Framingham, MA: Computerworld, 1997.

2. Hoover, Gary, Alta Campbell, and Patrick Spain. *Hoover's Handbook of American Business 1993*. Austin, TX: Reference Press, 1992.

3. Hoover, Gary, et al. *Hoover's Handbook of International Business 1995*. Austin, TX: Reference Press, 1994.

4. Hoover, Gary, et al. *Hoover's Guide to Computer Companies*. Austin, TX: Reference Press, 1996.

5. Jones, Capers. *Patterns of Software Systems Failure and Success*. Boston: ITCP, 1996.

6. Jones, Capers. *Applied Software Measurement*. 2nd ed. New York: McGraw Hill, 1996.

7. Rubin, Howard. *Worldwide Benchmark Report 1996*. Pound Ridge, NY: Rubin Systems, Inc.; 1996.

8. Jones, Capers, and Howard Rubin. *Software Assessments and Benchmarks*. Burlington, MA: SPR, Knowledge Base, vol. 5, no. 2. 1996.

9. Jones, Capers. *Software Quality and Productivity Today—The Worldwide Perspective*. Carlsbad, CA: Information Systems Management Group, 1993.

10. "15th Annual Ranking of the World's Largest Software Companies." *Software Magazine* (July 1997).

14 | Post-2000 Problem and Recovery Prognosis

IT IS NO SECRET that software is the most troubling technology of the twentieth century. A surprising aspect of the year 2000 problem is that the companies that solve this problem are going to end up knowing much more about their software than ever before. Even better, their software will be in much more stable and reliable condition than it is right now.

Recall that the year 2000 problem is only one instance of a large class of similar problems where storage limitations caused insufficient space to be reserved. The same tools that attack or solve the year 2000 problem can also be applied to the other instances so the software that is repaired should be more robust than it is now. Further, the detailed inventory of software portfolios, corporate databases, and repositories needed for year 2000 repairs will give corporations and government agencies a much improved ability to match their software projects to the needs of their operating units. With so many positive things awaiting year 2000 solutions, it is sad that so many corporations and government agencies have not addressed the problem vigorously, or even at all in many cases!

If aspects of game theory are applied to the year 2000 problem, the results indicate that a rapid and thorough attack on the year 2000 problem is the "minimax" solution—the solution that will give the best return for the lowest expense. Consider the following hypothesis: For every dollar spent on repairing the year 2000 problem, the value in terms of greater reliability and stability of software will probably return fifty cents in reduced maintenance costs for the applications in question. For every dollar *not* spent on repairing the year 2000 problem, the anticipated costs of litigation and potential damages will probably amount to more than $20.

The expenses of repairing the year 2000 problem are going to occur, like it or not. Since delays in attacking the year 2000 problem lower the probability of successful repairs and raise the probability of litigation and damage, the overall conclusion is that a rapid attack on the year 2000 problem is the best economic solution. However, it is now obvious that many companies and government agencies will not complete their year 2000 repairs before the end of the century. Indeed a number of enterprises will probably not even attempt to fix the problems at all before the turn of the century, but will simply wait and see what happens. Since it is only 1997 as this book is being written, the exact number of enterprises and applications that will have year 2000 hits after the turn of the century is still uncertain.

So far as can be determined, in all of human history there has never been a problem of the magnitude of the year 2000 problem where 100% preparedness occurred. Because of the uncertainty of the situation, it is well to deal with the unrepaired applications in terms of a "best-case," "expected-case," and "worst-case" set of scenarios. This section of the book addresses three important questions that urgently need answers.

1. How many applications will not be repaired before January 1, 2000?
2. What will be the damages associated with these unrepaired applications?
3. What will be the recovery costs after the unrepaired applications fail?

As shown earlier, the total number of software applications deployed in the United States is not known with certainty, but probably is in the range of 36,000,000. However, not all of these applications deal with dates or have any year 2000 problems embedded within them. Furthermore, building on the analysis that Kendall and Lamb[1] performed at eight IBM data centers, quite a high percentage of software applications installed in production libraries are actually dormant applications that have not been executed or run for several years, and indeed may never be run again. Their research suggests that if other companies follow the IBM pattern, about 50% of all installed US software applications are dormant and can be excluded from urgent year 2000 repairs. However, they state categorically that their research was limited to IBM data centers and that neither they nor anyone else really knows if their data can be assumed to be general.

The best-case scenario is that only about 25% of the installed applications in the United States are both active (rather than dormant) and have year 2000 hits. The expected-case scenario is that 50% of the applications have year 2000 hits, and the worst-case scenario is that 75% of the applications have year 2000 hits.

We should also consider the ranges of year 2000 discovery and repair activities. It would be nice to assume that the best case for the year 2000 problem is 100%, but unfortunately among our clients that is a very optimistic projection. In more realistic terms, the worst case for repairing year 2000 problems will be close to 0%, the expected case will be about 70%, and the best case will be lucky to top 95%. To deal with the probable damages and recovery costs of these software applications, it is necessary to consider the kinds of software that are likely to be affected by the year 2000 problem. There is no agreed-to taxonomy for software types, but the following general categories are fairly well understood.

MIS software is defined as software applications that deal with numerical and alphabetical information. Examples of MIS applications would be payroll systems, banking applications, insurance claims handling, tax calculations, and a host of others.

Systems software is defined as software that controls some kind of physical device. Examples of systems software would be computer operating systems such as MVS or DOS, telecommunication switching systems, manufacturing control systems, and process control systems.

Embedded software is defined as software that is actually contained within a physical device and is used to control or modify its operation. Examples of embedded software would be automobile fuel injection software, medical instrument controls, aircraft flight control software, the software inside a microwave oven, or the software controlling the time lock on a bank vault.

Commercial software is defined as software that is leased or marketed to consumers or to corporations. Examples of commercial software would be Microsoft Excel, Lotus, ACT, Quicken, Visual Basic, Netscape, SAP R/3, or my own company's CHECKPOINT and KnowledgePLAN software estimating tools, which were used for some of the calculations in this report.

Military software is defined as software that was developed in accordance with various military and defense standards such as the well-known DoD-STD-2167A or the more recent DoD-STD-498. Military software can be subdivided into logistics software,

weapons system software, and C^3 software. The military logistics software resembles civilian MIS applications. The military
weapons software is embedded in actual weapons systems such
as the Tomahawk cruise missile or the Mark 160 gun control system. Military C^3 software is concerned with the ability to coordinate military organizations and functions.

Scientific software is defined as software that deals with equations or
statistical information used primarily for research purposes.
Examples of scientific software would be special applications used
for analyzing seismic information, for astronomical purposes, or
for medical and genetic research.

End-user software is defined as software written for private use by
a knowledge worker who is not a professional programmer, but
rather who is in some other field of work such as accounting,
electrical engineering, law, or medicine.

The category "other" is for software that does not fit conveniently
into some of the other categories. Examples of "other" applications would include JAVA applets on the Web, some on-line computer games, software tools built for internal use such as test
tools, and even some proprietary year 2000 search-and-repair
engines that companies have built for dealing with the year 2000
problem.

Table 14.1 assumes a reasonable approximation of a best-case
scenario in that only about 25% of US applications are assumed to contain year 2000 problems. The critical aspect of this table is the assumptions made regarding the percentages of applications that contain year
2000 problems that will actually be fixed before the end of the century.
Note that Table 14.1 deals with unique applications. For example, there
are millions of customers using the Windows 95 software package, but
Windows 95 is essentially one application. This table does not address
how many specific customers are using an application, but rather how
many applications might exist and how many of these might contain
the year 2000 problem after the turn of the century.

Since the year 2000 event has not yet occurred, Table 14.1 is obviously somewhat speculative and has an unknown margin of error.
However, no one seriously doubts that as the sun rises on January 1,
2000, there will be a significant number of software applications that

Table 14.1: Probable Number of US Unrepaired Year 2000 Problems

Software Types	Active Applications with Year 2000 Problems	Applications Repaired in Time	Applications Not Repaired in Time	Unrepaired Applications in January 2000
Management information systems	4,687,500	82.00%	18.00%	843,750
Systems	1,250,000	77.00%	23.00%	287,500
Commercial (PC)	2,500,000	90.00%	10.00%	250,000
Commercial (mini)	1,250,000	95.00%	5.00%	62,500
Embedded	200,000	77.00%	23.00%	46,000
Commercial (mainframe)	1,125,000	96.00%	4.00%	45,000
End user	125,000	65.00%	35.00%	43,750
Military logistics	210,000	94.00%	6.00%	12,600
Scientific	28,125	80.00%	20.00%	5,625
Military weapons	30,000	96.00%	4.00%	1,200
Military command, control, and communication	15,000	97.00%	3.00%	450
Other	600,000	80.00%	20.00%	120,000
Total(T)/Average(A)	12,020,625(T)	85.75%(A)	14.25%(A)	1,718,375(T)

still contain two-digit date logic and will no longer function as intended. Furthermore, from more than 25 years of accumulated research[2] on the efficiency of finding errors of other kinds, the US average for "defect removal efficiency" is just about 85%, which makes Table 14.1 a reasonable extrapolation from known empirical studies.

For the United States as a whole, a little more than 1,700,000 unrepaired applications must, unfortunately, be regarded as the best-case scenario. The expected-case scenario is about 3,500,000 applications and the worst-case scenario could top 10,000,000 applications or a full one third of all applications in the United States! At a global level, the number of unrepaired applications on January 1, 2000, might be about 10,000,000 as a best-case scenario, 21,000,000 as a most likely scenario, and may go as high as 60,000,000 in the worst-case scenario. Let us now consider what kinds of damages are likely to occur on the dawn of January 1, 2000, from the applications that did not make the year 2000 cutoff date.

Damages from Unrepaired MIS Applications

The damages associated with unrepaired MIS applications include things such as paychecks with incorrect amounts, incorrect income tax records, tax bills with incorrect amounts, and annuities and interest rate miscalculations. Somewhat more serious problems might also include errors in the scheduling of airline flights or railroad travel errors. The recovery from missed year 2000 problems in the MIS domain will include recalling and reissuing the incorrect documents or checks. Corrections will also probably include recalculating bank balances, accrued interest rates, and probably removing penalties for things like late payments if they have been assigned incorrectly due to year 2000 errors.

One of the worst kinds of year 2000 problems would be the following scenario involving income tax reporting. While the IRS will probably be year 2000 compliant itself, there is a strong chance that a significant number of software-generated W2 and 1099 tax reporting forms, which are prepared by many thousands of companies and brokerages, will contain errors due to the year 2000 problem. These tax reporting errors, in turn, might trigger automatic penalties and possible audits by the IRS even though the individual tax payers themselves are not at fault. At the very best, the IRS will have a considerable amount of trouble validating whether or not tax payers have properly reported their 1999 and 2000 incomes. Basically the entire income tax system could be thrown out of kilter, and would perhaps stay that way for at least a year.

Another doomsday scenario involving the year 2000 problem would be programmed trading software that many brokerages use. These applications have already been accused of being capable of damaging the stock market by artificially creating trends based on incorrect assumptions. Imagine the consequences of these powerful applications running amok because of the year 2000 problem, and interfering with normal stock-trading practices.

Another possible form of year 2000 problem would be the accidental triggering of penalties that credit card companies, mortgage companies, and local tax agencies levy when payments are late or missed. It is conceivable that these penalties, most of which occur automatically and are software controlled, will accidentally be levied against unsuspecting individuals who actually paid on time or even early. Although these penalties might be removed or reversed by consumers, it will probably take individual actions on the part of affected consumers to recover from the year 2000 damage. There is a strong chance that many individual credit records might contain late payment notices accidentally sent to credit bureaus by software that contains the year 2000 problem. This, in turn, might affect the credit ratings of both consumers and companies, and affect their ability to borrow money.

Yet another kind of possible trouble from the year 2000 problem involves payment of traffic tickets, which occurs in very large numbers every day. If the local software dealing with traffic ticket payments contains the year 2000 problem, then a significant number of drivers might find themselves with penalties, or in some cases be prevented from renewing their driver's licenses or motor vehicle registrations. Although the drivers themselves may not be at fault, it is not an easy task to get a government agency to admit to or correct a mistake.

Damages from Unrepaired Systems Software

The kinds of problems that can occur from missed year 2000 hits in systems software are quite alarming. Some of the potential problems associated with systems software include:

- Shutdowns or malfunctions of:
  - nuclear power plants
  - electricity-generating plants
  - telephone switching systems
  - bank automated teller machines
  - badge-lock security systems
  - computer security systems
  - elevators in office buildings
  - electrical equipment
  - traffic light synchronization
  - hospital patient-monitoring devices
  - medical instruments
  - manufacturing assembly lines
- Failure of just-in-time deliveries of subcomponents or raw materials

The potential hazards from year 2000 problems in systems software reach the point of being life threatening and can certainly disrupt the daily activities of urban dwellers in the industrialized countries. Hopefully all essential services will be fully year 2000 compliant, but if they are not the consequences of protracted delays in the following services would be very disruptive:

- Electric power
- Telephone
- Air traffic control
- Railroad traffic control
- Manufacturing assembly lines
- Computer systems

The loss of these essential services for a period of several days or longer could do immense damage to both companies and consumers.

The kinds of recovery actions for systems software that fails due to the year 2000 problem will include emergency repairs or bypass masking of the affected software, and then restarting whatever physical device has been out of service. As many people know, restarting a complex physical device after an unplanned outage is not a trivial task and in some cases can take several days of around-the-clock work.

Damages from Unrepaired Embedded Software

Several years ago, there was a fire in my neighborhood that almost destroyed a neighbor's house. The investigation of the causes of the fire traced the problem to a malfunction in the embedded software controlling a microwave oven, which caused the oven to start and run spontaneously. Embedded software controlling complex physical devices is now so common that it is hard to enumerate all of the devices that are controlled by microcomputers and embedded software. In a civilian context, the possible year 2000 failures associated with embedded software might include situations similar to the one just described. Household appliances such as VCRs, television sets, or microwave ovens might work erratically if they are using automatic timers.

Embedded software is also a feature of modern automobile engines, brake systems, and electronics. Hopefully the year 2000 problem will not affect automotive safety. Other possible instances of year 2000 problems in a civilian context would be the on-board software governing aircraft hydraulic and engine performance. Some electric and utility meters also use embedded software, and there are some concerns as to whether rates will be correctly recorded after the turn of the century.

The exact nature of the recovery process for embedded software is uncertain and ambiguous, but will probably include recalls of the affected devices. Incidentally, if maintenance contracts include "on-site service," don't expect a service representative to show up at once. He or she will probably be swamped with service calls. Even making telephone contact with some vendors will be difficult due to the enormous volume of incoming calls (assuming the year 2000 problem has not shut down the phone systems).

Damages from Unrepaired Military Software

US military forces are the most computerized and software-intensive military organizations in the world. US armed services deploy and use more computers and software than the entire software consumption of at least half the countries in the world! This means that the year 2000 problem will be a significant issue for the US Army, Air Force, Navy, Marines, and Coast Guard, as well as for the Pentagon and Department of Defense executives. The implications of unrepaired year 2000 hits in a military context are quite serious. They include:

- Satellite positioning errors
- Encryption errors
- Shipboard nuclear shutdowns or malfunctions
- Weapons systems targeting errors
- Torpedo and cruise missile needing guidance repairs
- Military aircraft flight control problems
- Naval vessel recalls to port for upgrades
- Maintenance schedule miscalculations
- Compromised base security
- Command and control system malfunctions

Although the military implications of the year 2000 problem are not trivial, the Department of Defense and the military services are among the most active organizations in coming to grips with the year 2000 problem and have a better chance than most for getting the problems under control in time, although no organization as large as the US military is likely to achieve 100% year 2000 compliance.

Although not "military" in the sense of the Army, Air Force, and Navy, the security organizations of the world will also be severely impacted by the year 2000 problem. We will probably not read about what kind of year 2000 repair work is going on in the NSA, CIA, and similar agencies in other countries, such as the Mossad in Israel, but it is certain that these agencies will be quite active in making year 2000 repairs an urgent priority. The potential impact of the year 2000 problem on encrypted data is conceivably quite serious, and no other organizations in the world are so immersed in encrypted data as the NSA and CIA. Also, the impact of the year 2000 problem on global positioning satellites, weather satellites, radar satellites, communication satellites, the Hubble telescope, and other computer-driven objects floating in space may well prove to be both troublesome and difficult to repair.

However, the year 2000 problem is a global issue and it will involve the military software of Russia and the component countries of the former Soviet Union. In addition, the weapons systems of many other countries such as North Korea, Iran, and Iraq will probably contain the year 2000 problem, and these countries may or may not be able to deal with all of the military implications, or might even want to take advantage of some of them. It would not be surprising to see some kind of sudden military action occur on the night of December 31, 1999, due to the anticipated problems that the year 2000 problem will bring to various defensive software applications.

Repairs to military equipment actually deployed and in use is a very expensive proposition. As an example, it may be necessary to arrange special rotations of submarines, ships, and aircraft to repair facilities to make the necessary year 2000 repairs. The expenses in time, fuel, and human effort will be massive, and will probably be outside the scope of current budgets.

Damages from Unrepaired Commercial Software

While the major software vendors such as Microsoft, Oracle, IBM, SAP, Computer Associates, Novell, and others, are moving rapidly to achieve year 2000 compliance, the situation is not as clear with minor software vendors in niche markets. Some of the commercial software year 2000 actions are going to trigger massive expenses for their clients. Oracle, for example, has stated that they will achieve year 2000 compliance only for their most recent releases circa the end of 1997. Users of all earlier releases must upgrade to the latest release in order to achieve their own year 2000 compliance. Other vendors have announced similar policies, and the net affect will be a very expensive wave of migration to new releases primarily to gain year 2000 compliance.

Because the commercial software domain is so broad, it is not easy to generalize the kinds of problems that might occur. However, many commercial software packages use date and time logic, and hence are likely to produce erroneous results if they do not achieve year 2000 compliance. Recovery operations from commercial software will vary from package to package and vendor to vendor, but will probably include migration to a newer release of the offending package (assuming the vendor has a later release that is year 2000 compliant). Over and above this, recovery will also include redoing any work that was in error as a result of the noncompliance of the year 2000 problem.

Damages from Unrepaired Scientific Software

Unfortunately, my company has no immediate clients in the domain of scientific software, and hence we are unable to assess the potential for damages in this area. Some of the more obvious kinds of problems might include miscalculations of seismic results or errors in research programs involving long-range monitoring of sensors and signal processing. One would hope that all of the software concerning satellite positions and scientific instrumentation packages in space are fully year 2000 compliant, since there is no easy way of repairing equipment in orbit.

Damages from Unrepaired End-User Software

End-user applications are common and growing even more common. However, because they are often private property and not under the control of any corporate organization, there is no effective way of doing research into the numbers of end-user applications, their intended purposes, or the probable impact of the year 2000 problem.

Among our corporate clients, end-user applications are very common in accounting and financial services groups, where many controllers and financial personnel have used various macro languages to build customized reports and spreadsheet functions. Other end-user applications include decision-support tools used by executives in operating groups such as marketing, sales, manufacturing, or even human resources. Here, too, I do not have enough data available to judge the probable impact of being noncompliant for the year 2000 in the end-user domain. The entire topic of end-user software is difficult to evaluate because it is so personal and involves so many different people with so many different needs. Indeed, even the numbers and sizes of end-user applications are difficult to evaluate, to say nothing about the use of the applications.

Pattern of Expenses for Unrepaired Year 2000 Problems and Recovery Actions

From examining the implications of previous failures and outages of telephone switching systems, operating systems, network drivers, and the like, I have made some subjective judgments as to both the failure and recovery costs, assuming that a work month has an approximate burdened compensation rate of $8,400 in the United States (Table 14.2). This is not a bad value for software professionals, but probably over-states the situation for other kinds of occupations.

There is no real way of ascertaining what the immediate failure costs will be for the year 2000 problem, nor what the recovery costs will be either, because every factor in the equation is both independent and unproved and the final results are at the end of a long string of variable assumptions. Assuming that Table 14.2 is intended to be more or less a best-case scenario, the results are both alarming and somber. Recall from previous tables that the estimated cost for actual repairs of

Table 14.2: Probable Best-Case Costs for US Unrepaired Year 2000 Problems

Software Type	Unrepaired Applications in January 2000	Probable Damages per Application	Probable Recovery Costs per Application	Probable Damages and Recovery
Management information systems	843,750	$75,000	$150,000	$189,843,750,000
Systems	287,500	$125,000	$375,000	$143,750,000,000
Military logistics	12,600	$500,000	$1,000,000	$18,900,000,000
Military weapons	1,200	$2,000,000	$10,000,000	$14,400,000,000
Commercial (mainframe)	45,000	$100,000	$200,000	$13,500,000,000
Military command, control, and communications	450	$2,500,000	$15,000,000	$7,875,000,000
Embedded	46,000	$10,000	$50,000	$2,760,000,000
Commercial (mini)	62,500	$10,000	$20,000	$1,875,000,000
Commercial (PC)	250,000	$2,500	$5,000	$1,875,000,000
Scientific	5,625	$20,000	$40,000	$337,500,000
End user	43,750	$2,500	$5,000	$328,125,000
Other	120,000	$5,000	$10,000	$1,800,000,000
Total(T)/Average(A)	1,718,375(T)	$445,833(A)	$2,440,455(A)	$397,244,375,000(T)

the year 2000 problem in the United States was only about $70,000,000,000. This implies that the costs for damages and recovery of unrepaired applications will total to about $5.67 for every $1 spent on the repairs themselves! On a per capita basis, the damages and recovery costs from the year 2000 problem could amount to about $5,000 for every US citizen and more than $10,000 for every job holder in the United States. Of course it should not be forgotten that Table 14.2 is speculative, as are all other post-2000 estimates. Even so, it is a definite fact that these three phenomena will occur in January 2000.

1. There will be some software applications that are not year 2000 compliant.
2. There will be some damages from noncompliant software.
3. There will be some costs for recovering from non-compliant software.

The important question is what are the exact values of these three factual statements. The data presented here is only one possible scenario and there are many other possibilities. Unfortunately, quite a few of the possibilities are much worse than those in Table 14.2 and comparatively few of the possibilities are significantly better.

To illustrate how sensitive the assumptions are, Table 14.3 shows the probable US damages and recovery costs for the year 2000 problem when the percentage of problems found runs from a low of 75% to a high of 100% at 5% intervals. Because of the speculative nature of

Table 14.3: US Post-2000 Costs under Varying Percentages of Latent Year 2000 Software Problems

Percent Repaired	Percent Missed	Damage Costs per FP	Recovery Costs per FP	Post-2000 Total Cost per FP	Post-2000 Cost per LOC
75%	25%	$98.03	$237.46	$335.49	$3.35
80%	20%	$78.42	$189.96	$268.39	$2.68
85%	15%	$68.19	$165.19	$233.38	$2.33
90%	10%	$47.74	$115.63	$163.37	$1.63
95%	5%	$14.32	$34.69	$49.01	$0.49
100%	0%	$0.00	$0.00	$0.00	$0.00

FP = function point; LOC = lines of code.

Table 14.3, it only illustrates the data using cost per function point and cost per line of code. The LOC column is based on a simple ratio of 100 LOC per function point. Since languages can vary from this nominal value in both directions, it is merely a rough approximation. However, as you can see even from approximate information, if many more year 2000 problems slip through than the assumed value of 15%, then costs can rise steeply. On the other hand, if 10% or less slip through, the costs can also decline steeply.

Evaluating Pre-2000 and Post-2000 Software Costs for the United States

The estimates for post-2000 damages and recovery costs were not included in versions 1 through 6 of this book, because when they were prepared there was still some optimism that repairs might approach being universal. However, as the current book is being drafted in 1997 it is obvious that many enterprises will not finish their year 2000 repairs in time, and a significant number won't even attempt to do year 2000 repairs at all. Let us consider the costs of partial repairs combined with the costs of damages and recovery.

Table 14.4 builds on the earlier data of the approximate costs associated with attempts to repair the year 2000 problem, plus hardware upgrades and estimated litigation. However, Table 14.4 now includes estimates for the damages associated with unrepaired year 2000 applications and the costs of recovery from year 2000 problems such as restarting power plants, reissuing checks, and the like.

Note that Table 14.4 assumes that much of the work of year 2000 repairs will be done using in-house personnel, and the costs are based on function points deployed. (For a 10-year analysis of software updating and cumulative costs, refer to "Software Enhancement Modeling,"[3] which summarizes the factors that influence the maintenance costs of software applications as they grow old and evolve over extended periods.) Furthermore, Table 14.4 assumes a mixture of date field expansions, windowing, bridging, encapsulation, and other forms of masking that are less expensive than pure date field repairs themselves. Table 14.4 also assumes that dead code, which is no longer operational even though it is physically present in software applications, will not be part of the repair cost equation. However, if contractors or outsource vendors are used, this may not be a safe assumption. If external contractors are used and the costs are based on physical LOC then costs may be much higher than those shown here. For example, many year 2000 vendors

Table 14.4: Overall Total of US Pre-2000 and Post-2000 Repairs and Recovery[a]

Year 2000 Topic	US Year 2000 Cost Element	Cost per Function Point	Cost per Line of Code
Expenses prior to 2000			
Initial software repairs	$70,000,000,000	$41.13	$0.36
Secondary bad-fix software repairs	$7,000,000,000	$4.11	$0.04
Test library repairs	$10,000,000,000	$5.88	$0.05
Database repairs	$60,000,000,000	$35.25	$0.31
Hardware chip replacements	$10,000,000,000	$5.88	$0.05
Hardware performance upgrades	$20,000,000,000	$11.75	$0.10
Subtotal	$177,000,000,000	$103.99	$0.91
Expenses after 2000			
Litigation and damages	$100,000,000,000	$58.75	$0.52
Post-2000 damages	$116,075,625,000	$68.19	$0.60
Post-2000 recovery expenses	$281,168,750,000	$165.19	$1.45
Subtotal	$497,244,375,000	$292.13	$2.56
Total	$674,244,375,000	$396.12	$3.47

[a]Function points deployed in the United States = 1,702,125,000; lines of code deployed in the United States = 194,042,250,000.

are charging in excess of $1 per physical line of code, and some of these vendors are including both comments and dead code in their charge structures. Under these circumstances, external vendor costs might exceed in-house repairs by almost an order of magnitude.

In addition, Table 14.4 also attempts to normalize these cost elements using costs per function point and cost per LOC metrics. It should be noted that neither function points nor LOC has any actual relevance for some of the year 2000 cost elements, such as:

- Litigation
- Hardware upgrades
- Restarting power plants
- Reissuing checks and statements

However, once total costs for these activities have been accumulated using other means, then it is possible to express the results in a normalized fashion, even if neither function points nor LOC has any actual bearing on the costs themselves.

The function point totals were derived from analyzing the portfolios of our clients and then extrapolating those values to a national level. The source code values were derived by multiplying the function point total by an assumed expansion factor of 114 source code statements per function point, which is the same ratio used for the combination of languages shown in earlier tables. However, it cannot be overemphasized that cost per LOC is a very unreliable metric and it will fluctuate wildly from language to language.

For organizations with portfolios that consist primarily of recent COBOL applications, the costs can be much lower than those in Table 14.4 or indeed in most of the tables. But for organizations with portfolios that contain a diverse mixture of obscure languages, such as CORAL, BLISS, FORTH, CHILL, CMS2, Jovial, plus Assembly language the costs can be much higher due to the lack of available tools, trained personnel, and other issues. Even worse, many applications lack source code. For an overview of the tools and methods applied to legacy systems, refer to the SPR report on geriatric care for aging software.[4]

For large and multifaceted economic problems such as the year 2000 crisis, the accuracy of the predictions is questionable. About the only thing that is certain is that the year 2000 problem has already accumulated more costs than any other software problem in history, and many companies are only now beginning to address it.

Sources of Error in Year 2000 Cost Estimates

There are many possible sources of error in evaluating year 2000 repair costs, and it is appropriate to summarize a few of them since the world press tends to quote costs without regard for accuracy or error content.

Sources of Error in Software Year 2000 Repair Costs

The software costs for year 2000 repairs, in theory if not in practice, can be predicted with the greatest precision. For an individual company, the accuracy can probably come within ±15%. However for predictions at the levels of industries or countries, the accuracy is much lower and the range of possible errors can be ± 200% for the following reasons.

There are enormous variations in software compensation levels and also in software burden rates from region to region, company to company, and country to country. This fact alone can trigger variations of more than 100% in any single country, and obviously larger variations between countries. While source code sizes can be counted with reasonable precision for many common programming languages such as COBOL, determining code sizes is not without major sources of error. For some modern languages such as Visual Basic, the concept of lines of source code does not truly apply. Also, many older legacy applications are dormant and do not need repair. Even for active applications that do need repair, there are significant but sometimes unknown quantities of dead code, and also numerous blank lines and comment statements that do not need repair. Finally, for about 15% of aging legacy software, the source code is missing or not available, so code counts are only possible for object code, which may or may not be repairable at all.

Adding to the uncertainty of the cost data for source code year 2000 repairs are the varieties of year 2000 repair strategies, each of which have different costs associated with them: replacement, withdrawal without replacement, date field expansion, encapsulation, compression, windowing (fixed), windowing (sliding), and bridging.

Two other possible sources of error for year 2000 code repairs are bad-fix injections and year 2000 defect removal efficiency. For all known forms of software updates, a percentage of the changes include new errors. For year 2000 repairs, the probable bad-fix rate will run between less than 2% and more than 10%. For all known defect removal operations, the efficiency or number of bugs actually found is less than 100%. The US average against "normal" software bugs is about 85%; or, 85 out of every 100 bugs are found prior to release. The removal efficiency data for year 2000 repairs is uncertain, but is not likely to top 97% and may be lower.

Sources of Error in Test Library Year 2000 Repair Costs

The accuracy of repair costs for regression test libraries is unknown. For individual companies that keep accurate records of the number of test cases in their libraries, a precision of ±15% may be possible. However, many companies do not have any formal controls over their test libraries and hence do not know how many regression test cases they own. Many other companies don't even have regression test libraries, and hence the costs for regression testing may be zero, although that is an ominous situation for the products they will update.

For new year 2000 test cases some preliminary data was presented earlier in this book for predicting how many test cases might be created. Another troublesome topic, however, is the fact that the volume of errors in test cases is often greater than the volume of errors in the source code being tested. This is because test case production, unlike source code production, is almost never subject to formal quality control methods, the use of inspections, or to anything other than very casual development processes.

Sources of Error in Database Year 2000 Repair Costs

As discussed in previous chapters, the entire database and data warehouse domain has no quantification of any kind because of the lack of any form of data point metric for measuring the sizes of databases or normalizing the number of errors in databases during studies of data quality. This means that the entire cost structure of year 2000 database repairs is essentially unknown in any precise way, so the margins of errors for dealing with database repairs must exceed 200% in either direction.

Sources of Error in Litigation Year 2000 Costs

Because litigation involves human judgments and can include attorneys fees, damages, consequential damages, and punitive damages, no one can predict the legal costs within ±1,000%. The predicted litigation and legal costs in this book are about $100,000,000 for the United States and $300,000,000 for the world. In the remote event that 100% of global companies and government agencies achieve 100% year 2000 compliance, the year 2000 legal costs could be zero. Obviously this is a very unlikely scenario.

However, the Giga Group has predicted worldwide litigation expenses of a trillion dollars[5] which is the worst of the worst-case scenarios. It is almost as unlikely that the trillion-dollar figure will be correct as it is that the zero-dollar figure will be correct. The reason is that national governments are likely to intervene if litigation prospects become so enormous that they can shut down industries and damage national economies. It would not be surprising to see the industrialized countries begin to pass legislation that will cap or possibly even eliminate year 2000 damages. Capping year 2000 damages is a fairly reasonable scenario that has already occurred for other kinds of expensive lawsuits, and might be expected for the year 2000 case. Eliminating damages for year 2000 problems is so extreme a measure as to be highly improbable.

Sources of Error in Year 2000 Damage and Recovery Costs

Predicting the consequences of unrepaired year 2000 bugs is obviously quite unreliable, because the predictions are at the end of a long chain of assumptions, any one of which can contain significant errors. For example, to estimate the damages and recovery costs for the year 2000 problem you need to establish reasonable baselines involving topics such as (1) the number of year 2000 problems missed versus the number repaired, (2) the probability of certain kinds of damages from missed year 2000 problems, (3) the nature of the recovery stages. About the best that can be said of year 2000 damages and recovery expenses is that these costs will occur, and are probably going to be quite expensive.

Evaluating Global Pre-2000 and Post-2000 Costs

Because of the highly speculative nature of the post-2000 cost analysis, it is premature to attempt a country-by-country analysis. In general our European clients lag behind our US clients in year 2000 readiness.

The data shown in Table 14.5 is based on simple ratios of US results, and hence has a very large margin of error, which could be in either direction. The table assumes that the United States has about one ninth of the world's deployed software, so the global sizes in function points and LOC are derived merely by scaling up the US results by a factor of 6:1. The upper part of the cost data in Table 14.5 is essentially the same as the global data shown earlier except for the fact that it now shows normalized costs using both function points and LOC metrics. The lower portion of Table 14.5 is also scaled up from the US data using a simple ratio of 5:1. The disparity between size and possible damages is because of the enormous volume of military and systems software deployed in the United States. Note also that the costs for Table 14.5 are based on US dollars. A country-by-country analysis of year 2000 damages should be based on local values in terms of compensation, burden rates, inflation, and other financial factors. This book makes a general assumption that year 2000 repairs will be achieved on about 85% of software applications with the year 2000 problem, while 15% of applications will slip through and contain year 2000 errors on the morning of January 1, 2000.

The most significant point about Table 14.5 is the strong possibility that the post-2000 damages and recovery costs may exceed the pre-2000 repair costs. As this book is written, it actually expresses a reasonably optimistic best-case scenario in terms of the percentages of year 2000 problems that will not be repaired by the turn of the century.

This section on possible post-2000 damages and recovery costs concludes with a rough analysis of the distribution of our clients in terms of

Table 14.5: Global Total of Pre-2000 and Post-2000 Repairs and Recovery[a]

Year 2000 Topic	Global Year 2000 Cost Elements	Cost per Function Point	Cost per Line of Code
Expenses prior to 2000 AD			
Initial software repairs	$530,000,000,000	$51.90	$0.46
Secondary bad-fix software repairs	$50,000,000,000	$4.90	$0.04
Test library repairs	$75,000,000,000	$7.34	$0.06
Database repairs	$454,000,000,000	$44.45	$0.39
Hardware chip replacements	$76,000,000,000	$7.44	$0.07
Hardware performance upgrades	$150,000,000,000	$14.69	$0.13
Subtotal	$1,335,000,000,000	$130.72	$1.15
Expenses after 2000 AD			
Litigation and damages	$300,000,000,000	$29.38	$0.26
Post-2000 damages	$580,378,125,000	$56.83	$0.50
Post-2000 recovery expenses	$1,405,843,750,000	$137.66	$1.21
Subtotal	$2,286,221,875,000	$223.86	$1.96
Total	$3,621,221,875,000	$354.58	$3.11

[a]Global function points deployed = 10,212,750,000; global lines of code deployed = 1,164,253,500,000.

their year 2000 repair prognosis (Table 14.6), augmented by best-case and worst-case repair scenarios.

Since the year 2000 problem is a very large-scale problem involving thousands of enterprises and millions of individuals, it is not surprising that the overall spectrum of results would assume a more or less normal bell-shaped curve, with one end of the curve reflecting total year 2000 compliance and the other exhibiting zero year 2000 compliance. If the probable case becomes reality at the end of the century, then the year 2000 problem will have serious consequences that will affect business operations for several years into the next century, and will probably cause tax and revenue reductions from 1998 through 2005. If the best case becomes a reality at the end of the century, then the year 2000 problem will have some consequences, but the bulk of the trouble should be concentrated in the years 1998, 1999, and the first half of the year 2000 itself. Normal business operations, revenues and profits, and tax revenues should be back, more or less, to pre-2000 conditions by 2001.

Table 14.6: Estimated Numbers of Enterprises Achieving Year 2000 Compliance

Compliance	Probable	Best	Worst
Total compliance (100% repairs)	14%	55%	6%
Good compliance (>95% repairs)	20%	25%	12%
Average compliance (>85% repairs)	30%	10%	15%
Marginal compliance (>65% repairs)	16%	5%	30%
Poor compliance (<50% repairs)	13%	3%	22%
No compliance (0% repairs)	7%	2%	15%
Total	100%	100%	100%

If the worst case becomes a reality at the end of the century, the problems will be severe enough to damage national economies and the global economy for a period of 10 years or more from 2000 through at least 2010. Curiously, the worst-case situation may seem to be the best in 1998 and 1999 because companies will be skimping on year 2000 repair costs during those years and hence will not have such heavy year 2000 repair investments. The worst-case situation will trigger abrupt and severe damages to business operations, and severe reductions in tax revenues, severe repercussions in the stock and bond markets starting January 1, 2000. The worst-case scenario may well trigger a need for massive government intervention.

References

1. Kendall, Robert C., and E.C. Lamb. "Management Perspectives on Programs, Programming, and Productivity." In *Programming Productivity—Issues for the Eighties*, edited by Capers Jones, 201–212. Piscataway, NJ: IEEE Press, 1981.
2. Jones, Capers. *Software Quality—Analysis and Guidelines for Success.* ITCP, Boston: 1997.
3. Jones, Capers. "Software Enhancement Modeling." In *Software Maintenance: Research and Practice,* Vol. 1, 91–100. 1989.
4. Jones, Capers. *Geriatric Care for Aging Software.* SPR Knowledge Base, vol. 1 no. 1. Burlington, MA: SPR, 1994.
5. Testimony of Ann Coffou, Managing Director of Giga Information Group, before the US House of Representatives Science Committee. March 20, 1997.

15 | Defenses Against Unrepaired Year 2000 Problems

SINCE IT IS increasingly obvious that many enterprises will not achieve year 2000 compliance, it is now time to consider strategies for dealing with the chaotic computing and software situation that will occur at the end of the century. The fact that the year 2000 is also a leap year is an added piece of confusion on top of the already massive year 2000 problem. The enterprises that are effective in achieving year 2000 compliance will also be able to deal with the leap year situation, but the enterprises that lag in year 2000 readiness will probably lag in leap year readiness too, so the advice in this section to take action to minimize damages and recovery costs applies to both issues.

General Strategies as the Year 2000 Approaches

Although the year 2000 problem is of human origin, it is far more pervasive in the damages that will occur than many other problems created by our rather destructive species. In overall impact, the year 2000 problem should be viewed as being equivalent to a natural disaster such as major earthquakes, hurricanes, or droughts. Solving the year 2000 problem should transcend normal business and national competition, and there is every reason for urging organizations that are competitive in other domains to cooperate in bringing the year 2000 problem under control. Direct competitors in many major business sectors are all going to be affected by the year 2000 problem:

- Airlines
- Aircraft manufacturing
- Automobile manufacturing
- Banks
- Distribution (trucking, railroads)

- Insurance companies
- General manufacturing
- Retail and wholesale marketing
- State governments
- Urban governments

Since these vertical industrial groups all use software for similar if not identical purposes, it would be very cost effective if these industrial groups could share knowledge about the year 2000 problem, and possibly even share reusable year 2000 repair code segments. It would be highly desirable in the United States to suspend temporarily the various antitrust acts and allow competitors to work together on common year 2000 repair strategies and common tools. In fact, sharing year 2000 knowledge, tools, and code within vertical industries is the only known way of dealing with the year 2000 problem that does not lead to catastrophic expense levels for many individual companies. For example, consider the economies of scale if American Airlines, Continental Airlines, Delta Airlines, and all of the other major airlines were to pool their year 2000 knowledge and resources for the good of the entire industry.

Mutual year 2000 cooperation would be especially beneficial in the industries with the greatest year 2000 exposure and liabilities, such as banking and insurance. It would be highly advantageous for organizations such as JP Morgan, Citibank, Bank of America, First Union Bank, and so on, to consolidate their year 2000 repair efforts. This is also true for insurance organizations that handle property and casualty insurance, life insurance, and so forth. The same concept is true of many other industries. Sears Roebuck, JC Penney's, Wal-Mart, KMart and other retail establishments all use computers for the same purposes, and here too significant economies of scale might occur if they could work together on a common year 2000 containment strategy.

Unfortunately, this kind of large-scale cooperation is quite unlikely because of mutual distrust, government prohibitions, or the simple fact that the human species does not cooperate very well on large social and technical issues—no matter how valuable the results might be. The year 2000 problem is of such a vast magnitude that even global cooperation would be beneficial, but this is even harder to bring about than domestic cooperation among direct competitors. Possibly the national governments might establish year 2000 resource centers and allow direct competitors to participate, under temporary exemptions from antitrust penalties; however it is not very likely that governments will do this, or at least not in time for this kind of cooperation to bring the year 2000 problem under full control. Indeed, this kind of shared cooperation of year 2000 knowledge should already be in place to have a good chance of completing the year 2000 work by the end of the century.

As part of preparing for the year 2000 crisis, many corporations and government agencies have established year 2000 project offices and appointed fairly senior year 2000 project managers. These organizations are going to be more important after the year 2000 crisis than they are right now, before the crisis has occurred. Indeed, some of these year 2000 project offices may double in size after the year 2000 crisis has occurred.

No later than the year 1999 every major company and government agency should begin to publish the following information in their house journals and newsletters, and perhaps major national journals and newspapers as well: (1) their year 2000 compliance status (assuming the status is more or less on target and the year 2000 repairs are being made) and (2) the contact data for their year 2000 project office, including telephone numbers, email addresses, Web site URLs, and regular mailing address. The purpose of this is partly to reassure clients, shareholders, and suppliers, and partly to provide actual contact points in the event that all year 2000 repairs are not made in time and it is necessary to take corrective actions.

In addition, it would also be useful to extend the numerous published catalogs of year 2000 service providers to create a national or even international directory of year 2000 contacts within companies and government agencies. At the end of the century, year 2000 service providers will be only a small part of the year 2000 repair endeavor, and it will be much more important to know how to contact the year 2000 offices in companies such as AT&T, Computer Associates, IBM, Microsoft, SAP, and the like, plus the year 2000 project offices of the IRS, state departments of motor vehicles, city finance offices, and so forth. No doubt one or more of the current publishers of year 2000 service providers will add this second catalog to the set of available documents. In addition, one or more of the year 2000 Web sites will probably include year 2000 contact data, although the Web and Internet may be adversely affected by year 2000 problems, and possibly may be out of service or slow in the early days of January 2000.

The reason for creating a national year 2000 project office directory of year 2000 executives is so that when consumers, shareholders, clients, and suppliers become aware of year 2000 problems, they will not have to waste time trying to contact the appropriate year 2000 repair office. As stated, the year 2000 problem is a very pervasive one, and failure to achieve year 2000 compliance in any one company will very likely affect dozens of other companies, some government agencies, and perhaps hundreds or thousands of clients and shareholders. Starting in 1997 and certainly continuing through all of 1999, many business documents should probably include year 2000 contact data, such as:

- Annual reports
- Quarterly reports
- Annuities
- Bank statements
- Check registers
- Invoices
- Shareholders statements
- Tax statements
- Utility bills
- Withholding statements

Even if you think your organization is 100% compliant, there is a small chance of hidden year 2000 instances that will not show themselves until sometime in the next century. Indeed, even for companies that *do* eliminate the year 2000 problem in their own software and databases, they can still be affected if their subcontractors or their own service providers fail to make year 2000 repairs.

Corporate Year 2000 Defense Strategies

The SEC requires that public companies prepare a management report[1] with their filings of audited financial statements. The purpose of the management statement is to allow investors to consider the quality of earnings reported in audited financial reports. This regulation requires that management make known trends and future events that might affect the company's future earnings. Obviously the year 2000 problem falls under such an event and requires a management report. Further, when financial statements are audited, the audit report will also deal with the year 2000 effect on financial performance, and the audit statement will doubtless reflect the auditors' opinion of the prudence and thoroughness of the year 2000 responses.

The GAAS[2] requires that auditors detect and report on errors and irregularities. Failure to disclose year 2000 costs would certainly comprise an irregularity or an error. In addition, the FASB has made a controversial ruling that year 2000 repairs must be charged to current-year expenses.[3] The combination of these requirements, coupled with the high costs of the year 2000 repairs themselves, means that many public and private companies may have reduced or negative profitability during years 1997 through 2000, and probably during years 2001 and 2002.

Virtually all of the Fortune 500 companies and most smaller companies will be affected at the same time for the same reasons. The impact of these losses or reduced profits will no doubt affect stock prices, at least temporarily. Since so many companies throughout the world will be affected simultaneously, the net effect on stocks is difficult to predict. Probably there will be lowering of share values, which will be most severe for the companies that have lagged in their year 2000 preparations. There will no doubt be shake-ups in senior management, boards of directors, and other executive positions. Therefore it is prudent to be as proactive and cost effective as possible in dealing with the year 2000 problem. Disclose your strategy to investors in annual and quarterly reports.

The year 2000 problem is far too serious and vast to envision it as something that can give companies a competitive advantage, but without this being deliberately planned it will probably occur anyway. The companies that solve their year 2000 problems with a minimum of chaos, disruption, and costs will probably come out on top, while the companies that have botched it up will suffer fairly severely in terms of possible litigation, reduced earnings, and emergency recovery costs. At the corporate level, the year 2000 project offices will find themselves with widening sets of responsibilities as the end of the century approaches. Assuming that your own organization has successfully achieved year 2000 compliance, the role of the year 2000 project office will not be finished, but will broaden to ensure that year 2000 issues are under control in the enterprises with which your enterprise does business:

- Banks
- Subsidiaries
- Suppliers
- Subcontractors
- Clients
- Government agencies

If your enterprise is year 2000 compliant but your suppliers, customers, and government contacts are not, you will still face some major year 2000 expenses. It is advantageous for companies that have achieved year 2000 compliance to assist other enterprises in achieving this same status.

The peak period of activity for year 2000 project offices will probably be the last three months of 1999 and the first three months of the year 2000. During this critical six-month period, final testing of all year 2000 repairs will occur, cutting over to replacement applications will occur, and the most critical period for year 2000 damage control will occur. Expect the year 2000 project office to work almost around the clock from October 1999 through March 2000. Furthermore, the last three months of 1999 will probably be the peak time that a special kind of testing occurs—cross-enterprise testing for applications such as EDI, which link disparate enterprises.

Aspects of the year 2000 problem have been described as having a "domino effect" that will ripple through entire industries.[4] Some of the problems can affect companies that are already year 2000 compliant, if they share data or have EDI with organizations that are noncompliant.

Manual Backups for Automated Processes

Because a significant number of automated processes may be at least temporarily damaged or suspended when the year 2000 problem occurs, all organizations should prepare manual backup procedures for key business activities. Examples include the following:

- Banks may need extra tellers and extra accountants to handle manual transactions, assuming that automatic teller machines and other computerized systems are adversely affected.
- Retail stores and restaurants need a contingency plan in case credit card and check validations are suspended. (A cash-only policy may limit damages, but will offend customers.)
- Retail stores and restaurants should plan to have calculators available for cashiers, and should instruct them in the basics of totaling bills without using a computer.
- Police departments should prepare for extra shifts and extra duty, assuming that things such as traffic lights temporarily shut down.
- Fire departments should prepare for extra shifts and extra duty, assuming that the year 2000 problem triggers a number of false alarms from computerized fire detection systems.
- Electric power and telephone companies should prepare for 24-hour emergency repairs at the end of the century. (Hopefully the year 2000 problem will not occur at the same time as a major blizzard, but December 31 is a time of frequent, heavy snow.)

- Local governments should prepare to stay open all night on December 31, 1999, and January 1, 2000, because of the possibilities of unexpected problems with urban services.

No doubt in the last few months of 1999 every newspaper, television station, radio station, and Web site in the world will begin a year 2000 countdown, with additional information, advice, and warnings. The best case is that all major utilities and financial services organizations will be ready and waiting for the year 2000 problem with no disruptions. The expected- and worst-case scenarios are for severe business and commerce disruptions that could last somewhere between 24 hours and several months.

Advice for Noncompliant Companies

If your company has lagged behind in making year 2000 repairs or, worse, more or less ignored the year 2000 problem, there is a good chance that your corporate operations will be thrown into chaos at the end of fiscal year 1999 and again at the end of the 1999 calendar year. Indeed many of your business transactions may already be impacted, if you deal in long-term issues such as interest rates, credit card expiration, or long-range plans and budgets.

About the only good news for companies in this situation is that by the beginning of 1999 the major year 2000 repair companies will be at their peak in terms of expertise, and will perhaps have year 2000 special weapons and tactics teams available for emergency high-speed deployment. There is a small chance that you can deploy these "top-gun" year 2000 companies as late as 1999 and still succeed, assuming that the best year 2000 service providers are operating at peak efficiency and have available personnel. However, if your company made no serious attempt to achieve year 2000 compliance, you will almost certainly be sued by your shareholders, clients, and perhaps by suppliers or subcontractors.[5] If your company is a subcontractor, then expect a lawsuit by the prime contractor.

It will be very difficult to defend against year 2000 lawsuits because the issue is so well known and has generated so much publicity. It would hardly be possible to defend against a year 2000 lawsuit by saying, "I didn't realize the problem would occur," when every software magazine and many general magazines, plus radio and television shows, have discussed the year 2000 topic, to say nothing of the dozens of recently published books addressing the year 2000 problem. Further, if your company pursued a policy of "business as usual" and ignored the year 2000 problem, all legal defenses will be weakened by what will appear to be, and indeed may be, violation of fiduciary duty.

The most probable lawsuits will be for actual damages associated with the year 2000 problem. Note that before the end of the century there may be special year 2000 legislation enacted that might affect litigation, since several countries and state governments are considering this. Obviously your top executives might be sued for violation of fiduciary duty, and some members of your board of directors may face the same kind of lawsuit brought by shareholders because failure to achieve year 2000 compliance will lower the value of the company and its stock.[6] Incidentally, attempting to avoid year 2000 liabilities by retiring before the end of the century may not actually work. Any CEO or CIO who retires in 1998 or 1999 without having taken proper year 2000 precautions before retirement may well find that litigation will reach him or her anyway. This litigation may also occur even in the event of job changes or moves to other companies. Indeed, a prudent, "due diligence" activity for recruiting top executives from 1996 forward is to explore the exact nature of their year 2000 plans and activities. Top executives hoping to move up to CEO status who ignored the year 2000 problem will perhaps find themselves unemployed, as well as facing potential lawsuits. Indeed, if year 2000 negligence results in some kind of physical injury to employees or customers, even criminal charges are not beyond the scope of possible events.

No doubt the year 2000 problem will mean the end of the careers of a number of executives whose failure to take effective actions against such an obvious problem will damage their credibility in the eyes of boards of directors and shareholders. The major executive levels that may be sued for failing to deal effectively with the year 2000 problem include:

- CEOs
- CFOs
- CIOs
- Purchasing or contract administrators (if year 2000 vendors fail to perform)
- Chief legal counsel (for failure to provide adequate warnings)

There is not a lot of good news for noncompliant companies or the executives who direct them. Noncompliant companies should seek legal counsel from their corporate attorneys and should also explore the implications of declaring bankruptcy if the potential damages are likely to be severe.

Federal Government Year 2000 Defense Strategies

The year 2000 problem will reach a peak in a major election year, and it will probably not be a successful election year for many incumbents. Even if they are not personally involved, many incumbents will no doubt feel the wrath of voters if the year 2000 problem causes serious business disruption or problems in daily life, such as tax problems or electric power outages. The best strategy for incumbents who face reelection in or near the year 2000 is to be very visible and proactive in dealing with the year 2000 problem, starting ideally in 1996 but certainly running through the years 1997 through 1999. Any incumbent elected official who is caught napping by the year 2000 problem will justifiably be thrown out of office, and some may face even more serious consequences such as investigations into their poor performance.

The year 2000 problem will have an impact on every branch of the federal government.[7] As with corporations, every major operating agency and bureau of the federal government should publish the contact data for their year 2000 project offices. An overall federal register of year 2000 contact points should also be assembled, perhaps by the Office of Management and the Budget (OMB), or by the General Accounting Office (GAO). This registry needs to drop below the cabinet-level secretaries and should assemble a listing of the actual working groups at the regional and local level.

Ideally, all branches of the federal government will share information on the successes or problems they noted when using the various tools and service providers in the year 2000 domain. As progress occurs, each agency should report topics such as:

- Percent of applications now year 2000 compliant
- Percent of applications for which no updates were needed
- Percent of applications discovered to be dormant
- Percent of applications for which repairs were needed but will not occur in time
- Percent of dead code in active applications
- Recovery plans for unrepaired applications
- Tools used successfully for year 2000 work
- Tools that did not work as promised for year 2000 repairs
- Languages that were easy to repair
- Languages that were hard to repair
- Special or unusual year 2000 situations that were encountered
- Availability of reusable year 2000 repair routines

The last item on the list is of particular significance. Although many millions of software applications contain the year 2000 problem spanning a total of almost 500 programming languages, the actual number of ways the year 2000 problem occurs in software probably comprises less than a dozen variants. If the various federal agencies encapsulate their methods of making year 2000 repairs, a very cost-effective set of year 2000 repair routines might be made available and shared from agency to agency. In other words, the year 2000 problem is one of the best prospects since the software industry began to elevate software reuse from a theoretical construct to a viable undertaking.

At a practical level, although many federal agencies might be willing to make their year 2000 repair routines available to other agencies, it is not clear which agency or group should act as the year 2000 repository and clearinghouse. Perhaps an executive order might establish a year 2000 focal point, but a year 2000 reuse department would need an adequate budget, computers, staffing, and funding for the fiscal years of 1998 through at least 2001. As everyone knows, creating a new department in the federal government is usually not an overnight event and it is uncertain if the federal government could do this in time for it to be effective. Ideally, a federal software year 2000 reuse center would be announced in the summer of 1997, staffed in the autumn of 1997, and fully operational by the winter of 1997 or early spring of 1998.

Software reuse is a complex administrative task, since the users of the routines need to be recorded in case errors or recalls are necessary. However, the year 2000 problem is close to an ideal situation for establishing the nucleus of a federal software reuse program. Also, the reused routines need to be certified to near-zero defect levels, tested for viruses, and otherwise made safe for large-scale deployment. Because the year 2000 problem is so pervasive, and reuse could be so beneficial, a controversial suggestion would be for the Justice Department to relax antitrust regulations for companies in the same industry that want to cooperate on year 2000 repairs. Not only should the antitrust rules be temporarily relaxed for year 2000 work, but indeed the federal government should actively support large-scale year 2000 reuse with the full support of the Department of Commerce, Department of Justice, and other departments of the executive branch.

Starting in fiscal year 1998, every federal agency should include their year 2000 status and plans as part of both their budget requests and also their variance or progress reports. Presumably the OMB or the GAO can enforce this relatively commonsense directive, although an executive order may be needed to get things started.

The most troublesome federal agency in the minds of most US citizens is the IRS, and this bad reputation is endemic among the other revenue services of the industrialized countries. In spite of past lapses with software, the IRS has a fair chance of achieving year 2000 compliance. What is likely to cause immense grief for perhaps millions of taxpayers are the probable actions that the IRS might take if the W2 withholding data is incorrect or interest data reported on 1099 forms is incorrect. The IRS should publish a clear and comprehensive policy statement on how they will deal with income tax forms that are miscalculated due to the year 2000 problem. Hopefully individual taxpayers will not face audits or penalties because their employers, credit unions, banks, or brokers made mistakes in reporting earnings or interest due to the year 2000 problem. Incidentally, no one in Congress, the IRS, or other federal government agencies appear to have analyzed the probable reductions in corporate and personal income tax revenues in calendar years 1997 through 2000, and beyond.

The IRS should suspend section 482 of the IRC code for year 2000 tools, year 2000 software packages, and other aspects of dealing with the year 2000 problem.[8,9] Under IRC section 482, any division of a large corporation that receives year 2000 repair material from another division of the same company has to treat it as taxable income. This is basically a death blow to cost-effective year 2000 software reuse in the United States. Of course quite a few companies won't report year 2000 materials as taxable income, either by accident or design, but the whole IRC section 482 issue needs to be put aside for a problem as massive and expensive as the year 2000 problem.

Because of the FASB ruling on expensing year 2000 repair costs in the current year, coupled with the very high and unbudgeted nature of those costs, many corporations will report losses rather than profits from 1997 onward into the twenty-first century. As a result, corporate tax revenues may be reduced for quite a few consecutive years.

This same phenomenon, which could be serious at the federal level, could be even more serious at the state, province, county, and city levels. Reduced bond ratings and outright bankruptcies may well occur as local governments face the double or triple hit of their own year 2000 repairs coupled with reduced taxes plus possible litigation against them for their own noncompliance.

Another federal agency with major year 2000 exposure is the Federal Aviation Administration (FAA). All citizens would like to receive assurances from both the FAA and the airlines themselves that year 2000 problems will not disrupt air traffic control, in-flight aircraft instrumentation, or flight schedules. Starting no later than 1998 the FAA should issue an exact statement of year 2000 compliance (or noncompliance) and the probable effect on air travel, if any. The FAA statement should list year 2000 compliance for all major air carriers, and perhaps by type of aircraft if the on-board navigation or flight control software is being updated for year 2000 purposes.

Obviously every federal agency with substantial contact with US citizens should issue year 2000 compliance statements, and should attempt to reassure citizens that the government is taking effective steps to deal with the year 2000 problem. The role of Congress in the year 2000 situation is somewhat ambiguous. To date Congress has held hearings on the year 2000 problem and collected a substantial amount of information (some of it conflicting of course) about the year 2000 problem and its significance. The key issue is: What should Congress do now? At a minimum, individual senators and congressmen should issue public statements on the year 2000 prognosis within their own states and districts. If Congress wishes to go beyond just a general discussion of the year 2000 problem, some actions that might be considered would include:

- Providing low-interest year 2000 repair loans for small businesses through the Small Business Administration
- Passing protective legislation to minimize the risks to taxpayers from punitive IRS actions in the event that their withholding information or interest information is incorrectly reported due to year 2000 errors
- Providing some form of corporate income tax relief for businesses to compensate partly for the costs of the year 2000 repairs
- Passing special legislation to allow the costs of year 2000 repairs to be amortized across multiple years, instead of being treated as expenses in a single year as is currently the situation under the accounting standards
- Suspending antitrust laws for a five-year period for the specific purpose of sharing year 2000 repairs and technologies, regardless of competitive impacts (This is a controversial proposal but can anyone suggest a better alternative for dealing with the year 2000 crisis than by sharing year 2000 solutions within vertical industries where all competitors use software for virtually identical purposes?)
- Suspending section 482 of the IRC or barring the IRS from requiring that year 2000 repairs by one division of a company be treated as a taxable asset if used by other sections of the same company. In other words, if a division gives year 2000 repair tools or software packages to another division, it should not be treated as taxable income by the receiving division.

- Facilitating the creation and funding of a federal year 2000 repair reusability center, which would act as a repository and clearinghouse for year 2000 software routines in various languages
- Considering some kind of emergency financial relief package for states, small cities, and towns with year 2000 problems that may otherwise lead to urban bankruptcy or alarming tax increases
- Passing legislation to cap the anticipated wave of year 2000 damage suits, that will otherwise saturate court systems and possibly trigger waves of preemptive bankruptcies for many years into the next century

The role of the executive branch is also ambiguous for the year 2000 problem. President Clinton and Vice President Gore are personally interested in the year 2000 problem and have had meetings with Dr. Howard Rubin and other year 2000 consultants. However, there has been no visible outcome as a result of these meetings. Now that major journals such as *Newsweek* have started featuring the year 2000 problem, we will no doubt begin to see an increasing number of statements from the executive and legislative branches about their responses to the problem.

Since software is one of the key US industries, and one that cuts across and affects all other industries and government operations as well, the executive branch probably needs a permanent and fairly senior software advisor, similar to the science advisor in status and placement.

Military Year 2000 Defense Strategies

The year 2000 problems associated with military software will probably be shrouded with security issues and may never become public knowledge. However, the military implications of the year 2000 problems are just as severe as those of the civilian sector, and when weapons systems are involved, even more serious.

The year 2000 problem is obviously an interservice issue that affects all armed services and civilian workers too. Hopefully the year 2000 issue is no place for interservice rivalries, and every military service will cooperate and coordinate with other year 2000 groups across the US Army, Navy, Air Force, Marines, and Coast Guard. A strong recommendation is to establish an interservice year 2000 control board to coordinate both year 2000 repairs, and to establish year 2000 recovery programs for the instances in which year 2000 problems slip by and are not corrected. In all likelihood the interservice year 2000 control board would need funding through the end of fiscal year 2002 at the earliest, and possibly through year 2004.

Obviously a military year 2000 control board would serve as a repository and distribution point for reusable year 2000 repair software in a military context. The military services have long been somewhat different from the civilian world, and have used programming languages such as CMS2, Jovial, Ada 83, and the more recent Ada 95, which the civilian world uses only sparingly. It also would seem to be highly cost effective to create an interservice library of tested and reliable year 2000 repair routines in the more common military programming languages. For that matter, since much of the civilian year 2000 work centers around COBOL, it might also be useful for the military service to create or at least contract for year 2000 search-and-repair engines that support Ada, CMS2, Jovial, and other military software languages that the civilian sector does not use often enough to have made any commercial year 2000 tools.

The most troublesome year 2000 problems in a military context are those associated with ships, aircraft, and other weapons systems. Logistics and administrative software will be affected too, but the major issue is to minimize disruption in C^3 and be able to deploy tactical and strategic weapons systems. Since US military software systems are used throughout the globe, such as in the NATO countries, Japan, Israel, and South Korea, the success or failure of the US military forces in containing the year 2000 problem will have worldwide repercussions.

State and Local Government Year 2000 Defense Strategies

In the United States there are 50 state governments, close to 2,000 county governments, and perhaps 5,000 urban governments that use computers and software that might require year 2000 repairs. About 46 of the 50 US states have incomes that are large enough that they would be classified in the Fortune 500 set of companies if they were not governments. Unfortunately the year 2000 problem is going to have a very unpleasant impact on state, county, and local government incomes, and also on expenses. Governments at various levels are going to take a double hit (and possibly a triple hit) from the year 2000 problem.

- Their own year 2000 software repairs will be surprisingly large and may be unbudgeted. This may trigger a need for tax increases.
- The FASB ruling on expensing year 2000 repairs rather than amortizing them across several years will lead to many corporations

reporting profit and income losses for several years in a row, which will reduce the tax incomes of states, counties, and city governments (as well as of the federal government).

- If federal, state, county, and local governments are unsuccessful in achieving 100% compliance, they may be sued for damages by citizens, by class-action suits, or by companies within their geographic boundaries.

The overall impact of these hits can lead to unpleasant consequences for various government levels, including:

- Lowering of municipal bond ratings
- Need for higher sales, income, and personal property taxes
- Possible bankruptcy of city, county, and perhaps state governments

Since all state and most urban governments are headed by elected officials, the adequacy of state and local year 2000 responses will play a major role in elections. At the moment, officials who are proactive and successful in dealing with the year 2000 problem will have a better chance of reelection than those who stumble. However, no matter how good the year 2000 plans may be, the costs are going to be so expensive at state and local government levels that voters will no doubt be outraged when they see the costs showing up in higher taxes, reduced services, or both.

Many individual states and some counties and cities now have well-formed year 2000 containment plans, and some are even ahead of schedule in achieving year 2000 compliance. However, the software used by every state is quite similar, as are the software applications used at lower levels of government such as counties and urban areas. All of these government levels use software for purposes such as:

- Budget and expense control
- Police and fire department administration
- Payroll and pension
- School funding
- Construction and maintenance of government buildings
- Taxation and revenue
- Disbursements and payments
- Courts and correctional institutions
- Services (health care, unemployment, and so on)

Because the software applications at state, county, and urban areas are often similar, here too a centralized repository of reusable year 2000 repair routines would seem to be economically advantageous. The problem with this approach is that each individual government is equipped to handle their own year 2000 problems, but not to help out in repairing the year 2000 problems of outside government agencies in distant states and cities. Perhaps the various associations of state governments and urban governments can find some way of establishing an overall year 2000 coordination and reuse center to share tools, methods, and approaches across the separate administrative and geographic boundaries. An extreme example of very wide-scale cooperation would be the joint hiring of year 2000 service providers to handle both unique year 2000 repairs and also to assist in the deployment of reusable year 2000 software repair routines. For example, many urban police and fire departments use the same applications, or similar applications with functionality that resembles every other agency of the same class. This approach might offer significant economies of scale. However, monitoring contract performance and ensuring oversight would not be an easy task if, for example, 100 major cities spread across 50 states were to attempt to pool their year 2000 tools and year 2000 repair routines.

Even without the year 2000 problem as a catalyst, it would be very cost effective for state governments, county governments, and municipal governments to pool some of their technological resources. As the situation stands, however, we have 50 state software organizations that are essentially duplicating one another's software work with little or no lateral coordination. At the levels of counties and cities, we have the same sort of independent redundant effort with little or no cooperation or coordination, only with 500 or so replicas instead of 50 replicas that occur at the state level.

Personal Year 2000 Defense Strategies

Perhaps the best way to deal with personal defense strategies about the year 2000 problem is to start with some of the defensive actions that I am considering.

- Keep paper backup records of bank balances, credit card balances, investments, and bills for telephone, water, electricity, gasoline, cable television, car payments, mortgage payments, Internet service, and so forth.
- If you receive any strange communications from companies or government agencies in which a date of 00 is cited, contact the issuing office and try and get the error corrected. For example, you might get a bill or invoice that asserts that you are 99 years late for a payment of some kind.

- Check with your personal bankers and brokers to ascertain their year 2000 status. There is no value in checking before early 1999, because the final status will not be known until then. The more proactive banks and financial institutions will not only know their status, but will probably have major ads and even billboards saying things like, "Acme National Bank Is Year 2000 Compliant," to assure customers that they have things under control.
- Look for announcements by your local telephone and electric companies or contact their consumer liaison offices to find out if they will be year 2000 compliant.
- If you are taking prescription medicines, be sure to have your prescriptions refilled before the end of the century. Check with your pharmacy about year 2000 compliance and when your next prescription refill dates will come up.
- If your home uses oil heat and you depend on computer-controlled automatic deliveries by your oil company, check with your oil company to be sure that their delivery schedule software packages are year 2000 compliant. January 2000 is not a good time to run out of heating oil.
- Some of the year 2000 problems with electrical generating equipment may cause voltage fluctuations and even changes in electrical frequency from 60 Hz to something else. While surge protectors might help, they also might not be sufficient. Check announcements from your power company about year 2000 compliance. If they don't know their status, you may want to consider unplugging electrical equipment that might be running at midnight on December 31, 1999, such as computers, stereo equipment, refrigerators, and other items.
- Check with company controllers and financial groups to ascertain that your income tax information will be handled correctly for 1999 and 2000.
- If you discover in January 2000 that your income tax withholding (W2 forms) or interest calculations (1099 forms) are in error, contact both the originating offices to report the error, and also a tax attorney or certified tax preparation specialist to ensure that the errors will not affect your personal tax status. You might also call the IRS or equivalent organization since they will probably have a year 2000 contact point available.
- In the first quarter of year 2000, check your credit rating to ensure that no adverse credit information has been filed against you due to year 2000 problems. It would be prudent to check in the last quarter of 1999 and keep a copy of that report also.

- If your company has badge-lock security systems on the doors, check with your security group to be sure that the software controlling your entry and exit points is year 2000 compliant, and that it will also work on February 29, 2000.
- If you work in a large office building with elevators, check with your building maintenance or security office to see how they plan to handle elevator inspections. Some elevators keep computerized records of inspection dates and will shut down if the inspection date has passed. Moving from 1999 to 2000 will probably precipitate an indication that the inspection period has passed, thus causing the elevators to descend to the first floor and shut down.
- If your office computer systems and networks use security systems, check with your system administrator to find out if your security packages are year 2000 compliant and won't lock you out on either January 1, 2000, or on February 29, 2000.
- Keep some emergency funds available in the form of travelers checks, cash, or both, in case automatic teller machines and credit card processing are affected for the first week of January 2000.
- Attend town meetings and raise the question of year 2000 compliance with local governments. In particular, inquire how much the year 2000 repairs will cost and from what source the funds or budget have been provided.
- If you need to renew your driver's license, your automobile registration, or have any other business with state and local governments in December 1999 or January 2000, try and get it done as early as possible, say the first week of December, since the offices will perhaps be swamped with calls and requests for year 2000 information as the end of the year approaches.
- Check for FAA, airline, and rail travel announcements about year 2000 compliance in the last few months of 1999.
- If you plan to travel over the New Year holiday, check with travel agents and airlines to be sure that schedules for arrivals and departures will handle year 2000 and leap year situations successfully. This is especially true for European travel, since Western Europe is lagging in year 2000 repairs.
- If you plan to travel by automobile, fill up your gas tank on or before December 31, 1999, in case electrical power shuts down or gasoline credit card-reading instruments become inoperative.
- Check the year 2000 announcements on local television and radio, and also in local newspapers. As the end of the century approaches, these

channels of information will devote increasing amounts of airtime and column space, and will have much better information available, than is currently the case.

These are merely precautionary measures and do not actually indicate that the problems will occur. Hopefully all major banks, utilities, airlines, and local governments will achieve a level of year 2000 compliance that these precautions will prove to be unnecessary. However, it is better to take early precautions and not need them rather than discovering after January 1, 2000, that you should have been more careful.

References

1. SEC. SEC release no. 6835. Washington, DC: Government Printing Office, 1996.
2. GAAS. GAAS no. 53. Washington, DC: Government Accounting Standards Board, 1997.
3. FASB. *Financial Accounting Standards Board (FASB) Emerging Issues Task Force (EITF) Report 98-14.* Norwalk, CT: 1966.
4. Freeman, Leland, and Larry Meador. *Year 2000: The Domino Effect.* Newton, MA: Datamation, 1997.
5. Jinnett, Jeff. "Legal Issues Concerning the Year 2000 'Millennium Bug.'" *The Computer Lawyer,* vol. 16, 20–200. New York: 1996.
6. Peraino, Vito. "Corporate Directors' Liability and the Year 2000 Problem." *Delaware Corporate Litigation Reporter,* February 17, 1987: 19874.
7. Hearings before the US House of Representatives Science Committee. March 20, 1997.
8. Paul, Joan. *International Tax Consequences of Year 2000 Fix Costs.* Article of the month on Peter de Jager's year 2000 Web site: http://www.year2000.com, July 1997.
9. IRS. IRC 482 and Treasury regulations 1.482.1–1.482.8. Washington, DC: Government Printing Office, 1997.

Summary and Conclusions

The year 2000 problem is rapidly approaching and is one of the most critical issues ever faced by the software industry or by any industry for that matter. Because the year 2000 problem has been developing for more than 25 years and affects many aging legacy applications, the one-time costs for year 2000 repairs are going to be alarmingly high. However, the year 2000 problem cannot be ignored and will not go away by itself. The best response to the year 2000 problem is a rapid and energetic attack as early as possible. The worst response is to ignore the problem or to understate its importance. Since it is obvious that not every company will achieve year 2000 compliance, it is now time for every company, every government agency, and every citizen to begin to consider defensive strategies and guard against possible damages from unrepaired year 2000 problems.

The information presented in this book is believed, by me, to have a large but unknown margin of error. However, even uncertain data is better than none when it comes to dealing with a problem as severe as the year 2000 problem. By the time better data can be assembled, it will be too close to the year 2000 event for the data to have any practical value. The only other alternative is to present preliminary data, because the overall indications are that the year 2000 problem will be extremely serious.

Perhaps the best advice for dealing with the year 2000 problem may be to mirror the advice of Zen Buddhism: "Do not depend upon books and words because they only point the way. You must work out your own salvation with diligence."

Appendix A: Sources of Information in this Book

The data in this book comes from a variety of sources, but much of the information stems from the software assessment and benchmark studies performed by my company. On a monthly basis, my colleagues and I collect software data from three to four enterprises on 15 to 20 projects from each enterprise. (My company, SPR, Inc., builds and markets software cost-estimating tools: SPQR/20 in 1985, CHECKPOINT in 1989, and KnowledgePLAN in 1997. These tools estimate both new development projects, and also maintenance and enhancement projects such as the software repairs associated with the year 2000 problem.) Since our estimating methods support cost estimates for all known programming languages and combinations of languages, we have long been collecting information on programming languages, and also on the numbers of programmers that use various languages. The list of languages in Appendix D is a sample of some of the many languages used throughout the world that will have year 2000 implications.

Our main consulting business is the collection of data on factors that influence the outcomes of software projects for better or for worse. Our knowledge base comprises about 7,000 projects from 600 enterprises, and continues to grow at a rate of 50 to 70 projects each month. The data spans clients from the United States and 22 other countries at last count. Since our data from the year 2000 projects of our clients indicated a serious perturbation of the software industry, it was decided to consolidate some of the many pieces of information that are relevant to the year 2000 problem and make them available in one place. After the first version of this year 2000 report was assembled in the summer of 1996, it became obvious to me that the cost elements of the year 2000 problem were much more extensive than just the software repairs themselves. It is necessary to deal with software repairs, database repairs, test library repairs, hardware upgrades, litigation, possible damages, and a host of other topics. As a result, the manuscript on the year 2000 problem grew from fewer than 30 pages to more than 300 book pages as new year 2000 information became available. When the manuscript reached this size, it became too large for a simple technical report or Web publication, so a book-length treatment was adopted.

Function Point versus LOC Metrics

We use both function points and LOC metrics in our productivity and quality analysis. However, the LOC metric is a very bad choice for large-scale studies involving multiple languages. The major problems with LOC metrics are widely known, such as the inability to deal with noncoding work and the fact the LOC metrics penalize high-level languages. In fact the 50% annual increase in usage of function point metrics is due primarily to the fact that LOC metrics are so hazardous for serious economic and quality analysis.

Many of my previous books such as *Applied Software Measurement* (McGraw-Hill, 1996) and *Software Quality—Analysis and Guidelines for Success* (ITCP, 1997) illustrate and give examples of the hazards of using LOC metrics so it is not necessary to replicate the examples. The major hazards of LOC metrics include:

1. LOC metrics do not support activity-based costing.
2. LOC metrics do not support cross-language productivity comparisons.
3. LOC metrics do not measure economic productivity.
4. LOC metrics do not measure requirements or design quality.
5. LOC metrics do not measure noncode work such as specifications.
6. LOC metrics do not measure indirect work such as project management.
7. LOC metrics cannot be used to track the growth rate of requirements.
8. LOC metrics penalize high-level languages.
9. LOC metrics have wider ranges of variation than function point metrics.
10. LOC metrics have no formal training or certification examination.
11. LOC metrics have no standard definition.
12. LOC data mixes physical lines and logical statements in random ways.
13. LOC metrics cannot be used at all for certain languages such as Visual Basic.
14. LOC metrics are not sensitive to dead code.
15. LOC metrics have random variations based on programming styles.

The first five versions of this manuscript did not use LOC data at all, but we received so many requests from readers who had seen other reports such as the Gartner Group's interesting report on the year 2000 problem (Gartner Group, 1996) that used LOC that it was decided to include some LOC data, with the caveat that the data in this report is only for a selected set of programming languages since it is impossible to use LOC data for all languages in an accurate way.

The mathematical problem of dealing with productivity measures across multiple languages is exactly the same as dealing with cost measures when multiple currencies are involved. It is not possible to make direct comparisons between unlike currencies such as dollars, yen, pounds, and deutsche marks without converting all values to a common base. Similarly, it is not possible to make direct comparisons between unlike languages such as Assembly, C++, COBOL, and SMALLTALK without converting all of the values to a common base. Unfortunately, much of the software literature fails to realize that direct conversions of unlike languages are economically invalid, even though they are easy to perform mathematically.

The many problems with LOC metrics do not imply that function point metrics are a perfect choice for software economic studies. However, function point metrics stay constant regardless of the programming language or language(s) used, and hence are more stable for large-scale economic studies involving multiple programming languages. Further, function point metrics support activity-based costing and can deal with noncoding work such as requirements, specifications, project management, and the like.

Function point metrics do have their own set of troubles, and it is only fair to state some of them:

1. Function point metrics in the United States and the United Kingdom are not the same. (This book uses United States function points, version 4 rules, defined by the IFPUG. The method commonly used in the United Kingdom is termed *Mark II function points,* and they differ from US function points by about 20%.)

2. Function point metrics are inaccurate for small maintenance projects below 10 function points in size, which is where many year 2000 repairs will be found.

3. Function point metrics are more difficult to quantify than LOC metrics, although for estimating purposes they can be quantified directly from requirements and specifications.

Neither function points nor LOC can handle every aspect of the year 2000 problem. For example, neither metric can be used for database repairs, hardware upgrades, litigation, and test library repairs.

Demographic Data

The demographic data used in this report has a high margin of error, but is probably no worse than any other software demographic data. In 1982 I was assistant director of programming technology at ITT Corporation's Programming Technology Center in Stratford, Connecticut. ITT was planning a major venture into the software market and commissioned a study of global software demographics.

For the United States, SRI (formerly Stanford Research Institute in California) was commissioned to perform a study of software personnel, while John Freer, a former IBM marketing manager, was commissioned to perform a similar study for Europe. I was charged with exploring the global industries and enterprises that had the largest software populations. Once the original demographic data was collected in 1982, it seemed useful to keep it refreshed and to update it from time to time. In 1993 much of this demographic data was published as part of global study of software populations in the book *Software Productivity and Quality Today—The Worldwide Perspective* by the Information Systems Management Group of Carlsbad, California.

The origin of much of the demographic data in this book differs from a number of other studies and government reports on software populations, because it is based on the counts of software personnel employed by our major clients, rather than on census data. Additional demographic data on software specialization was published in 1995 in *Patterns of Software Systems Failure and Success* by the International Thomson Computer Press. This latter data was part of a multiclient study and dealt with the large number of specialized occupations that have sprung up in the software domain, such as testing specialist, quality assurance specialist, Web master, database administrator, and the like.

The research was partly derived from a special study of software occupation groups commissioned by AT&T and involving other large organizations such as the US Air Force, IBM, Texas Instruments, and some others. This study covered the topic of software roles and software specialties in large enterprises.

In our client organizations there are many technical workers who earn their livings writing software but whose academic backgrounds are electrical engineering, mathematics, statistics, or something other than computer science or software engineering. Many of these de facto programming personnel identify themselves by their academic degrees, rather than by their actual work building software. For example, a major automotive company has several hundred automotive and electrical engineers developing software for engine controls, brake systems, and so forth, who refuse to identify themselves as "programmers" or "software engineers," even though that is what they do.

At approximately two-year intervals the demographic data is updated using government reports, industry studies, and in-house studies performed by our client organizations. Since software employment is skewed toward large corporations and large government groups, our data is concentrated on the software populations of the Fortune 500 and Forbes 500 classes of companies. Tables A.1 and A.2 illustrate a 1997 view of US software populations working in large organizations. In these two tables some of the data is derived from the 1997 edition of *Forbes® Top Companies—The Forbes® Annual Review of Today's Leading Businesses* (John Wiley and Sons, 1997) as the base for the industry rankings. However, additional data for outsourcing, year 2000 repairs, and government agencies at various levels was added from other sources. Table A.1 simply ranks estimated 1997 US software employment in descending order by industry.

Table A.1: Approximate US Software Employment in Forbes 500 Enterprises and Government Organizations

Industry	Enterprises	Total Employment	Software Employment
Government, federal	98	2,881,000	144,050
Outsourcing, MIS	5	375,000	105,000
Aerospace and defense	12	1,100,000	77,000
Telecommunications	30	1,000,000	75,000
Retailing, drugs and discount	11	1,200,000	66,000
Automobiles/trucks	5	1,250,000	62,500
Government, military	5	1,000,000	60,000
Government, urban	1,250	1,100,000	49,500
Retailing, department stores	7	850,000	42,500
Electrical equipment	8	700,000	42,000
Computers, processors	16	550,000	38,500
Finance, regional banks	95	300,000	33,000

Continued on next page

Table A.1: Approximate US Software Employment in Forbes 500 Enterprises and Government Organizations, continued

Industry	Enterprises	Total Employment	Software Employment
Supermarkets and convenience stores	16	800,000	32,000
Food products	20	600,000	30,000
Travel, airlines	9	500,000	30,000
Government, state	50	600,000	30,000
Finance, multinational banks	8	250,000	27,500
Travel, hotels	8	600,000	27,000
Energy, oil	9	330,000	23,100
Health, drugs	23	375,000	22,500
Electric utilities	55	370,000	22,200
Outsourcing, year 2000	250	55,000	22,000
Beverages	6	360,000	21,600
Chemicals, diversified	9	300,000	21,000
Restaurants	3	300,000	21,000
Insurance, property and casualty	20	170,000	20,400
Automotive parts	11	400,000	20,000
Finance, lease and finance	19	200,000	20,000
Government, county and province	750	400,000	20,000
Health, healthcare	18	320,000	19,200
Computers, peripherals	30	230,000	18,400
Business supplies	8	300,000	18,000
Tobacco	6	300,000	18,000
Insurance, diversified	9	150,000	18,000
Personal products	11	230,000	16,100
Business services	13	150,000	15,000
Energy, other	20	200,000	14,000
Advertising and publishing	15	200,000	14,000
Heavy equipment	8	270,000	13,500
Health, medical supplies	13	225,000	13,500
Retailing, apparel	5	220,000	13,200
Paper and lumber	13	260,000	13,000
Insurance, life and health	23	100,000	12,000
Metals	19	200,000	12,000
Travel, railroads	8	200,000	12,000
Outsourcing, systems	7	20,000	11,000
Finance, brokerage	10	100,000	11,000

Continued on next page

Table A.1: Approximate US Software Employment in Forbes 500 Enterprises and Government Organizations, continued

Industry	Enterprises	Total Employment	Software Employment
Computers, software	14	16,000	10,400
Industrial equipment	7	130,000	9,100
Travel, shipping	6	150,000	9,000
Photography and devices	3	145,000	8,700
Chemicals, specialized	19	120,000	8,400
Broadcasting and movies	12	120,000	8,400
Retailing, specialty	7	130,000	7,800
Outsourcing, commercial	20	19,000	7,500
Packaging	8	110,000	6,600
Food wholesalers	5	100,000	6,000
Retailing, home improvement	5	100,000	6,000
Home furnishings	7	110,000	5,500
Energy, gas	5	70,000	4,900
Construction	10	100,000	4,500
Clothing	5	70,000	4,200
Appliances	3	100,000	4,000
Finance, thrift institutions	23	30,000	3,300
Retailing, electronics	6	50,000	3,000
Retailing, home shopping	3	50,000	3,000
Recreation equipment	3	50,000	2,500
Totals	3,215	24,361,000	1,590,050

MIS = management information systems.

Table A.2 uses the same information as Table A.1, but sorts the information into alphabetic sequence and then aggregates related sub-industries such as government, insurance, and finance into major industrial groupings. Both tables have an unknown margin of error and both concentrate on the larger enterprises in which many software personnel are employed. However, both tables are relevant to the year 2000 problem even though the data is not precise, because the year 2000 problem is most widespread in the industries with the greatest concentrations of software personnel.

Table A.2: Approximate US Software Employment in Forbes 500 Industries and Major Industrial Groupings

Industry	Enterprises	Total Employment	Software Employment	Industry Groupings	Group Totals
Advertising and publishing	15	200,000	14,000		
Aerospace and defense	12	1,100,000	77,000		
Appliances	3	100,000	4,000		
Automobiles/trucks	5	1,250,000	62,500		
Automotive parts	11	400,000	20,000	Automotive	82,500
Beverages	6	360,000	21,600		
Broadcasting and movies	12	120,000	8,400		
Business, services	13	150,000	15,000		
Business, supplies	8	300,000	18,000		
Chemicals, diversified	9	300,000	21,000		
Chemicals, specialized	19	120,000	8,400	Chemicals	29,400
Clothing	5	70,000	4,200		
Computers, peripherals	30	230,000	18,400		
Computers, processors	16	550,000	38,500		
Computers, software	14	16,000	10,400	Computers	67,300
Construction	10	100,000	4,500		
Electrical equipment	8	700,000	42,000		
Energy, electric utilities	55	370,000	22,200		
Energy, gas	5	70,000	4,900		
Energy, oil	9	330,000	23,100		
Energy, other	20	200,000	14,000	Energy	64,200
Finance, brokerage	10	100,000	11,000		
Finance, lease and finance	19	200,000	20,000		
Finance, multinational banks	8	250,000	27,500		
Finance, regional banks	95	300,000	33,000		
Finance, thrift institutions	23	30,000	3,300	Finance	94,800
Food products	20	600,000	30,000		
Food wholesalers	5	100,000	6,000		
Government, county and province	750	400,000	20,000		
Government, federal	98	2,881,000	144,050		
Government, military	5	1,000,000	60,000		
Government, state	50	600,000	30,000		

Continued on next page

Table A.2: Approximate US Software Employment in Forbes 500 Industries and Major Industrial Groupings, continued

Industry	Enterprises	Total Employment	Software Employment	Industry Groupings	Group Totals
Government, urban	1,250	1,100,000	49,500	Government	303,550
Health, drugs	23	375,000	22,500		
Health, healthcare	18	320,000	19,200		
Health, medical supplies	13	225,000	13,500	Health	55,200
Heavy equipment	8	270,000	13,500		
Home furnishings	7	110,000	5,500		
Industrial equipment	7	130,000	9,100		
Insurance, diversified	9	150,000	18,000		
Insurance, life and health	23	100,000	12,000		
Insurance, property and casualty	20	170,000	20,400	Insurance	50,400
Metals	19	200,000	12,000		
Outsourcing, commercial	20	19,000	7,500		
Outsourcing, MIS	5	375,000	105,000		
Outsourcing, systems	7	20,000	11,000		
Outsourcing, year 2000	250	55,000	22,000	Outsourcing	145,500
Packaging	8	110,000	6,600		
Paper and lumber	13	260,000	13,000		
Personal products	11	230,000	16,100		
Photography and devices	3	145,000	8,700		
Recreation equipment	3	50,000	2,500		
Restaurants	3	300,000	21,000		
Retailing, apparel	5	220,000	13,200		
Retailing, department stores	7	850,000	42,500		
Retailing, drugs and discount	11	1,200,000	66,000		
Retailing, electronics	6	50,000	3,000		
Retailing, home improvement	5	100,000	6,000		
Retailing, home shopping	3	50,000	3,000		
Retailing, specialty	7	130,000	7,800		

Continued on next page

Table A.2: Approximate US Software Employment in Forbes 500 Industries and Major Industrial Groupings, continued

Industry	Enterprises	Total Employment	Software Employment	Industry Groupings	Group Totals
Retailing, supermarkets and convenience stores	16	800,000	32,000	Retailing	173,500
Telecommunications	30	1,000,000	75,000		
Tobacco	6	300,000	18,000		
Travel, airlines	9	500,000	30,000		
Travel, hotels	8	600,000	27,000		
Travel, railroads	8	200,000	12,000		
Travel, shipping	6	150,000	9,000	Travel	78,000
Totals	3,215	24,361,000	1,590,050	—	—

MIS = management information systems.

Over and above the major companies and government agencies shown in Tables A.1 and A.2 there are close to 30,000 smaller organizations in the United States that also employ software professionals. Almost another 500,000 software personnel work in these small organizations.

Note that Tables A.1 and A.2 include a number of occupational groups and do not deal just with "programmers," which is too narrow a term. The occupations include all those for which some form of ability to write software is part of the job:

- Application programmer
- Maintenance programmer
- Maintenance specialist
- Programmer
- Programmer/analyst
- Software engineer
- Software project manager
- Software quality assurance specialist
- Systems programmer
- Testing specialist

I do not regard this demographic information as being particularly accurate, but one important fact can be derived from it whether it is accurate or not: Software is a very ubiquitous occupation and permeates both US and global industries to a degree that was never imagined even 30 years ago. The pervasive impact of software is one of the prime reasons why the year 2000 problem is a very serious one. If software and computers were rare and used only for specialized purposes, the year 2000 problem would be a significant but minor annoyance. But computers and software now drive business, manufacturing, government, and military operations to a very large degree. This elevates the year 2000 problem and makes it a global concern in industrialized countries.

Appendix B: Additional Sources of Information Regarding the Year 2000 Software Problem

Because of the magnitude and seriousness of the year 2000 problem, the opinions and data of a single organization such as SPR should be confirmed or challenged by means of using multiple sources. This section includes contact information for other independent research organizations that have been addressing aspects of the year 2000 problem. Readers are urged to contact any or all of these data sources for alternate evaluations of the year 2000 problem. This set of contacts deals primarily with organizations that are not direct vendors of year 2000 services and tools, since these organizations may have a vested interest in their own products. The emphasis in this section is on organizations that can provide information about the costs and schedules of making year 2000 repairs. Both nonprofit and profit-making organizations are cited.

Applied Computer Research, Inc. (ACR)

ACR is a well-known seminar and publishing company that produces a number of useful catalogs that support the software domain: catalogs of software executives, catalogs of software tools, and now a catalog of year 2000 resources and service providers. ACR is a for-profit organization located in Phoenix, Arizona. They publish a number of newsletters and hold conferences on a variety of software topics. The ACR Year 2000 Resource Guide catalog was produced by Laura Hadley and Alan Howard, who is principal at ACR.

```
ACR
PO Box 82266
Phoenix, AZ 85071-2266
Phone:      800-234-2ACR
Web site:   http://www.acrhq.com
```

Association of Information Technology Professionals (AITP)

The AITP, formerly the Data Processing Management Association (DPMA), is a well-known nonprofit association of software managers and professional personnel. Like most software-oriented nonprofits, the AITP has been aware of, and is moving toward, sharing information on the year 2000 problem. The AITP sponsor regional and national year 2000 conferences and are publishing a book of collected year 2000 articles. (See the entry for Dick Lefkon.)

AITP
50 Busse Highway
Parkridge, IL 60068
Phone: 800-224-9371
Fax: 847-825-1693
Web site: http://www.AITP.Org

de Jager, Peter

Peter de Jager is an independent Canadian consultant, speaker, and collector of data on the year 2000 problem. Peter runs a very popular year 2000 Web site (http://www.year2000.com), and is a frequent contributor of articles and lectures on the year 2000 problem. Since Peter has specialized in year 2000 economic issues, he is a good source of practical information.

Peter de Jager
22 Marchbank Crescent
Brampton, Ontario L6S 3B1
Canada
Phone: 905-792-8706
Fax: 905-792-9818
Email: pdjager@hookup.net
Web site: http://www.year2000.com

Digital Consulting, Inc. (DCI)

DCI is a well-known software conference and seminar company founded by George Schussel. DCI, a for-profit organization, is primarily a conference group, with a smattering of management consulting as well. DCI sponsors a number of large conferences on the year 2000 issue in the United States and abroad.

Digital Consulting, Inc.
204 Andover Street
Andover, MA 01810
Phone: 978-470-3880
Fax: 978-470-0526
Web site: http://www.DCI.Expo.COM

Financial Accounting Standards Board

One of the major issues with the year 2000 problem is how the costs are going to be handled on corporate books, since they will not be trivial. The FASB sets US accounting standards and is currently in the process of ruling on year 2000 expenses. There is some concern that the method they are considering might be harmful to the US software industry and indeed to US business in general.

FASB
401 Merritt 7
PO Box 5116
Norwalk, CT 06856
Phone: 203-847-0700

Florida Information Resource Commission

The state of Florida has produced a well-thought-out year 2000 response plan that can serve as a model for other state, provincial, and urban governments. However, quite a few states now have fairly well-planned year 2000 containment strategies. The key issue, however, is whether year 2000 costs will raise taxes, and this topic is not usually discussed.

Office of the Executive Director
Suite 235
4050 Esplanade Way
Tallahassee, FL 32399-0950
Phone: 904-488-4494
Fax: 904-922-5929
Email: douglaj@irc.state.fl.us
Web site: http://mail.irm.state.fl.us/yr2000.html
Point of Contact: John Douglas, Interim Executive Director

Gartner Group

The Gartner Group is a for-profit research corporation that collects data on a wide variety of topics. The Gartner Group has produced a report similar to this one on the global impact of the year 2000 problem (Hall, B., and Schick, K. *Year 2000 Crisis—Estimating the Cost.* Stamford, CT: Gartner Group, 1996). Be aware that the Gartner approach is to use LOC rather than function point metrics.

Gartner Group
Gartner Park
Top Gallant Road
Stamford, CT 06904
Phone: 203-964-0096
Fax: 203-324-7901
Email: info@gartner.com
Web site: http://gartner.com

Giga Group

The Giga Group is a direct competitor of the Gartner Group. Interestingly, both Giga and Gartner were founded by the well-known entrepreneur Gideon Gartner. (Yet another competitor in the information market, Meta Group, was founded by ex-employees of the Gartner Group, so Gideon Gartner can be credited with creating a significant subindustry all by himself.) The Giga Group collects data on year 2000 costs. Ann Coffou, a managing director at Giga, is the source of the widely quoted statement that year 2000 litigation costs will be a trillion dollars.

Giga Information Group
One Kendall Square, Building 1400
Cambridge, MA 02139
Phone: 617-577-9595
Web site: http://www.gigasd.com

Hayes, Ian

Ian is head of Clarity Consulting, and has been speaking and writing on the year 2000 issue for some time.

Clarity Consulting
40 South Street, Suite 104
Marblehead, MA 01945-3274
Phone: 781-639-1012
Email: 70661.1063@compuserve.com

Humphrey, Watts

Watts is the well-known originator of the Software Engineering Institute (SEI) capability maturity model. He is also the author of a number of best-selling books on software engineering and software management topics. He has recently begun to speak on the year 2000 problem at major conferences. Due to his reputation in the software industry his views carry significant weight. Watts is now an SEI fellow, but is no longer located on the SEI campus in Pittsburgh.

Email: Watts@SEI.CMU.EDU

IBC USA Conferences, Inc.

IBC is a commercial conference organizer that hosts a number of software-related events. Like most conference houses, IBC has started running a series of regional year 2000 events. Unlike some year 2000 conferences, IBC tends toward vertical themes for specific industries such as insurance, banking, and financial services.

IBC USA Conferences, Inc.
225 Turnpike Road
Southborough, MA 01772-1749
Phone: 508-481-6400
Fax: 508-481-7911
Email: inq@ibcusa.com
Web site: http://www.io.org/-ibc/vendor2000/

The Information Technology Association of America (ITAA)

The ITAA is a nonprofit association of software vendors that has formed a year 2000 task force under the chairmanship of Peter Sheridan of Viasoft. The ITAA has published a useful although incomplete catalog of year 2000 vendors. Heidi Hooper (703-284-5312 or hhooper@-itaa.org) is the contact cited in the ITAA year 2000 vendor catalog.

ITAA
1616 N. Fort Myer Drive
Suite 1300
Arlington, VA 22209
Phone: 703-522-5055
Fax: 703-525-2279
Web site: http://www.itaa.org

Jinnett, Jeff

Jeff Jinnett is one of an increasingly large number of practicing attorneys who are beginning to specialize in the legal aspects of the year

2000 problem. While there are many good attorneys who are conversant with year 2000 issues, not all of them are good at public speaking or writing for the popular press, and Jeff Jinnett does both of these well. His normal practice is computer law for the firm of LeBoeuf, Lamb, Greene & MacRae in New York. He has published a number of interesting articles on the year 2000 legal issues in the context of corporate liabilities and the personal risks faced by corporate executives.

Jeff Jinnett
LeBoeuf, Lamb, Greene & MacRae LLP
125 West 55th Street
19th Floor
New York, NY 10019
Phone: 212-424-8292
Fax: 212-424-8500
Email: jinnett@llgm.com

Ken Orr Institute

Ken Orr, the founder and chairman of the Ken Orr Institute, is a well-known author and lecturer on a variety of software topics. He has been a frequent keynote speaker at year 2000 conferences and has performed a number of consulting studies on the year 2000 issue. Ken also explores issues in the data warehouse domain. His conclusion is that US companies may not be moving fast enough to solve the year 2000 problem before the end of the century.

Ken Orr Institute
534 South Kansas
Topeka, KS 66603
Phone: 913-357-0003
Fax: 913-357-8446
Web site: http://www.kenorrinst.com

Kendall, Robert

Robert Kendall is now an independent consultant, after retiring from the IBM corporation. While at IBM Kendall performed a large-scale analysis of the mainframe software in eight IBM data centers. This study found, surprisingly, that dormant or inactive programs that had not been run in more than a year comprised more than half of the entire software portfolio. Assuming other corporations have a similar ratio of dormant-to-active applications, this study may be relevant to the year 2000 problem by allowing enterprises to delay or avoid spending money to update dormant applications. However, it proved to be very difficult to separate the active portions from the dormant portions of software portfolios.

Phone: 914-226-2419
Email: Bobkend@AOL.com

Lefkon, Dick

Dick Lefkon is one of the pioneers of the year 2000 topic. He led perhaps the first year 2000 date conversion in history, circa 1984. He is also the chairman of the year 2000 committee of the AITP, which was formerly the mainframe group of the DPMA.

Lefkon and his colleagues Kathryn D. Jennings and Patrick J. Hagan have produced what is one of the most useful and perhaps the largest year 2000 source book yet published. This is a resource book published by the mainframe special interest group of the AITP and is entitled *Year 2000: Best Practices for Y2K Millennium.* (The book is subtitled "Panic in Year Zero" and the back cover is a movie poster from the 1950's horror film of that name starring Ray Milland, Jean Hagan, and Frankie Avalon.) The AITP also supports year 2000 conferences in the New York area.

SIG Mainframe of the AITP
PO Box 885 Wall Street Station
New York, NY 10005
Phone: 800-665-2315

Meta Group

The Meta Group was founded by ex-employees and officers of the Gartner Group, and is the third information services company derived from the pioneering concept of Gideon Gartner. The Meta Group also collects data on the year 2000 problem, and has licensed some of the studies and data collected by Dr. Howard Rubin.

Meta Group
208 Harbor Drive
PO Box 120061
Stamford, CT 06912-0061
Phone: 203-973-6700

MITRE Corporation

The MITRE Corporation is a nonprofit, government-sponsored research institute that deals with a large number of military technology questions. The US Department of Defense sponsored a study of the military and defense implications of the year 2000 problem. The MITRE study of the year 2000 issue is specialized, but very thorough. The research was headed by Thomas Backman of MITRE's Bedford laboratory. The MITRE year 2000 research is somewhat alarming because it deals with the impact of the problem on satellites, military aircraft, military logistics, ships, weapons systems, and a number of other areas in which failures can range from serious to catastrophic.

MITRE Corporation
202 Burlington Road
Bedford, MA 01730-1420
Phone: 781-271-2725
Fax: 781-271-6239
Email: tkb@mitre.org
Web site: http://mitre.com

National Software Council (NSC)

The NSC is a fairly new nonprofit organization created to assist the US software industry in maintaining a favorable balance of trade. The NSC is still feeling its way in terms of missions, but the year 2000 problem is obviously one that falls within the NSC purview. However, the NSC is not overburdened with funds and resources. The current NSC president (1997) is Larry Bernstein, formerly of AT&T.

National Software Council
PO Box 4500
Alexandria, VA 22303
Phone: 703-742-7111
Fax: 703-742-7200
Email: lbernstein@worldnet.att.net

Peraino, Vito

Vito Peraino is a practicing attorney in Los Angeles. He is a frequent author on the legal aspects of the year 2000 problem, and has also appeared on radio talk shows. Because the legal implications of the year 2000 problem are massive, it is very useful to include attorneys as part of all major year 2000 upgrade plans.

Hancock, Rothert & Bunshoft LLP, Attorneys
515 S. Figueroa Street
19th Floor

Los Angeles, CA 90071
Phone: 213-623-7777
Fax: 213-623-5405

Rubin Systems, Inc.

Howard Rubin is a well-known software lecturer, author, and researcher on a wide variety of topics. He is also the designer of the ESTIMACS software cost-estimating tool and a tenured professor of software engineering at Hunter College. Howard is a frequent keynote speaker at year 2000 conferences and has accumulated a solid body of data on the year 2000 issue. He has performed an independent study on the performance degradation associated with careless year 2000 repairs and has reached a conclusion similar to the one in this report.

Dr. Howard Rubin
5 Winterbottom Lane
Pound Ridge, NY 10576
Phone: 914-764-4931
Fax: 914-764-0536
Email: 71031.377@compuserve.com

Society of Information Management

SIM is a nonprofit association aimed at the software management community. SIM has a year 2000 working group that is accumulating data and information on the year 2000 problem. The co-chairman is Dr. Leon Kappelman of the University of North Texas.

Dr. Leon A. Kappelman
Associate Professor, Business Computer Information Systems
College of Business Administration
University of North Texas
PO Box 305249
Denton, TX 76203
Phone: 940-565-3110
Fax: 940-565-4935
Email: kapp@unt.edu
Web site: http://www-LAN.UNT.EDU/COBA/BCIS/faculty/
           kappelma/

Software Productivity Group (SPG)

SPG is a for-profit conference, seminar, research, and publication company. Among their various offerings is the well-known software journal

Application Development Trends. SPG also sponsors a variety of conferences and seminars on year 2000 issues. SPG and the next company in this listing, Software Productivity Research (SPR), have similar names, but have no direct business relationship. This same statement is also true for the Software Productivity Consortium (SPC), SEI, and Software Research Associates. We all have the word *software* as part of our corporate names, but we are not related in any business sense.

Software Productivity Group, Inc.
386 West Main Street, Suite 2
Northboro, MA 01532
Phone: 508-393-7100
Fax: 508-393-3388

Software Productivity Research, Inc. (SPR)

SPR, established in 1984, is a for-profit research, development, and management consulting company located in Burlington, Massachusetts. Capers Jones, the author of this book, is the SPR Chairman. SPR has been actively collecting data on the economic impact of the year 2000 problem, as evidenced in this book.

Software Productivity Research, Inc.
1 New England Executive Park
Burlington, MA 01803-5005
Phone: 781-273-0140
Fax: 781-273-5176
Email: Capers@spr.com
Web site: http://www.spr.com

SPR

This company and the previous company, Software Productivity Research, Inc., share the same acronym but do not have any direct business connection. This company was formed in 1973 and is a midwestern corporation specializing in maintenance, renovation, and year 2000 software updates. The president is Rob Figliulo. Both SPRs collect data on the year 2000 issue, and both are occasionally mistaken for the other. Fortunately there is no direct competition between the two SPRs and sometimes the two have cooperated on various software topics.

SPR
2105 Spring Road
8th Floor

Oak Brook, IL 60521
Phone: 708-990-2040
Fax: 708-990-2062
Web site: www.sprinc.com

Software Technology Support Center (STSC)

STSC is a nonprofit organization funded by the US Air Force and located at Hill Air Force Base in Ogden, Utah. STSC performs research on a variety of software-related topics, including the year 2000 problem. STSC is also the publisher of the interesting military software journal *Crosstalk*. One of the STSC year 2000 researchers, Bryce Ragland, has written a useful book that is being published by McGraw-Hill as this book is being written *(The Year 2000 Problem Solver: A Five-Step Disaster Prevention Plan)*.

Software Technology Support Center
ALC/TISE
7278 Fourth Street
Hill AFB, UT 84056-5205
Phone: 801-777-8068
Fax: 801-777-8069
Email: stscols@software.hill.af.mil
Web site: http://www.stsc.hill.af.mil

Strassmann, Paul

Paul Strassmann is the former CIO of the Department of Defense and a very well-known author and speaker on software matters. Because of Paul's prior work as one of the world's most highly visible CIOs, he is in frequent contact with senior executives and is able to address a number of large-scale economic issues. Paul is one of the leading figures in research on software economic topics, and a pioneer of serious research on ways of dealing with the value of software and computers. Paul's work is characterized by a significant volume of empirical data, and his analysis of the year 2000 situation is very significant. From a sociological point of view, Paul Strassmann's access to top executives is likely to be more effective in making year 2000 issues visible than similar work by other year 2000 researchers.

Strassmann, Inc.
Phone: 203-966-5505
Fax: 203-966-5506

Email: Paul@strassmann.com
Web site: http://www.strassmann.com

Ulrich, William

William Ulrich is a well-known public speaker and author on year 2000 issues. He is head of the Tactical Strategy Group.

Tactical Strategy Group, Inc.
2091 Park Avenue South
Suite C3
Soquel, CA 95073
Phone: 408-464-5344
Email: tsginc@cruzio.com

WSR Consulting Group

WSR Consulting Group occupies an interesting niche: management, technology, and litigation consulting. The founder and president, Warren Reid, is not an attorney but rather a management consultant who specializes in intellectual property and software litigation. Warren frequently works as an expert witness in arbitration and litigation involving software issues. Obviously the year 2000 problem will be a fruitful domain for litigation. Warren is a frequent writer and speaker at year 2000 events, and tends to stress the legal issues, of which other speakers and authors may not be aware.

WSR Consulting Group
4273 Noeline Avenue
Suite 200
Encino, CA 91436
Phone: 818-986-8842
Fax: 818-986-7955
Email: consult@primenet.com

Y2K Investor; WBZS AM730, Washington, DC

This is an interesting business radio show for the Washington, DC, audience. As the name implies, the show is slanted toward investment opportunities in the year 2000 problem domain. However, the show also features guests who are year 2000 managers and executives from both private industry and government agencies. The co-hosts are John Anthony Keyes and Ed Mulhall. Tony Keyes is writing a book on year 2000 investment opportunities, which is an interesting slant on the issue.

The Y2K Investor
PO Box 178
Brooksville, MD 20933
Phone: 301-924-6643
Web site: http://www.y2kinvestor.com

Year 2000 Group (the Information Management Forum)

The Atlanta-based Year 2000 Group, a subsidiary of the Information Management Forum, is one of more than a score of special-interest organizations formed to share knowledge and ideas about dealing with the year 2000 crisis. Similar groups can be found in most large cities. This group is a for-profit organization, but many of the local year 2000 groups are nonprofit organizations. Jim Jones (no relation to the author, Capers Jones) is the contact point for the Year 2000 Group. This particular organization is a bit unusual in that many of its members are from the Fortune 500 class of companies, such as IBM, General Motors, Ford, Coca Cola, and the like.

The Year 2000 Group
4380 Georgetown Street
Suite 1002
Atlanta, GA 30338
Phone: 770-455-0070
Fax: 770-455-0082
Email: timf@mindspring.com
Web site: http://infomgtforum.com

Yourdon, Ed

Ed Yourdon is a well-known author and software management consultant. He is a frequent keynote speaker at major conferences and respected opinion setter on many software topics. He is also the editor of *American Programmer* magazine, which has already had several special issues on the year 2000 software problem. In addition, Yourdon is at work on a new book on the year 2000 problem. Since his books are among the top sellers in the software world, his new book on the year 2000 problem is anxiously awaited.

Phone: 212-769-9460
Email: Ed@yourdon.com
Web site: http://www.yourdon.com

Zvegintzov, Nicholas

Nicholas Zvegintzov is one of the pioneers of research in software maintenance technologies, and has been publishing and speaking on maintenance topics for more than 20 years. He is a frequent speaker and writer on the year 2000 problem, and he takes the position that the software industry may be getting what it deserves for not paying sufficient attention to maintainability. He also cautions companies and individuals to be very careful of false claims and exaggerated promises. Zvegintzov is often a chairman or program committee member of maintenance conferences, and is the publisher of many articles and several books.

Phone:	718-816-5522
Fax:	718-816-9038
Email:	72050.570@compuserve.com

Appendix C: Web Sites Containing Year 2000 Information

The year 2000 problem is the first major business issue where the Internet and the World Wide Web have been available as information resources. As a research tool for year 2000 issues, the Web is proving to be invaluable. The operations method of the Web is to link from site to site. So, beginning at almost any of the more popular year 2000 Web sites makes it feasible to move from site to site, although some of the specialized legal and governmental Web sites are not linked to the common year 2000 general information sites.

The de Jager Year 2000 Web Site

The "mother of all year 2000 Web sites" is probably the one originated by the well-known year 2000 consultant Peter de Jager. The URL of this famous site is http://www.year2000.com. This site contains links to almost every other known Web site with year 2000 information and hence is an excellent starting place for acquiring perhaps more information about the year 2000 problem than many people realize even exists. The organization of the Web site changes from time to time, but includes the following direct links:

- Year 2000 vendors, organized alphabetically
- Year 2000 articles and reference materials
- Year 2000 user groups
- Year 2000 news clips of late-breaking news
- Year 2000-related stock quotes

Although this Web site is one of the best available, it still has some gaps and omissions that may eventually be completed. For example, this Web site is skimpy on cost and economic data. It also emphasizes MIS year 2000 issues rather than military software, systems software, embedded software, and the other "technical" forms of software.

The Gartner Group Web Site

The Gartner Group is a well-known information services company that was one of the pioneer sources of year 2000 cost data. Gartner year 2000 costs are the most widely cited of any current software cost information.

Gartner's year 2000 research is expanding on a daily basis, and their reports cover a wide variety of year 2000 topics, including accounting issues, tax issues, performance issues, and a host of others. The URL of the Gartner Web site is http://gartner.com. Note that not all of Gartner's year 2000 data is available to casual browsing, since some of the more interesting studies are reserved for Gartner Group clients. Even so, this is a useful stop for research on the year 2000 problem.

The General Services Administration (GSA) Web Site

The federal government is obviously going to be affected by the year 2000 problem. The GSA is the federal agency that acts as a purchasing agent and clearinghouse for software and computers, and hence has a Web site with considerable information on year 2000 issues. The URL of this Web site is http://itpolicy.gsa.gov. Some of the more interesting year 2000 information on this Web site includes excerpts from the congressional testimony on the year 2000 problem held by Congressman Horn and Congresswoman Morella in March 1997.

The ITAA Web Site

The ITAA is one of the larger nonprofit associations exploring the year 2000 problem, although most other software associations are doing year 2000 research too. The ITAA Web site has lists of vendors, study groups, and other relevant data. The URL of this Web site is http://www.itaa.org. This site is representative of a number of nonprofit Web sites dealing with year 2000 issues.

The SPR Web Site

The SPR Web site is the repository for much of the information in this book dealing with function points. The SPR Web site also points to many other metric and measurement Web sites, most of which use function point data for a variety of business and technical purposes. The URL of the SPR Web site is http://www.spr.com. Included in this site is an annotated bibliography of software management books with links to many book publishers, book stores, and book marketing sites such as Amazon, Computer Literacy, and SoftPro.

Appendix D: Languages Affected by the Year 2000 Problem

Some of the journal articles on the year 2000 problem have mistakenly asserted that COBOL is the primary language affected by dates and the year 2000 crisis. Even the well-known *Newsweek* year 2000 cover story of June 2, 1997, contained incorrect information on the percentage of applications in COBOL that would be affected. Although COBOL is a widely used programming language, no more than about 30% to 35% of the software needing year 2000 repairs is written in COBOL.

Following COBOL are the C and C++ languages, and Assembly language, each of which will comprise about 10% of the year 2000 repairs. After COBOL, C, C++, and Assembly languages are considered, almost 500 other languages may have year 2000 date references. This situation is critical, because most of the year 2000 tool and service providers are concentrating on COBOL or one of the high-use languages, while literally hundreds of languages have no tools, few trained programmers, and little or no support for finding and fixing the year 2000 problem.

Table D.1 is a large list of languages that is included simply to make plain to journalists and other information companies that COBOL is only the tip of the year 2000 iceberg. It is a dangerous mistake to concentrate only on COBOL and ignore the hundreds of other languages with year 2000 implications.

The languages in Table D.1 are sorted alphabetically. The Level column reflects the relative power of each language versus basic assembly language. The original meaning of *level* in this context is the number of statements in basic assembly language needed to replicate the functionality of one statement in the language under discussion. Thus for a level-3 language such as COBOL, it would require three assembly statements to generate the functionality of one COBOL statement.

The Low, Average, and High columns describe the number of logical source code statements that are equivalent to one function point. The Average column is the base used for *backfiring* or direct conversion of source code statements into equivalent function point values. Note that logical statements rather than physical LOC are assumed, which means that blank lines, comments, dead code, and other extraneous physical lines are not counted.

Table D.1: Alphabetical List of Software Languages Subject to Year 2000 Problems

ID	Language	Level	Low	Average	High
1	1032/AF	20.00	—	16	—
2	1st generation default	1.00	200	320	400
3	2nd generation default	3.00	55	107	165
4	3rd generation default	4.00	45	80	125
5	4th generation default	16.00	10	20	30
6	5th generation default	70.00	2	5	6
7	AAS Macro	3.50	—	91	—
8	ABAP/4	20.00	—	16	—
9	ACCEL	17.00	—	19	—
10	Access	8.50	—	38	—
11	ACTOR	15.00	—	21	—
12	Acumen	11.50	—	28	—
13	Ada 83	4.50	60	71	80
14	Ada 95	6.50	—	49	—
15	ADR/DL	8.00	—	40	—
16	ADR/IDEAL/PDL	16.00	14	20	30
17	ADS/Batch	16.00	—	20	—
18	ADS/Online	16.00	—	20	—
19	AI shell default	6.50	30	49	65
20	AI SHELLS	6.50	—	49	—
21	ALGOL 68	3.00	—	107	—
22	ALGOL W	3.00	—	107	—
23	AMBUSH	10.00	—	32	—
24	AML	6.50	—	49	—
25	AMPPL II	5.00	—	64	—
26	ANSI BASIC	5.00	35	64	100
27	ANSI COBOL 74	3.00	65	107	170
28	ANSI COBOL 85	3.50	—	91	—
29	ANSI SQL	25.00	—	13	—
30	ANSWER/DB	25.00	—	13	—

Continued on next page

Table D.1: Alphabetical List of Software Languages Subject to Year 2000 Problems, continued

ID	Language	Level	Low	Average	High
31	APL 360/370	10.00	12	32	45
32	APL default	10.00	10	32	45
33	APL*PLUS	10.00	—	32	—
34	APPLESOFT BASIC	2.50	—	128	—
35	Application Builder	16.00	—	20	—
36	Application Manager	9.00	—	36	—
37	APS	19.00	—	17	—
38	APT	4.50	—	71	—
39	APTools	16.00	—	20	—
40	ARC	6.50	—	49	—
41	Ariel	3.00	—	107	—
42	ARITY	6.50	—	49	—
43	Arity PROLOG	5.00	—	64	—
44	ART	6.50	—	49	—
45	ART Enterprise	7.00	—	46	—
46	Artemis	8.00	—	40	—
47	ART-IM	7.00	—	46	—
48	ASI/INQUIRY	25.00	—	13	—
49	AS/SET	17.00	—	19	—
50	ASK Windows	7.00	—	46	—
51	Assembly (basic)	1.00	237	320	416
52	Assembly (macro)	1.50	170	213	295
53	Associative default	5.00	35	64	85
54	Autocoder	1.00	225	320	400
55	AWK	15.00	—	21	—
56	Aztec C	2.50	—	128	—
57	BALM	3.00	—	107	—
58	BASE SAS	6.00	—	53	—
59	BASIC A	2.50	70	128	165
60	Basic assembly	1.00	200	320	450
61	Berkeley PASCAL	3.50	—	91	—
62	BETTER BASIC	3.50	—	91	—
63	BLISS	3.00	—	107	—
64	BMSGEN	9.00	—	36	—
65	BOEINGCALC	50.00	—	6	—
66	C (default value)	2.50	60	128	170
67	C Set 2	3.50	—	91	—
68	C++ (default value)	6.00	40	53	140
69	C86Plus	2.50	—	128	—
70	CA-dBFast	8.00	—	40	—

Continued on next page

Table D.1: Alphabetical List of Software Languages Subject to Year 2000 Problems, continued

ID	Language	Level	Low	Average	High
71	CA-EARL	11.50	—	28	—
72	CAST	6.50	—	49	—
73	CBASIC	3.50	—	91	—
74	CDADL	16.00	—	20	—
75	CELLSIM	7.00	—	46	—
76	Centerline C++	6.00	—	53	—
77	CHILI	3.00	—	107	—
78	CHILL	3.00	60	107	143
79	CICS	7.00	—	46	—
80	CLARION	5.50	—	58	—
81	CLASCAL	4.00	—	80	—
82	CLI	10.00	—	32	—
83	CLIPPER	17.00	—	19	—
84	CLIPPER DB	8.00	—	40	—
85	CLOS	15.00	—	21	—
86	CLOUT	8.00	—	40	—
87	CMS2	3.00	70	107	135
88	CMSGEN	17.00	—	19	—
89	COBOL	7.00	65	46	150
90	COBRA	16.00	—	20	—
91	CodeCenter	9.00	—	36	—
92	Cofac	9.00	—	36	—
93	COGEN	9.00	—	36	—
94	COGNOS	9.00	—	36	—
95	COGO	4.50	—	71	—
96	COMAL	4.00	—	80	—
97	COMIT II	5.00	—	64	—
98	Common LISP	5.00	—	64	—
99	Concurrent PASCAL	4.00	—	80	—
100	CONNIVER	5.00	—	64	—
101	CORAL 66	3.00	—	107	—
102	CORVET	17.00	—	19	—
103	CorVision	22.00	—	15	—
104	CPL	2.00	—	160	—
105	CSL	6.50	—	49	—
106	CSP	6.00	—	53	—
107	CSSL	7.00	—	46	—
108	CULPRIT	25.00	—	13	—
109	CxPERT	6.50	—	49	—
110	CYGNET	17.00	—	19	—

Continued on next page

Table D.1: Alphabetical List of Software Languages Subject to Year 2000 Problems, continued

ID	Language	Level	Low	Average	High
111	Data base default	8.00	25	40	55
112	Dataflex	8.00	—	40	—
113	Datatrieve	16.00	—	20	—
114	dBase III	8.00	25	40	47
115	dBase IV	9.00	—	36	—
116	DCL	1.50	—	213	—
117	Decision support default	9.00	20	36	40
118	DEC-RALLY	8.00	—	40	—
119	DELPHI	11.00	—	29	—
120	DL/1	8.00	—	40	—
121	DNA-4	17.00	—	19	—
122	DOS batch files	2.50	—	128	—
123	DTABL	7.00	—	46	—
124	DTIPT	7.00	—	46	—
125	DYANA	4.50	—	71	—
126	DYNAMO-III	7.00	—	46	—
127	EASEL	11.00	—	29	—
128	EASY	6.50	—	49	—
129	EASYTRIEVE +	25.00	—	13	—
130	Eclipse	6.50	—	49	—
131	EDA/SQL	27.00	—	12	—
132	ED-Scheme 3.4	6.00	—	53	—
133	EIFFEL	15.00	—	21	—
134	ENFORM	7.00	—	46	—
135	English-based default	6.00	35	53	90
136	Ensemble	11.00	—	29	—
137	EPOS	16.00	—	20	—
138	Erlang	8.00	—	40	—
139	ESF	8.00	—	40	—
140	ESPADVISOR	6.50	—	49	—
141	ESPL/I	4.50	55	71	95
142	EUCLID	3.00	—	107	—
143	EXCEL 1-2	51.00	—	6	—
144	EXCEL 3-4	55.00	—	6	—
145	EXCEL 5	57.00	—	6	—
146	EXPRESS	9.00	—	36	—
147	EXSYS	6.50	—	49	—
148	Extend. Common LISP	5.75	—	56	—
149	EZNOMAD	9.00	—	36	—

Continued on next page

Table D.1: Alphabetical List of Software Languages Subject to Year 2000 Problems, continued

ID	Language	Level	Low	Average	High
150	Facets	16.00	—	20	—
151	FactoryLink IV	11.00	—	29	—
152	FAME	9.00	—	36	—
153	FileMaker Pro	9.00	—	36	—
154	FLAVORS	11.00	—	29	—
155	FLEX	7.00	—	46	—
156	FlexGen	11.00	—	29	—
157	FOCUS	8.00	—	40	—
158	FOIL	6.00	—	53	—
159	Forte	18.00	—	18	—
160	FORTH (default)	5.00	27	64	85
161	FORTRAN 66	2.50	75	128	160
162	FORTRAN 77	3.00	65	107	150
163	FORTRAN 90	4.00	—	80	—
164	FORTRAN 95	4.50	—	71	—
165	FORTRAN default	3.00	75	107	160
166	FORTRAN II	2.50	75	128	160
167	Foundation	11.00	—	29	—
168	FOXPRO 1	8.00	—	40	—
169	FOXPRO 2.5	9.50	—	34	—
170	FRAMEWORK	50.00	4	6	10
171	G2	6.50	—	49	—
172	GAMMA	20.00	—	16	—
173	Genascript	12.00	—	27	—
174	GENER/OL	25.00	—	13	—
175	GENEXUS	21.00	—	15	—
176	GENIFER	17.00	—	19	—
177	GeODE 2.0	20.00	—	16	—
178	GFA Basic	9.50	—	34	—
179	GML	7.00	—	46	—
180	Golden Common LISP	5.00	25	64	80
181	GPSS	7.00	—	46	—
182	GUEST	11.50	—	28	—
183	Guru	6.50	—	49	—
184	GW BASIC	3.25	63	98	135
185	Haskell	8.50	—	38	—
186	High C	2.50	—	128	—
187	HLEVEL	5.50	—	58	—
188	HP BASIC	2.50	—	128	—

Continued on next page

Table D.1: Alphabetical List of Software Languages Subject to Year 2000 Problems, continued

ID	Language	Level	Low	Average	High
189	HTML 2.0	20.00	10	16	23
190	HTML 3.0	22.00	9	15	21
191	Huron	20.00	—	16	—
192	IBM ADF I	16.00	—	20	—
193	IBM ADF II	18.00	—	18	—
194	IBM Advan. BASIC	3.25	—	98	—
195	IBM CICS/VS	8.00	30	40	50
196	IBM Compiled BASIC	3.50	60	91	130
197	IBM VS COBOL	3.00	—	107	—
198	IBM VS COBOL II	3.50	57	91	134
199	ICES	4.50	—	71	—
200	ICON	4.00	—	80	—
201	IDMS	8.00	—	40	—
202	IEF	23.00	10	14	22
203	IEW	23.00	11	14	23
204	IFPS/PLUS	10.00	—	32	—
205	IMPRS	8.00	—	40	—
206	INFORMIX	8.00	—	40	—
207	INGRES	8.00	—	40	—
208	INQUIRE	25.00	—	13	—
209	INSIGHT2	6.50	—	49	—
210	INSTALL/1	20.00	—	16	—
211	INTELLECT	6.00	—	53	—
212	INTERLISP	5.50	—	58	—
213	Interpreted BASIC	3.00	70	107	160
214	Interpreted C	2.50	—	128	—
215	IQLISP	5.50	—	58	—
216	IQRP	25.00	—	13	—
217	JANUS	4.50	—	71	—
218	JAVA	6.00	40	53	140
219	JCL	1.45	—	221	—
220	JOSS	3.00	—	107	—
221	JOVIAL	3.00	70	107	165
222	KAPPA	8.00	—	40	—
223	KBMS	6.50	—	49	—
224	KCL	5.00	—	64	—
225	KEE	6.50	—	49	—
226	Keyplus	8.00	—	40	—
227	KL	5.00	—	64	—

Continued on next page

Table D.1: Alphabetical List of Software Languages Subject to Year 2000 Problems, continued

ID	Language	Level	Low	Average	High
228	KLO	5.00	—	64	—
229	KNOWOL	6.50	—	49	—
230	KRL	5.50	—	58	—
231	KSH	15.00	—	21	—
232	Ladder Logic	9.00	—	36	—
233	LAMBIT/L	5.00	—	64	—
234	Lattice C	2.50	—	128	—
235	Liana	2.50	—	128	—
236	LILITH	4.50	—	71	—
237	LINC II	23.00	—	14	—
238	LISP default	5.00	25	64	80
239	LOGLISP	5.50	—	58	—
240	LOOPS	15.00	—	21	—
241	LOTUS 123 DOS	50.00	4	6	12
242	LOTUS Macros	3.00	—	107	—
243	LUCID 3D	51.00	—	6	—
244	LYRIC	6.00	—	53	—
245	M	20.00	—	16	—
246	macFORTH	5.00	—	64	—
247	MACH1	8.00	—	40	—
248	Machine language	0.50	—	640	—
249	Macro assembly	1.50	130	213	300
250	MAESTRO	20.00	—	16	—
251	MAGEC	20.00	—	16	—
252	MAGIK	15.00	—	21	—
253	MAKE	15.00	—	21	—
254	MANTIS	8.00	—	40	—
255	MAPPER	6.00	—	53	—
256	MARK IV	8.00	—	40	—
257	MARK V	9.00	—	36	—
258	MATHCAD	60.00	—	5	—
259	MDL	9.00	—	36	—
260	MENTOR	6.00	—	53	—
261	MESA	3.00	—	107	—
262	Microfocus COBOL	4.00	45	80	127
263	microFORTH	5.00	—	64	—
264	Microsoft C	2.50	—	128	—
265	MicroStep	16.00	—	20	—
266	Miranda	8.00	—	40	—

Continued on next page

Table D.1: Alphabetical List of Software Languages Subject to Year 2000 Problems, continued

ID	Language	Level	Low	Average	High
267	Model 204	8.50	23	38	43
268	MODULA 2	4.00	70	80	90
269	MOSAIC	50.00	—	6	—
270	MS C ++ V. 7	6.00	—	53	—
271	MS Compiled BASIC	3.50	60	91	130
272	MSL	5.00	—	64	—
273	muLISP	5.00	—	64	—
274	MUMPS	17.00	—	19	—
275	NASTRAN	4.50	—	71	—
276	NATURAL 1	6.00	43	53	77
277	NATURAL 2	7.00	—	46	—
278	NATURAL Construct	13.00	—	25	—
279	Natural language	0.10	1,800	3,200	5,000
280	NETRON/CAP	17.00	—	19	—
281	NEXPERT	6.50	—	49	—
282	NIAL	6.50	—	49	—
283	NOMAD2	8.00	30	40	55
284	Nonprocedural default	9.00	23	36	40
285	Notes VIP	9.00	—	36	—
286	Nroff	6.00	—	53	—
287	OBJECT Assembler	5.00	—	64	—
288	Object LISP	11.00	—	29	—
289	Object LOGO	11.00	—	29	—
290	Object PASCAL	11.00	—	29	—
291	Object-oriented default	11.00	13	29	40
292	Objective-C	12.00	17	27	38
293	ObjectVIEW	13.00	—	25	—
294	OGL	4.00	—	80	—
295	OMNIS 7	8.00	—	40	—
296	OODL	11.00	—	29	—
297	OPS	7.00	—	46	—
298	OPS5	5.50	—	58	—
299	ORACLE	8.00	—	40	—
300	Oracle Developer/2000	14.00	—	23	—
301	Oscar	3.00	—	107	—
302	PACBASE	22.00	12	15	24
303	PACE	8.00	—	40	—
304	PARADOX/PAL	9.00	—	36	—
305	PASCAL default	3.50	50	91	125

Continued on next page

Table D.1: Alphabetical List of Software Languages Subject to Year 2000 Problems, continued

ID	Language	Level	Low	Average	High
306	PC FOCUS	9.00	—	36	—
307	PDL Millennium	15.00	—	21	—
308	PDP-11 ADE	6.00	—	53	—
309	PERL	15.00	—	21	—
310	Persistance Object Builder	15.00	13	21	31
311	PILOT	6.00	—	53	—
312	PLANIT	6.00	—	53	—
313	PLANNER	5.00	—	64	—
314	PLANPERFECT 1	45.00	—	7	—
315	PLATO	6.00	—	53	—
316	PL/I	4.00	65	80	95
317	PL/M	4.50	—	71	—
318	PL/S	3.50	47	91	143
319	polyFORTH	5.00	—	64	—
320	POP	5.50	—	58	—
321	POPLOG	5.50	—	58	—
322	Power BASIC	6.50	—	49	—
323	PowerBuilder	20.00	—	16	—
324	POWERHOUSE	23.00	—	14	—
325	PPL (Plus)	8.00	—	40	—
326	Pro-C	12.00	—	27	—
327	PRO-IV	5.50	—	58	—
328	Problem-oriented default	4.50	50	71	90
329	Procedural default	3.00	50	107	175
330	Professional PASCAL	3.50	—	91	—
331	Program Gen. default	20.00	10	16	20
332	PROGRESS V4	9.00	—	36	—
333	PROLOG default	5.00	35	64	90
334	PROSE	3.00	—	107	—
335	PROTEUS	3.00	—	107	—
336	QBasic	5.50	—	58	—
337	QBE	25.00	—	13	—
338	QMF	22.00	—	15	—
339	QNIAL	6.50	—	49	—
340	QUATTRO	51.00	—	6	—
341	QUATTRO PRO	51.00	—	6	—
342	Query default	25.00	9	13	20
343	QUICK BASIC 1	5.00	45	64	105
344	QUICK BASIC 2	5.25	40	61	100

Continued on next page

Table D.1: Alphabetical List of Software Languages Subject to Year 2000 Problems, continued

ID	Language	Level	Low	Average	High
345	QUICK BASIC 3	5.50	38	58	90
346	Quickbuild	11.50	—	28	—
347	Quick C	2.50	—	128	—
348	QUIZ	22.00	—	15	—
349	RALLY	8.00	—	40	—
350	RAMIS II	8.00	30	40	50
351	RapidGen	11.50	—	28	—
352	RATFOR	3.50	—	91	—
353	RDB	8.00	—	40	—
354	REALIA	7.00	—	46	—
355	Realizer 1.0	8.00	—	40	—
356	Realizer 2.0	9.00	—	36	—
357	RELATE/3000	8.00	—	40	—
358	Reuse default	60.00	3	5	8
359	REXX (MVS)	4.00	—	80	—
360	REXX (OS/2)	7.00	—	46	—
361	RM BASIC	3.50	—	91	—
362	RM COBOL	3.00	—	107	—
363	RM FORTRAN	3.00	—	107	—
364	RPG I	4.00	50	80	115
365	RPG II	5.50	40	58	85
366	RPG III	5.75	37	56	80
367	RT-Expert 1.4	5.50	—	58	—
368	SAIL	3.00	—	107	—
369	SAPIENS	20.00	—	16	—
370	SAS	10.00	—	32	—
371	SAVVY	25.00	—	13	—
372	SBASIC	3.50	—	91	—
373	SCEPTRE	4.50	—	71	—
374	SCHEME	6.00	—	53	—
375	Screen painter default	57.00	—	6	—
376	SEQUAL	27.00	—	12	—
377	SHELL	15.00	—	21	—
378	SIMPLAN	9.00	—	36	—
379	SIMSCRIPT	7.00	35	46	60
380	SIMULA	7.00	—	46	—
381	SIMULA 67	7.00	—	46	—
382	Simulation default	7.00	30	46	65
383	SMALLTALK 286	15.00	—	21	—

Continued on next page

Table D.1: Alphabetical List of Software Languages Subject to Year 2000 Problems, continued

ID	Language	Level	Low	Average	High
384	SMALLTALK 80	15.00	—	21	—
385	SMALLTALK/V	15.00	12	21	30
386	SNAP	4.00	50	80	115
387	SNOBOL2-4	2.50	—	128	—
388	SoftScreen	23.00	—	14	—
389	SOLO	5.50	—	58	—
390	SPEAKEASY	9.00	—	36	—
391	Spinnaker PPL	9.00	—	36	—
392	S-PLUS	10.00	—	32	—
393	Spreadsheet default	50.00	3	6	9
394	SPS	1.00	—	320	—
395	SPSS	10.00	—	32	—
396	SQL	25.00	7	13	15
397	SQL-Windows	27.00	—	12	—
398	Statistical default	10.00	20	32	40
399	STRATEGEM	9.00	—	36	—
400	STRESS	4.50	—	71	—
401	Strongly typed default	3.50	45	91	125
402	STYLE	7.00	—	46	—
403	SUPERBASE 1.3	9.00	—	36	—
404	SURPASS	50.00	—	6	—
405	SYBASE	8.00	—	40	—
406	Symantec C++	11.00	—	29	—
407	SYMBOLANG	5.00	—	64	—
408	Synchroworks	18.00	—	18	—
409	SYNON/2E	17.00	—	19	—
410	System-W	9.00	—	36	—
411	Tandem Access. Lang.	3.50	—	91	—
412	TCL	5.00	—	64	—
413	TELON	20.00	13	16	20
414	TESSARACT	8.00	—	40	—
415	THEMIS	25.00	—	13	—
416	THE TWIN	50.00	—	6	—
417	TI-IEF	23.00	10	14	22
418	Topspeed C ++	11.00	—	29	—
419	TRANSFORM	22.00	—	15	—
420	TRANSLISP PLUS	5.75	—	56	—
421	TREET	5.00	—	64	—
422	TREETRAN	5.00	—	64	—

Continued on next page

Table D.1: Alphabetical List of Software Languages Subject to Year 2000 Problems, continued

ID	Language	Level	Low	Average	High
423	TRS80 BASIC II,III	2.50	80	128	170
424	TRUE BASIC	5.00	—	64	—
425	Turbo C	2.50	—	128	—
426	TURBO C++	6.00	23	53	80
427	TURBO EXPERT	6.50	—	49	—
428	Turbo PASCAL >5	6.50	—	49	—
429	Turbo PASCAL 1-4	4.00	55	80	115
430	Turbo PASCAL 4-5	4.50	—	71	—
431	Turbo PROLOG	4.00	—	80	—
432	TURING	4.00	—	80	—
433	TUTOR	6.00	—	53	—
434	TWAICE	6.50	—	49	—
435	UCSD PASCAL	3.50	—	91	—
436	UFO/IMS	9.00	—	36	—
437	UHELP	10.00	—	32	—
438	UNIFACE	20.00	—	16	—
439	UNIX Shell Scripts	3.00	—	107	—
440	VAX ACMS	5.50	—	58	—
441	VAX ADE	8.00	—	40	—
442	VECTRAN	3.00	—	107	—
443	VHDL	17.00	—	19	—
444	Visible C	6.50	—	49	—
445	Visible COBOL	8.00	—	40	—
446	Visicalc 1	35.00	5	9	15
447	VisualAge	15.00	—	21	—
448	Visual Basic 1	8.50	25	38	45
449	Visual Basic 2	9.00	23	36	40
450	Visual Basic 3	10.00	20	32	37
451	Visual Basic DOS	8.00	—	40	—
452	Visual C++	9.50	—	34	—
453	Visual COBOL	16.00	—	20	—
454	VisualGen	18.00	—	18	—
455	Visual Objects	20.00	—	16	—
456	VS-REXX	10.00	—	32	—
457	VULCAN	5.00	—	64	—
458	VZ Programmer	9.00	—	36	—
459	WARP X	8.00	—	40	—
460	WATCOM C	2.50	—	128	—
461	WATCOM C/386	2.50	—	128	—

Continued on next page

Table D.1: Alphabetical List of Software Languages Subject to Year 2000 Problems, continued

ID	Language	Level	Low	Average	High
462	Waterloo C	2.50	—	128	—
463	Waterloo PASCAL	3.50	—	91	—
464	WATFIV	3.75	—	85	—
465	WATFOR	3.50	—	91	—
466	WHIP	3.50	—	91	—
467	Wizard	11.50	—	28	—
468	XLISP	5.00	—	64	—
469	YACC	6.00	—	53	—
470	YACC++	6.00	—	53	—
471	ZBASIC	3.50	—	91	—
472	ZIM	17.00	—	19	—
473	ZLISP	5.00	—	64	—

My colleagues and I at SPR have been maintaining this table for almost 10 years, and continue to remain surprised that so many new programming languages continue to be developed. Between two and five new programming languages have been reported to SPR every month for more than a 10-year period! There is no indication that the rate of new languages is decreasing, and so far as I can tell the creation of new programming languages will probably continue well into the next century. Further, new versions of existing languages come out at frequent intervals. From the standpoint of someone trying to create a census of programming languages, the combination of new languages and revisions to current languages indicates that programming language development is one of the most dynamic and rapidly changing domains in all of software.

Appendix E: Annotated Bibliography of Year 2000 Books

Over the summer of 1997 at least half a dozen new year 2000 books will be published, and by the end of 1997 the total number of year 2000 books in print may be approaching 20. All major publishers have two or three such books planned or in production. Some of the books that will soon be published are by very well-known software and year 2000 experts such as Ed Yourdon. The current listings are only samples to illustrate the type of information available.

De Jager, Peter, and Richard Bergeon. *Managing 00: Surviving the Year 2000 Computing Crisis.* New York: John Wiley & Sons, 1997.

Peter de Jager was one of the first—and has been one of the most articulate—year 2000 specialists. Richard Bergeon is a technical year 2000 specialist at Data Dimensions and is also well known in the year 2000 arena. Together they have written one of the most comprehensive and readable year 2000 books in this emerging domain. Peter and Richard cover many aspects of the year 2000 issue: software repairs, repairs to databases, hardware upgrades, possible litigation, and more.

In addition to being an author of this book and many articles on the year 2000, Peter de Jager founded one of the largest Web sites of year 2000 data, and is a prolific speaker at year 2000 conferences. Much of the attention that the world press is now focusing on the year 2000 problem stems from Peter's tireless proselytizing. His book is one of the best overall treatments of the subject, and should be read by every year 2000 manager, as well as by executives who need to understand the implications of this problem for their corporations and themselves.

Jones, Keith. *Year 2000 Software Crisis Solutions.* Boston: ITCP, 1997.

Keith Jones' book is aimed primarily at MIS and the COBOL programming language, although other kinds of software and other languages are discussed too. Unlike some other year 2000 books, this one does not assume that date field expansion is the only available year 2000 repair strategy. The book contains examples and very useful discussions of a variety of year 2000 masking strategies such as bridging, windowing, encapsulation, and data duplexing.

Because cost information on the year 2000 problem is fairly difficult to obtain, this book also contains information on probable year 2000 expenses. One notable feature is that it contains the first known attempt to correlate the Gartner Group's method of sizing year 2000 costs based on LOC metrics and my method of attempting to size year 2000 costs based on function point metrics. Although these two methods use different metrics and tackle the year 2000 problem from very different sets of data, the overall results are actually fairly similar when examined carefully. Jones' book also places year 2000 repairs in a social and organizational context, and contains very interesting suggestions on organizing year 2000 repair teams, reporting progress to management, and many other day-to-day issues that confront real-life year 2000 project managers.

Kappelman, Leon, ed. *Solving the Year 2000 Problem.* Boston: ITCP, 1997.

Dr. Leon Kappelman has long been associated with practical research on the year 2000 problem, and was the co-chairman of the SIM year 2000 research group. Dr. Kappelman's book is a very useful combination of empirical data, case studies, and thoughtful articles written by a number of year 2000 experts.

The primary information that sets this book apart from many others is the wealth of practical, empirical data on actually solving the year 2000 problem derived from companies that are ahead of the year 2000 learning curve. Another useful attribute of this book, which is also rare in the year 2000 literature, is the extensive tables derived from large-scale surveys of hundreds of year 2000 managers in many companies.

Kappelman's book concentrates on the year 2000 problem in the United States and is sparse in dealing with the international implications of the year 2000 problem. Except for this minor caveat, this book is filled with solid, practical data and is a welcome addition to the year 2000 section of a software manager's library.

Lefkon, Dick, ed. *Year 2000 Best Practices for Y2K Millennium Computing: Panic in Year Zero.* New York: AITP, 1997.

The AITP is an offshoot of DPMA and is the SIM devoted to mainframe computing and software. In spite of the book's strange subtitle and curious back cover, it is a very useful compendium of year 2000 source material. It contains short excerpts, from 1 to no more than 40 pages, from more than 100 researchers and organizations. It contains a great deal of useful data on year 2000 costs, various strategies for containing the year 2000 problem, legal implications, and other relevant matters. The fact that this massive book totals 919 pages of rather small type indicates the enormous quantity of information starting to be published about the year 2000 problem and its many manifestations.

Murray, Jerome T., and Marilyn J. Murray. *The Year 2000 Computing Crisis.* New York: McGraw-Hill, 1996.

This year 2000 book was published in 1996 and was one of the first commercial books to deal directly with the impact of the year 2000 problem. Since the book was no doubt started in 1994 and 1995, the book assumes that the year 2000 problem will be solved and does not indulge in the frantic warnings of impending doom and disaster that tend to be features of more recent year 2000 books.

The book is aimed at MIS, and assumes that date field expansion will be the primary year 2000 repair strategy. Within these two criteria, the book is very solid and readable, and contains examples of the kinds of code changes necessary to correct the year 2000 problem. The authors' view of the year 2000 problem is practical, and their advice on and examples of repairs are both sound. A companion disk is included that contains usable sample code. The disk contains year 2000 correction code in Assembly, COBOL, and RPG.

One scholarly feature that this book contains, which is missing from essentially all other books on the year 2000 problem, is a very interesting historical perspective on the measurement of time, with detailed discussions of the problems that the designers of the Julian and Gregorian calendars were attempting to solve. Knowing the history of time measurement does not have any immediate impact on the year 2000 problem itself, but it is somewhat comforting to know that time problems have been occurring for thousands of years and we are not the only generation to experience business and technical problems because of the technical difficulty of measuring and recording time accurately. This is a technically sound book with useful historical background information.

Ragland, Bryce. *The Year 2000 Problem Solver.* New York: McGraw-Hill, 1997.

Bryce Ragland is a software researcher at the well-known Air Force STSC at Ogden Air Force Base. Based on his extensive military software background, Bryce has produced a solid, general-purpose year 2000 book that avoids the narrow focus of some other authors who assume that the year 2000 problem will affect only COBOL applications dealing with finance. Bryce's book contains some very useful advice about checking out personal computers, and some year 2000 containment strategies for real-time, systems, and embedded software. Information systems in COBOL are not ignored, but they are not given any more emphasis than is needed for a topic that comprises only about 30% of the overall year 2000 problem.

Robbins, Brian, and Howard Rubin. *The Year 2000 Planning Guide.* Pound Ridge, NY: Rubin Systems, Inc., 1997.

Brian Robbins is the Vice President of Chase Manhattan Bank and is responsible for their year 2000 repair work. Dr. Howard Rubin is a well-known management consultant, author, and lecturer on a variety of software topics including the year 2000 problem. This collaborative book is based in part on the actual repair work at Chase Manhattan Bank, and in part on the work of other year 2000 authors. It includes case studies from a number of companies at various stages of year 2000 readiness.

Dr. Rubin is one of the top software metrics experts, and hence his reports and articles usually contain more quantified information than many other authors. This book is no exception, and Dr. Rubin provides a number of examples of year 2000 cost-estimating methods and a substantial set of cost data derived from actual companies' year 2000 repair work. Since this book is derived in part from the actual year 2000 repair work in a major corporation, some of the information on how to establish a year 2000 project office, how to establish multidisciplinary year 2000 committees, and many other topics reflect the real-world needs of many large corporations.

The year 2000 problem does not just affect financial software, but is a very pervasive problem that can affect building security, telephone systems, elevators, electric power, assembly lines, and many diverse physical appliances. The Robbins/Rubin book deals with all of the diversity of the year 2000 problem, and hence has much broader relevance than just a treatise on changing source code from two-digit to four-digit formats. It is a very useful book for year 2000 project managers because it shows how large corporations are dealing with the multi-faceted aspects of the year 2000 crisis.

The book is published in notebook format, and contains a mixture of articles, linking materials, presentation materials, and various tables and graphs containing quantified information. While the organization of the book is not perfect in terms of rapid access to the information, the information itself is very useful to those seeking solid cost information as well as "how-to" information on preparing for year 2000 readiness.

Ulrich, William M., and Ian S. Hayes. *The Year 2000 Software Crisis: Challenge of the Century.* Upper Saddle River, NJ: Yourdon Press (Prentice Hall), 1997.

William Ulrich is a very well-known speaker at year 2000 conferences, and Ian Hayes has long been associated with software management consulting topics. Together these two authors have produced a solid book that is a good introduction to the topic for those seeking to understand some of the broad impacts of the year 2000 problem. Although the book is very readable and covers many year 2000 topics, some of the more interesting, newer subjects such as bridging, encapsulation, windowing, and data duplexing are not supported with any quantitative data. In fact, this book shares a common problem with many other year 2000 books in that it is very short on quantification of year 2000 cost information.

Glossary

Activity-based costing denotes estimating or collecting cost data at a very granular level, rather than at the project level. In a year 2000 software repair context, the major activities will include triage (separating software projects into those that need or don't need repair), searching for year 2000 hits in the software that needs immediate repairs, repairing the year 2000 hits (or masking them), testing the repaired application, and repairing bad fixes that accidentally introduced new errors.

Backfiring denotes calculating the function point total for an application by direct mathematical conversion from source code statements. For example, COBOL applications contain an average of 106.7 logical source code statements in the procedure and data divisions for every function point. Backfiring is the most widely used method for creating function point totals for aging legacy applications and hence is very common in a year 2000 context.

Bad-fix injection defines a very common software problem. Each time a bug or defect is repaired in a software application there is a chance that a new bug or defect will be introduced *by the repair*. The US average for bad fixes is roughly 7%, and there is no reason to think that year 2000 repairs will be lower and some reason to think that year 2000 repairs may be higher.

Bad test cases are a common but poorly understood software phenomenon. Test cases are just as likely to contain bugs or errors than the software packages for which the test cases have been created to test. In fact, the few studies of this phenomenon indicate that the number of errors in test cases may often be greater than the number of errors in the source code. In a year 2000 context, this means that a significant number of test cases (perhaps 5%) will themselves contain errors.

Blank lines are software programs and systems that, like printed documents, often use blank lines to separate paragraphs. Although there are wide variations in the number of blank lines in a software program, about 7% blank lines is a typical value. In a year 2000 context blank lines are significant because some year 2000 outsourcers and contractors base their costs on a count of physical LOC, in which case clients will be billed for blank lines in software applications.

Bridging is a hybrid form of a solution to the year 2000 problem. This method deals with the fact that some applications are already year 2000 compliant and use four-digit year dates while others are not yet compliant and use two-digit year dates. The bridging method is based on an external rule-based software package that allows program logic to be converted into four-digit form, but databases and files can use either two-digit or four-digit formats. The external bridge tool contains a "window" that dynamically converts two-digit dates into the correct four-digit century format when the application is run.

Century compliant means that software applications can successfully run without failures or disasters in both the twentieth and twenty-first centuries. An implicit meaning of the phrase *century compliant* is that years will be recognized in full, four-digit format such as 1999 and 2000 instead of 99 and 00. The phrase does not mean that all date fields must actually be expanded to four-digit form, since windowing, encapsulation, and other masking approaches can also lead to century compliance.

Comments statements are nonexecutable remarks that programmers insert into their applications as tips or reminders for the benefit of future generations of programmers when the application needs to be changed. Comments usually explain what a routine is supposed to do, or cautions about things that maintenance programmers need to understand. Although the volume of comments can run from zero to almost half the total number of physical LOC, the US average is about 15% comments. In a year 2000 context comments are significant because some year 2000 outsourcers are basing their charges on gross physical lines, which means that clients are being charged for comments statements even though they have no direct impact on year 2000 processing.

Compression is a year 2000 repair strategy that does not expand date fields from two-digit format, but substitutes some kind of code in the year field to indicate century. This method is questionable since there are no standards for what code should be used, and the method may create unpredictable side effects.

Consequential damages is a legal expression for payments for the loss caused by business or physical problems that a technical problem like the year 2000 situation may cause. For example, suppose a company is using a $500 cost-estimating tool to bid on a $10,000,000 contract and an error in the cost-estimating tool causes the company to lose the job. If they sue the vendor, they may be awarded some portion of the lost $10,000,000 opportunity rather than just having their $500 refunded. The concept of consequential damages has seldom been invoked for software lawsuits, but the year 2000 problem may change this situation.

Cost per function point denotes one of several methods of normalizing software costs. Cost per line of code is the other widely used method. Cost per function point has the advantage of being economically valid for noncoding activities such as project management and requirements analysis. Cost per function point is also accurate for economic studies involving multiple programming languages. Year 2000 software repairs often range between about $25 and $85 per function point based on number of year 2000 hits, complexity, and other factors. Cost per function point does not work for database repairs and is also not suited for topics such as hardware upgrades or litigation costs.

Cost per line of code is currently the most common method for normalizing software year 2000 repairs, although this method does not work at all for database repairs, hardware upgrades, test library repairs, litigation preparation, and a number of other year 2000 cost elements. However, cost per line of code is the dominant charging method used by year 2000 outsourcers and contractors, whose fees tend to range between about $0.75 per line of code and $2.50 per line of code. These fees are often based on gross physical lines, which means that clients will be charged for blank lines, comments, and dead code. When used as an internal charge method for in-house year 2000 repairs, costs range from perhaps $0.25 to $1.15 per gross physical line of code.

Cyclomatic complexity is the number of edges, minus the number of nodes, plus two, of a graph of software control flow. In essence cyclomatic complexity seeks to measure the number of branches in the control flow of an application. Software with no branches at all has a cyclomatic value of 1. Empirically, modules and programs with high cyclomatic complexity levels (20 and up) are harder to modify safely than applications with low values. In a year 2000 context, applications with high levels of cyclomatic complexity will be more difficult to modify and to test, and will have a higher bad-fix injection rate than applications with low values for cyclomatic complexity.

Database year 2000 repairs is a generic term for dealing with year 2000 hits in databases, rather than in source code. Because repairing databases via date field expansions is so difficult and expensive, a variety of alternative methods are coming into use, such as data duplexing, bridging, windowing, and encapsulation.

Data duplexing is a form of database year 2000 processing for batch transactions rather than on-line transactions. As year 2000 repairs proceed, some software applications will become year 2000 compliant and will use four-digit date fields, while others will still be unrepaired and use two-digit date fields. Using data duplexing, databases are duplicated—one version has two-digit date fields and the other version has four-digit date fields—but all other data is identical. This strategy allows software using either two-digit or four-digit dates to execute by simply assigning the correct database to the application.

Data point is a hypothetical software metric that is assumed to be equivalent for function point metrics for software. As this book is being written, research on data point metrics are underway, but no formal definitions have been published. Some of the component parts of a data point metric being evaluated include logical files (as with function points); entities, or the number of "things," contained in the database; relationships among the entities; attributes or the number of qualifications per entity; inquiry types (as with function points); and interfaces.

Data quality applies to the absence of errors in databases. However, without a normalizing metric such as a data point it is difficult to ascertain how many errors databases actually contain. It is suspected that databases are even more error prone than software, but this is only speculation since there are no metrics available for normalizing database errors.

Date field expansion is a common form of year 2000 repair. This term denotes expanding two-digit date fields such as "97" for 1997 into four-digit format (using 1997). Date field expansion is a permanent form of repair, but is also among the most expensive of the year 2000 repair strategies. For database repairs, date field expansion is so troublesome and expensive that alternatives such as bridging or data duplexing are now the most common approaches.

Dead code is routines and subroutines that exist in software applications but are never executed. As software applications are modified and updated, it is a common practice for programmers to leave old code present in the application, but to disable the entry and exit points so the old code is no longer usable. The rationale for this practice is that some of the new updates may not work, and if they have to be removed leaving in the old code is the safest policy. For aging legacy applications (10 to 20 years old), sometimes more than 30% of the entire volume of code can be dead. In a year 2000 context, the fact that dead code is common may lead to substantial costs if year 2000 contractors or outsource vendors are used, since charges may be based on a count of gross physical LOC, which includes dead code as well as active code.

Defect removal efficiency is the percentage of bugs or errors removed prior to release of a software package. Removal efficiency is calculated by keeping track of all bugs found prior to release versus the bugs reported after release for a fixed time period, such as six months. If the prerelease bugs in an application total 90 and the clients find 10 bugs in the first six months, then the defect removal efficiency for this example would be 90%. In a year 2000 context, this is an important concept because unless year 2000 repairs are 100% efficient, there will still be problems. The actual removal efficiency of year 2000 defects is not known, but the US average for other kinds of defects is only about 85%. There is some reason to think that year 2000 repairs will be higher than this, but it is unlikely that they will achieve 100%.

Directors' liability indicates that corporate directors have a legal responsibility to behave prudently and act in the best interest of shareholders. In a year 2000 context, the phrase may soon be invoked in lawsuits by shareholders who feel that the value of their shares have been reduced by either (1) failure to take effective action to repair year 2000 problems or (2) the high costs of the year 2000 repairs themselves.

Dormant application is software that may be present in corporate libraries or portfolios, but that is no longer executed or used. Obviously, dormant applications should be identified and removed from consideration for year 2000 repairs. The incidence of dormant applications is surprisingly high and may approach 50% of all software.

Embedded data is data that is "hard coded" in a software application, rather than being stored in an external database or file. Embedded data is significant in a year 2000 context because it may not be easy to find and isolate.

Embedded software is software that resides inside a physical device, which it then controls. For example, appliances such as microwave ovens contain embedded software, as do automobiles, cameras, and many other consumer appliances. In a year 2000 context, it may be necessary to replace hardware chips since embedded software often cannot be modified or updated.

Encapsulation is one of the many masking approaches that are being used to make temporary repairs to software for the year 2000 problem. A common form of encapsulation is an external software routine that shifts dates downward by 28 years as they enter an application and upward by 28 years when they leave. Thus the year 1997 would be converted into 1969 on entering, and converted back to 1997 on leaving. This is a temporary repair for the year 2000 problem. A period of 28 years is selected because that period brings the days of the week and the dates of the month into correct synchronization.

European currency conversion is the work of converting software applications so that they support a new common currency for the European Community. The planned start date for the completion of the currency conversion is January 1, 1999, but this date is unlikely to be achieved. Since there are not enough resources for currency conversion and year 2000 repairs simultaneously, the two problems are in sharp conflict in Western Europe.

Fiduciary duty is the legal obligation of corporate executives to behave prudently and act in the best interest of shareholders. If shareholders feel that the value of their stock has been damaged by imprudent actions, then executives may be sued for violation of fiduciary duty. Failure to repair the year 2000 problem may lead to many such lawsuits for CEOs, CFOs, CIOs, vice presidents of software engineering, vice presidents of quality, corporate counsel, and other top-ranking officers.

Function point is a synthetic metric used to determine the size of an application without regard to the amount of source code or the programming language used to encode the application. Function points were invented by A. J. Albrecht of IBM and were made part of the public domain in October 1979. Function points are derived from the weighted totals of five external attributes: (1) inputs to the application, (2) outputs from the application, (3) inquiries that can be made against the application, (4) logical files maintained by the application, and (5) interfaces between the application and the outside world. The definition of function points and the rules for counting them are determined in the United States by the IFPUG. Other countries have similar organizations, and there are also variant function point metrics such as the British Mark II function point, which differs from the US function point. The ISO is working on a standard for function point sizing, but it is not available at the time that this book is being written.

Leap year is a calendar year that contains February 29th. The rules for calculating leap years make the year 2000 a leap year, which adds another problem to the already serious basic year 2000 problem. A year is a leap year if it is divisible by four unless it ends in 00. However years ending in 00 are leap years if they are divisible by 400, which makes the year 2000 a leap year. There is one exception, which is that the year 3600 will not be a leap year. The reason for leap years is to synchronize calendars with the actual rotation of the earth around the sun.

Legacy application is any kind of software that has been in use long enough so that maintenance is no longer performed by the original personnel who built the application. Thus this phrase can apply to software that is less than a year old and also to applications that are more than 20 years old. For many legacy applications older than about 10 years, the source code may be missing or the compiler may no longer operate. This adds difficulty to year 2000 repairs.

Line of code (logical) is one of the variations used to count source code volumes. A count of logical statements in an application is based on formal rules and is concerned with the way source code statements are terminated. The string of instructions BASE = 0: BASE = HOURS * RATE: PRINT BASE would comprise three logical statements even though the statements occupy only one physical line. The colon is used to terminate the first two statements. The rationale for counting logical statements is that this method reflects the thought processes and work of writing computer programs. Depending on the rules of specific languages, counts of logical statements and counts of physical LOC may be identical or may vary by several hundred percent in either direction.

Line of code (physical) is one of the variations used to count source code volumes. The string of instructions BASE = 0: BASE = HOURS * RATE: PRINT BASE would comprise one physical line even though it contains three separate logical statements. The colon is used to terminate the first two statements, but when counting physical lines only a carriage return is used. The rationale for counting physical lines is that this method is very easy to do. Depending on the rules of specific languages, counts of logical statements and counts of physical lines of code may be identical or may vary by several hundred percent in either direction.

Masking denotes a variety of methods for working around the year 2000 problem without actually having to expand the date fields. Examples of masking approaches include bridging, compression, data duplexing, encapsulation, and windowing. Each of these, in turn, has yet other variants such as the windowing approach, which has both fixed and sliding variations. Masking is a convenient term for dealing with any or all of these disparate methods.

Missing source code is active, executable software for which the source code is no longer available. The source code may have been lost or it may be so old that the original compiler used to create the application no longer works. If applications with missing source code need year 2000 repairs, then the repairs must be made against the object code, masking must be used, or the application must be replaced. About 15% of applications tend to have missing source code, but for applications more than 10 years old, the incidence can approach or exceed 50%.

Object code is the compiled, executable code that actually operates on a computer. The source code and object code of software applications are not always kept together, which can lead to a situation where the object code continues to operate but the source code is lost or can no longer be compiled. In a year 2000 context, this greatly increases repair difficulty. However, several tools are being tested that assert that they can repair year 2000 problems in object code, although the efficiency and effectiveness of these tools is not yet confirmed.

Performance is the speed at which computer software operates. This term is significant in a year 2000 context because some of the repair alternatives such as bridging and windowing may degrade software performance to unacceptable levels. The degradation of performance is most likely to affect applications with very high rates of throughput, such as credit card processing or airline reservation systems.

Portfolio is all of the software owned by an enterprise, including custom software and leased or purchased software packages. End-user software is normally excluded from this term, as are embedded applications such as software-controlled elevators and faxes. Portfolio size can be measured using function points, physical LOC, logical statements, or all three methods.

Professional malpractice is the performance of a knowledge worker that violates the accepted canons of the occupation and that may also cause harm to a client. The term *professional malpractice* has long been applied to formal professions such as doctors and attorneys, but has seldom been applied to software managers or technical workers due to the fact that software is not recognized as a true profession. However, in a year 2000 context, where lawsuits are likely to be plentiful, it is quite likely that several variants of professional malpractice claims will occur: (1) against software managers who fail to deal with the year 2000 problem, and (2) against year 2000 tool and service vendors who claim to have fixed the year 2000 problems, but do not do so successfully.

Regression testing is a common kind of testing associated with maintenance and enhancements of existing software. The word *regression* means to go back. Regression tests are run to ensure that all prior software features are still operational. In a year 2000 context, regression testing will be a key defense against bad fixes, performance degradation, and other accidental byproducts of hasty year 2000 repairs. However, it is important to realize that regression tests themselves may need year 2000 repairs. If current regression tests look for dates at all, they look for two-digit date fields.

Test library repair is the need to fix year 2000 problems in test cases, as well as in source code and in databases. If current test cases look for dates at all, they look for two-digit date fields. Thus when applications are repaired and the dates are converted into four-digit format, many test cases will return error messages. Therefore not only software itself, but many existing test cases will need to be repaired. This form of year 2000 problem is not widely covered in the year 2000 literature, but may amount to as much as 10% to 15% of software repair costs, although it may be less than that for companies that don't have formal test libraries.

Triage is used in medical practice, usually in the context of medicine or the aftermath of earthquakes, tornadoes, or major disasters. The term *triage* denotes the categorization of patients into three distinct categories: (1) those who need immediate medical attention to survive, (2) those who probably will not survive whether they get medical attention or not, and (3) those who will survive without needing immediate medical attention. In a year 2000 software context, the same term is used with software applications that (1) need immediate repairs, (2) cannot be repaired and must be replaced, and (3) can continue to operate without immediate year 2000 repair work.

Windowing is one of several alternatives to expand date fields from two-digit to four-digit form. The windowing concept is based on the fact that in every 100-year period, any two-digit number will occur only once. When used with software for year 2000 purposes, a hundred year window is selected and then incoming dates are assigned to either the twentieth or twenty-first century based on assumptions of the meaning of the two-digit date. Suppose 1930 is selected as the base date in a 100-year window. Any incoming date that is greater than 30 such as 40 would be assigned to the twentieth century as 1940. Any incoming date that is less than 30 such as 20 would be assigned to the twenty-first century as 2020. Windows can either be fixed or sliding, and serve to delay the need for actual date field expansions. However, windowing requires care and consistency, and may also degrade performance levels.

Year 2000 removal efficiency is the percentage of year 2000 problems actually repaired in any given application or in an overall portfolio. The obvious goal is to achieve 100% year 2000 repair efficiency. However, for repairing other kinds of software problems the US average is only about 85%. As this book is being written, there is not enough empirical data to assign year 2000 removal efficiency levels. However, there is no reason to think that year 2000 repairs will routinely achieve 100%, although rates in excess of 95% may occur.

Year 2000 repair engine is an automated tool, usually a software tool, that a vendor asserts can fix the year 2000 problem in software applications. While a number of year 2000 repair engines are on the commercial market, their effectiveness is currently unknown. That is, it is unclear if these tools can repair 100% of year 2000 problems, and the actual repair value is still not available. For the 500 or so programming languages in which the year 2000 problem may exist, automated repair tools have been announced for less than 10, with COBOL having more than any other language.

Year 2000 search engine is an automated tool, usually a software tool, that a vendor asserts can find year 2000 problems in source code (or, less commonly, in object code). Many vendors have year 2000 search engines available for common languages such as COBOL and C. However there are more than 500 programming languages that may contain year 2000 problems, and there are no known commercial search engines available for more than 450 of these. Also, the efficiency and effectiveness of year 2000 search engines is unknown. It is probable that less than 100% of actual year 2000 problems can be found, but the actual value is not yet determined.

Year 2000 specialists is a phrase describing one of the fastest-growing occupations in human history. Year 2000 specialists are programmers or consultants who devote themselves to finding and fixing the year 2000 problem in software, test libraries, databases, or wherever the problem resides. As this book is being written in 1997, year 2000 specialists are approaching 10% of the software population of the United States. By the end of 1998, year 2000 specialists might exceed 50% of the software population of the United States, and the numbers could grow to more than 75% by the end of 1999. This is an ephemeral occupation, and the need for year 2000 specialists will probably disappear by about 2005.

Index